Re-embodying
Pastoral Theology

Re-embodying Pastoral Theology

Ritual Care for Moral Injury in Veterans

Johann Choi

LEXINGTON BOOKS/FORTRESS ACADEMIC
Lanham • Boulder • New York • London

Published by Lexington Books/Fortress Academic
Lexington Books is an imprint of The Rowman & Littlefield Publishing Group, Inc.
4501 Forbes Boulevard, Suite 200, Lanham, Maryland 20706
www.rowman.com

86-90 Paul Street, London EC2A 4NE, United Kingdom

Copyright © 2024 by The Rowman & Littlefield Publishing Group, Inc.

All rights reserved. No part of this book may be reproduced in any form or by any electronic or mechanical means, including information storage and retrieval systems, without written permission from the publisher, except by a reviewer who may quote passages in a review.

British Library Cataloguing in Publication Information Available

Library of Congress Cataloging-in-Publication Data

Names: Choi, Johann, 1981– author.
Title: Re-embodying pastoral theology : ritual care for moral injury in veterans. / Johann Choi.
Description: Lanham : Lexington Books, Fortress Academic, [2024] | Includes bibliographical references and index. | Summary: "Re-embodying Pastoral Theology uses the problem of moral injury in veterans to propose a pastoral theology that recognizes ritual as the means by which the Christian community addresses the body in pastoral care. The author endeavors first to re-think moral injury and then to re-embody the field of Pastoral Theology"— Provided by publisher.
Identifiers: LCCN 2024009068 (print) | LCCN 2024009069 (ebook) | ISBN 9781978717107 (cloth) | ISBN 9781978717114 (epub)
Subjects: LCSH: Moral injuries. | Psychic trauma—Social aspects. | War—Moral and ethical aspects. | Pastoral care.
Classification: LCC BF175.5.P75 C47 2024 (print) | LCC BF175.5.P75 (ebook) | DDC 259.086/97—dc23/eng/20240430
LC record available at https://lccn.loc.gov/2024009068
LC ebook record available at https://lccn.loc.gov/2024009069

♾️™ The paper used in this publication meets the minimum requirements of American National Standard for Information Sciences—Permanence of Paper for Printed Library Materials, ANSI/NISO Z39.48-1992.

Contents

Acknowledgments   vii

Introduction   1

Chapter 1: Moral Injury as a Pastoral Theological Construct   11

Chapter 2: Ritual and the Problem of Moral Injury   49

Chapter 3: Contributions from Moral Injury and Ritual Care
Literature for a Pastoral Theological Approach to Moral Injury   77

Chapter 4: Non-humanistic Ritual Care for Moral Injury: A Pastoral
Theological Commentary   111

Chapter 5: Sin and Pastoral Theology   177

Appendix A: Solidarity in Sin in the Early Church   185

Appendix B: The Universality of Kill-Trauma   189

Bibliography   199

Index   207

About the Author   213

Acknowledgments

The *Mystical Body of Christ* is one of the doctrines to which I appeal in this book. One of my assertions is that the inherent solidarity of humankind is made manifest in that one cannot do such harm to another, as take a person's life, without feeling that something of one's own life is disrupted. Moreover, this very principle of solidarity—that in a sense I am not my own apart from the other—demands that all others see that they too are implicated in the acts of such an individual as a combat veteran. Moral injury is so devastating in part because individual perpetrators tend to (and wrongly) bear the full weight of their actions alone.

There may be something inauspicious about beginning this book by comparing it to a moral injury; however, in a similar way this project—born from my doctoral dissertation—would not have come about without an elaborate network of people in my life, not all of whom were necessarily involved in my research. Not only my professors and scholarly interlocutors, but so too my friends and family can (or will have to?) take credit for these pages presented here. Just some of these conspirators will be named here.

First, I am indebted to my dissertation committee members for their obvious and direct contributions to the outcome of this project. Dr. Karen Scheib, my advisor, gave me my first lesson in pastoral care at Emory when I arrived for my interview as an applicant and she greeted me outside the meeting room, grasped my shoulders, and told me that everything was going to be okay. That I completed both my dissertation and this book is a testament not just to her gift at prognosticating, but her measurable investment into this project. Dr. L. Edward Phillips can be credited for my foray into liturgical studies, which has played a central role in this book. By introducing me to the study of early Christian liturgies, he has enriched both my scholarly life as well as my personal devotional life. Dr. Elizabeth Bounds was so gracious to be part of my committee and lend her expertise despite never having met me in person until the day of my dissertation defense (up until that point we

viii   *Acknowledgments*

had always communicated by email). I counted myself lucky to find at Emory the rare theological scholar with serious academic interest in moral injury.

The less obvious partners in making this book possible are those graduate school friends, who made little or no direct scholarly contribution to my research. They nevertheless were the intellectual and social ground in which the seeds of this book and I were sown in those doctoral program years. Mike Suh, Devin White, and Matthew Pierce are people with whom I had met individually many a time for talks in which we solved all the world's problems. Each of these classmates sharpened me with their exercises of intellect, charity, and humor. It is an added bonus that my wife absolutely adores all of their wives.

The following have contributed nothing to this project and most of them will have no clue as to what this book is about. They have nevertheless contributed to my very being in such a way that it is obvious that I could not even be myself without them, let alone be the person to undertake this project. Daniel Lee, one of my oldest friends, is the only person other than my wife that truly understands me in this world. I have to thank his wife, Jennifer, and his boys (Jacob, Jeremiah, and Caleb) for making him a better person, as I could not do it. My brother's (Eugene) ambition, inventiveness, and drive to pursue his passions continue to inspire me and make me proud. I am lucky to have a father (a.k.a. Anpanman) who bucked the trend of his generation when it came to parenting by being funny, affectionate, open-minded, and supportive of me in all I did. My mother, now sixteen years deceased, started me on this journey by passing down to me her faith—still the greatest gift of my life. My late grandfather, the artist and Korean religion scholar Ryu Dong Shik, is the model of the man I continue to aspire to be. Most importantly, I wish to thank my wife. Meeting her was an unequivocal turning point in my life. She helped me find my courage, balance, and sense of adventure. We have moved too many times and found ourselves in some unexpected places. It was never easy, but I was always at home because she was next to me.

Introduction

My work as a chaplain in VA (Veterans Affairs) hospitals has been the impetus for this study. I worked for the VA prior to and alongside my graduate studies in Religion. I then served four years as an Air Force chaplain and returned to working as a VA chaplain post-separation from the military. Like any person working with veterans, I was already keenly aware of matters related to Post Traumatic Stress Disorder (PTSD). Yet in the course of my work I began encountering another related phenomenon, both in the literature and in the lives of the veterans I met—the problem of moral injury (MI). I had been told that people typically become morally injured not because their lives have been threatened, but, more often than not, because they have perpetrated harm against another.

The notion that someone could be deeply traumatized for hurting another intrigued me for a number of reasons. First, I was surprised that a person would enlist in the military, aware that her job could require her to kill someone in war, think that it was morally acceptable to do so, and then come away feeling inconsolably guilty after having committed the act. Second, I was intrigued by the medical world's decision to investigate clinically matters of morality, an area that seemed more fitting for the field of theology or ethics. Finally, the sheer novelty of this condition and the relative paucity of research on the topic drew me to direct my research interests accordingly.

From that point on, certain key questions and texts led me to my decision to pair a pastoral theological investigation of moral injury with ritual. From my first year as a chaplain, I had noticed the monopoly that psychotherapeutic literature and theories tended to hold in shaping pastoral theology. This observation led me to wonder whether the practice of pastoral care had adequate resources for addressing the body in addition to the mind and emotions. At a time when patristic theology, and particularly the writings of the Desert Fathers, was swirling about in my head, it seemed appropriate that a Christian practice of care would attend to both the body and the soul.[1] What connected this question to the matter of moral injury was a book by trauma psychiatrist Bessel van der Kolk, *The Body Keeps the Score* (2015). In this book, the psychiatrist relates how trauma imprints in the brain and the body.

2 *Introduction*

He also explains how bodily practices, including participation in drama and moving meditation, can assist in trauma recovery. This is the point at which I became convinced that I had to revisit ritual as a pastoral theological modality and that an investigation into moral injury would be a relevant context for doing so.

WHICH MORAL INJURY AND WHICH RITUAL?

To say that ritual would be one answer to moral injury is not a new idea. Intuitively, some psychiatrists have sent their morally injured patients to their priests, with beneficial results.[2] Some chaplains and pastoral theologians have proposed liturgies and rituals specially crafted for those suffering from moral injury and PTSD. The few who have actually followed through and used such rituals for veterans have likewise found them to be helpful in their recovery.[3]

Despite a general consensus amongst specialists across disciplines that a ritual of some sort would be helpful for veterans suffering from moral injury, one cannot assume too quickly that such specialists share a common understanding of what it means to employ rituals in the care of the morally injured. These clinicians and theologians represent a greater diversity of views and opinions than might first seem to be the case. Though these differences may be slight, they are not insignificant when considered from a pastoral theological perspective. A measure of nuance is also lacking when those voices propose the "ritual" care of veterans, as such suggestions are typically no more than a brief side note or afterthought. It is as if to say that any ritual, so long as somebody formulates one, would be sufficient. This complicates the task of getting at the heart of what these individuals mean by ritual and the reasons for which they view ritual to be helpful for the care of veterans. Nevertheless, a general pattern emerges from a review of statements regarding ritual in moral injury literature. Below, I first summarize the two broad types of rituals this literature offers as examples for use in the ritual care of morally injured veterans. I then provide a brief summary of the three most common reasons people give for why ritual should be employed in such cases.

CALLS FOR RITUALS

The two types of rituals commonly prescribed for cases of moral injury are the Christian rites of reconciliation and the more transcultural and less definitive rite of purification. Naturally, Christian rites are those most often referenced by pastoral theologians. These rituals are those already available and found in the history of the church. Christopher Grundy,[4] Rita Brock and

Introduction 3

Gabriella Lettini, and Warren Kinghorn[5]—all theologically trained in the Christian tradition—make some reference to the ancient penitential practices of the church as they relate especially to Christians who have participated in war. Brock writes,

> Christian churches in the first millennium required anyone who 'shed human blood' to undergo a rehabilitation process that included reverting to the status of someone who had not yet been baptized and was undergoing training in Christian faith. Now long in disuse, this ancient form of quarantine was required because early Christians understood that killing or participating in war, regardless of reasons, injured [the] souls of those who fought. Returning soldiers were commonly expected to spend at least a year among the order of penitents.[6]

While no theologian has actually advocated for this particular penitential system to be reintroduced, this commonly cited historical reference serves as an illustration of how the church can be a site where veterans make confession, do penance, and receive absolution for the guilt associated with participation in war. As alluded to above, psychiatrist Jonathan Shay has even sent his Catholic patients to see their priests for confession. Ironically, none of the above-mentioned theologians are in fact Catholic, and there is an obvious challenge for the many Protestants who do not have the liturgical infrastructure that allows for priestly absolution.[7]

While Shay appeals to the Christian rite of reconciliation for his patients, ultimately what he seeks is a type of purification ritual. Though, conceptually, purification rituals may have some overlap with the Christian rites, the calls for purification are distinctive in that they are not necessarily tied to any one tradition but are a response to a perceived universal human need for cleansing after war. Shay writes, "What I have in mind is a communal ritual with religious force that recognizes that everyone who has shed blood, no matter how blamelessly, is in need of purification. Those who have done something blameworthy require additional purification and penance, if their religious tradition provides for it."[8] Therefore, Shay is not tied to a Christian ritual as such, but recommends a purification ritual with "religious force."

Comparative and ethnographic studies of various indigenous cultures seem to have spawned this desire for a purification ritual in the West. Arthur Hadley's *Straw Giant* is a prominent text that, for example, inspired Dave Grossman's view on the matter. Hadley's study of "warrior societies" led him to conclude that all such "societies, tribes, and nations incorporate some form of purification ritual for their returning soldiers, and this ritual appears to be essential to the health of both the returning warrior and the society as a whole."[9] Others have also recognized this impulse within "warrior societies," among them journalist Sebastian Junger, who mentions the Yanomami and

4 *Introduction*

the Comanche in his article on the moral burdens of war,[10] and anthropologist Paul Granjo, who has written about the Mozambican cleansing rituals in the *Armed Forces & Society* journal.[11] What these theorists see in their observations of purification and penitential rites, whether in Catholic churches or "warrior cultures," is not a particular rite that they wish to appropriate, but an essential cultural practice noticeably absent within modern American society.

THE RATIONALE FOR RITUAL

The reasons for why ritual appears to be helpful to many in the case of moral injury generally fall into three not unrelated categories. First, physician-theologian Warren Kinghorn seems to suggest that a means for reconciliation following participation in war may be a moral and theological necessity.[12] Second, psychiatrist Jonathan Shay and psychotherapist Edward Tick note the limitations of psychotherapy to deal with such issues related to morality and guilt.[13] Third, counselor and military veteran Dave Grossman and psychologists Laurie Slone and Matthew Friedman tout the cathartic and therapeutic benefits of rituals.[14] To this, I might add that liturgical scholar Christopher Grundy suggests the importance of rituals for *transitioning* military personnel into civilian life. When he describes what "transitioning" entails, he essentially summarizes the points above.[15]

Despite a seeming consensus that a ritual for warriors returning from war would be a good idea, there has been no extensive investigation—let alone any pastoral theological investigation—into *why* rituals are an appropriate and effective response to moral injury, and *what* kind of ritual would be most appropriate. Even though Kinghorn sees some ritual of confession and forgiveness to be a necessity, he does not articulate any theological reasons why. Also, as Grossman and Slone and Friedman tout the benefits of ritual for coping with grief,[16] managing guilt and stress, and overall health,[17] one encounters the issue of the purpose of rituals and whether instrumentalizing them solely for practical benefits is appropriate. The nebulous quality of these discussions regarding ritual and moral injury reflects the relative newness of moral injury as a construct, and the relatively late and scant contributions of theological reflection on the matter. It is at this nexus that this study finds its entrée into the discussion.

Introduction

APPROACH AND METHODOLOGY

The primary purpose of this study is to understand moral injury and the appropriate response to it from a pastoral theological perspective. In the course of this exploration, I will be reconsidering ritual as a form of pastoral care, as the one task is ingredient in the other. As ritual offers a fitting response to the particular needs of a moral injury, this form of trauma provides an ideal test case, as it were, for highlighting the significance of ritual care. The purpose is not to arrive at some definitive treatment plan for moral injury. Rather, I seek to answer those questions posed above, that is: What is moral injury from a pastoral theological perspective? How might ritual be a fitting pastoral response to it? What kind of ritual would be most appropriate in response to moral injury?

The definitions of moral injury that ground most explorations of the topic today spring from doctors and psychologists, in short from those who formulated this construct as a consequence of what they saw in clinical practice. Chaplains and pastoral theologians have almost wholly taken for granted and taken over these terms and definitions from the clinical world. That I approach these topics primarily from a pastoral theological perspective, therefore, is one of the novelties of this study.[18] As the study unfolds, the implications of starting from this different point should be evident.

For the sake of achieving precision, clarity, and consistency, I pursue an understanding of moral injury and ritual explicitly from within the Christian context. In other words, I am not going to complicate this study by trying to achieve an ecumenical or transcultural understanding of terms that would endeavor to offer approaches to moral injury and ritual agreeable to all. Non-confessional approaches are appropriate for the work of chaplains and clinicians in secular settings. Much of the study of moral injury has been done in this mode. At the same time, these appeals to non-confessional understandings of morality and transcultural "purification rites," while necessary in some settings, have led to much of the imprecision, nebulousness, and inconsistency of ideas and terms when discussing these topics. This study aspires to avoid this impasse.

To seek a narrowly Christian approach to this study would also be an honest and familiar one for me, as a Christian. Given the nature of this study, it would be relevant to share that I am, more specifically, an ordained Anglican chaplain. My liturgical-theological interests, however, extend beyond this one tradition, as this study will show.

The reader will find that these pages refer frequently to Alexander Schmemann's text, *For the Life of the World* (1973), and that they cite the research of Catholic thinkers. This focus may be expected for a book committed to *ritual* forms of care, given the centrality of the *Divine Liturgy* and *Mass* within the Eastern Orthodox and Roman Catholic churches. That the Mass serves as something of an anchor in Catholic thought is reflected in the work of Catholic ethicists like William T. Cavanaugh, who frames questions of war from a distinctively liturgical perspective. Conversely, this study singles out Eastern Orthodox liturgical theologian Alexander Schmemann due to his sacramental view of the world beyond the church, such that even *worldly* tasks and events can be read through the lens of the liturgy. Such perspectives will be helpful as I interface one model of ritual care with moral injury and demonstrate how the liturgy can function as pastoral care, not the least for the morally injured.

The pastoral methodological approach for this study will be in the form John Swinton's "revised model of mutual critical correlation."[19] Swinton follows Deborah van Deusen Hunsinger who uses the "Chalcedonian Pattern" (regarding the two natures of Christ) as a model for relating theology and psychology.[20] Swinton explains his method as such: "[A]lthough qualitative research data is both logically independent of and dependent on theological categories in different ways, theological categories are by definition both logically prior to and independent of psychological categories with respect to their significance."[21] In accordance with this method, I will hold theology close yet logically prior to its discursive partners in the social sciences. This is made manifest in a number of ways throughout the study. For one, as I translate a largely clinical construct into theological terms, I trade the therapeutic aims in the various medical and psychotherapeutic treatment plans I evaluate for a Christian one. Later, as I assess various models of ritual pastoral care in chapter 3, the logical prioritization of theological aims will determine from which models in particular I draw as I propose an approach to ritual care. This will lead to my argument in favor of *theocentric* liturgies as opposed to *humanistic* ones.[22] The use of Swinton's methodological approach is perhaps most pronounced in chapter 4 where I provide a pastoral theological commentary on an ancient penitential rite, utilizing various social scientific perspectives. My primary theological sources will be in the areas of pastoral theology, liturgical theology, and historical theology. From the social sciences I will be drawing primarily from psychology and ritual studies. Following Swinton's claim, the sciences in my study are intended to "offer complementary knowledge which will enhance and sharpen our theological understandings."[23]

Introduction 7

CHAPTER OUTLINE

The remainder of this study will be divided into five chapters and arranged as follows:

Chapter 1 focuses on understanding moral injury from a pastoral theological perspective. The chapter opens with a general note on why trauma in general, and moral injury in particular, ought to be regarded as an issue worthy of greater pastoral attention. Following this, I review various definitions and understandings of moral injury across disciplines. After gaining a sense of the *status quaestionis*, I close the chapter by proposing a definition of moral injury in which I seek to understand the phenomenon from a theological perspective. By doing so, I couch moral injury in the theological language of sin. This establishes the foundation upon which the remainder of my research sits.

After posing moral injury as a pastoral theological issue in chapter 1, chapter 2 is dedicated to understanding ritual as a fitting pastoral response to this problem. The chapter opens with a definition of such terms as "ritual" and "worship" that are to be the presumed understandings of these terms throughout this study. The remaining and vast majority of the chapter, however, is divided into two interrelated parts. The first details the unique challenges that moral injury offers for conventional approaches to pastoral care. The second provides an argument for why rituals circumvent some of these issues and furnish a means of addressing the pastoral needs of the morally injured.

Chapter 3 offers an investigation of two bodies of literature that culminates in my proposal of three principles for a ritual approach to pastoral care. In the course of the chapter, I conduct a summary and analysis of material related to the care of veterans suffering from moral injury or combat-related guilt, as well as literature in which ritual/liturgy/worship and pastoral care intersect. Having established moral injury as a pastoral issue and ritual as a proper pastoral response, this chapter provides a summary of how the two have been approached to date. From and in response to this material, I propose three principles that should undergird a ritual approach to pastoral care. By presenting these principles I am establishing where I stand in light of the range of approaches to ritual care evaluated in the earlier sections. These principles will serve as the basis for the pastoral theological commentary and analysis conducted in the following chapter.

Chapter 4 presents a pastoral theological commentary on St. Gregory's third century 'graded' penitential rite. The chapter is intended to illustrate the concrete application of the principles proposed, as well as provide a synthesis of all the previous chapters, using this historical rite as a model. The chapter begins with a historical analysis of the penitential rite with a view toward its use as a means for pastoral care. The remaining more substantial portion

8   *Introduction*

of the chapter involves a pastoral theological commentary on each of the stages of the rite itself. My exploration of this rite will illustrate the principles I have posited and detail the means by which such practices could speak to the particular needs of the morally injured. Throughout this task I will be in conversation with various disciplines, including psychotherapy, psychiatry, ritual studies, and liturgical theology.

Chapter 5 offers some concluding thoughts regarding the potential implications that the proposed approach to moral injury and ritual has for the field of pastoral theology. I suggest here some possible areas for future exploration in light of the claims advanced in this study.

I feel compelled to close this introduction by noting one final critical resource that leaves its imprint on just about every page of this book and yet cannot be cited as readily: the voices of the scores of veterans with whom I have met as a chaplain over the years in chapel offices, psychiatric wards, emergency rooms, outpatient clinics, intensive care units, nursing homes, rehabilitation programs, and even at a county jail. Not all of them have been morally injured, though too many of them have. Their words and stories will at times be included in the body of the pages or in footnotes. Naturally, their names will not be included. At other times their stories are simply presupposed behind an argument. It is they who are the impetus and the driving force of this book. And it is they to whom I ultimately introduce the reader in the following pages.

NOTES

1. For my understanding of "soul," I lean upon St. Gregory of Nyssa, who states, "The soul is . . . a living and intellectual existence which by itself gives to the organic body the power of life and reception of sense-impressions as long as the nature which can receive these maintains its existence." [*On the Soul and Resurrection* (Crestwood, NY: St. Vladimir's Seminary Press, 1993), 37–38.]

2. Jonathan Shay, *Odysseus in America: Combat Trauma and the Trials of Homecoming* (New York: Scribner, 2010), 153. In a phone conversation with Dr. Shay on January 22, 2016, I asked him about the impact of this practice of sending vets to do confession through their priests. He remembers one vet who they encouraged to see their priest and so the vet reconnected with a family priest. Shay says there is no one "landmark moment after which now everything has changed from what has been before," but he says there was a clear change in the man's demeanor. Psychiatrists Mardi Horowitz and George F. Solomon have also concluded that "the classical maneuvers of the Catholic Church for the reduction of guilt"—referring to confession, atonement or penance, and restitution—can be very helpful to returning soldiers. They have decided that such "maneuvers are classical because they work comparatively well." See Bernard Joseph Verkamp, *The Moral Treatment of*

Returning Warriors in Early Medieval and Modern Times (Scranton, PA: Univ. of Scranton Press, 1993), 109, see also 111; Mardi J. Horowitz and George F. Solomon, "A Prediction of Delayed Stress Response Syndromes in Vietnam Veterans," *Journal of Social Issues* 31, no. 4 (1975): 78–79. My own experience as a Protestant chaplain offering a time of confession for a veteran yielded similar results. The veteran wished to fulfill step five of the twelve-step program and upon finishing his confession he stated that a huge weight was lifted from him. Like many veterans' stories of combat, most of these experiences were never shared with anyone.

3. I have in mind David Bachelor, a United Methodist minister and former military chaplain, whose "Warrior Wash" ministry offers morally injured veterans a ritual of cleansing. In my conversation with him he has validated that veterans have changed noticeably for the better following participation in his rite.

4. Christopher Grundy, "Basic Retraining: The Role of Congregational Ritual in the Care of Returning Veterans," *Liturgy* 27, no. 4 (2012): 32.

5. Warren Kinghorn, "Combat Trauma and Moral Fragmentation: A Theological Account of Moral Injury," *Journal of the Society of Christian Ethics* 32, no. 2 (Fall/Winter 2012): 68.

6. Rita Nakashima Brock and Gabriella Lettini, *Soul Repair: Recovering from Moral Injury after War* (Boston, MA: Beacon Press, 2013), xvii–xviii.

7. That being said, Kinghorn notes that there have been "only sporadic efforts among Catholics to encourage these practices." [Kinghorn, "Combat Trauma and Moral Fragmentation," 69–70.] To this I will add that actual participation in the Rite of Reconciliation for any reason is generally low for the Catholic Church, further diminishing its force within the tradition. The Center for Applied Research in the Apostolate (CARA) at Georgetown University conducted a survey of Catholics in 2005 and 2008. The survey asked how often one participated in the Sacrament of Reconciliation or Confession. Only two percent of the population stated "once a month or more," while the categories of "less than once a year" and "never" combined for 75 percent of all respondents. [http://cara.georgetown.edu/reconciliation.pdf]

8. Shay, *Odysseus in America*, 245.

9. David Grossman, *On Killing: The Psychological Cost of Learning to Kill in War and Society* (Boston: Little, Brown, 1996), 271–72.

10. Sebastian Junger, "Veterans Need to Share the Moral Burden of War," *The Washington Post*, May 26, 2013.

11. Paulo Granjo, "The Homecomer: Postwar Cleansing Rituals of Mozambique," *Armed Forces & Society* 33, no. 3 (2007): 382–95.

12. Kinghorn, "Combat Trauma and Moral Fragmentation: A Theological Account of Moral Injury," 68.

13. Shay, *Odysseus in America*, 152, and Edward Tick, "Healing the Wounds of War," *Parabola Magazine*, October 31, 2014, 121.

14. Grossman, *On Killing*, 271–73, and Matthew J. Friedman and Laurie B. Slone, *After the War Zone: A Practical Guide for Returning Troops and their Families* (Cambridge, MA: Da Capo Lifelong, 2008), 114.

15. Christopher Grundy, "Basic Retraining: The Role of Congregational Ritual in the Care of Returning Veterans," *Liturgy* 27, no. 4 (2012): 27–36.

16. Friedman and Slone, *After the War Zone*, 114.

17. Grossman, *On Killing*, 271–73.

18. Larry Kent Graham's book, *Moral Injury: Restoring Wounded Souls* (2017), does explore moral injury from a pastoral theological perspective and even touches upon the role of rituals in healing. The text, however, explores moral injury more as a general construct and does not explicitly engage any of the clinical studies or texts discussed here. Moreover, moral injury in *veterans* is not Graham's primary concern or framework for understanding this construct as it is in this study.

19. John Swinton and Harriet Mowat, *Practical Theology and Qualitative Research* (London: SCM Press, 2011), 80.

20. Swinton and Mowat, *Practical Theology and Qualitative Research*, 80.

21. Ibid., 83.

22. In chapter 3 I make a distinction between what I call *theocentric* and *humanistic* rituals. There I describe "humanistic liturgies" as ad hoc liturgies designed to address emergent pastoral situations with the primary aim of providing some therapeutic or practical benefit for its central participants.

23. Ibid., 85.

Chapter 1

Moral Injury as a Pastoral Theological Construct

Many of the landmark studies related to moral injury have been conducted by clinicians like the aforementioned psychiatrist Jonathan Shay and psychotherapist Edward Tick. It is such persons in the clinical world who first articulated calls for a ritual response to moral injury. One of the overarching tasks of this book is to investigate this perceived need for ritual care in moral injury from a pastoral theological perspective. The assumption and driving force of this particular chapter is that one must understand moral injury, as well as its effects on both the individual and community, in order to offer an appropriate pastoral response to it. Central to this task is formulating a theological definition of moral injury. Though various attempts at coming to a definition have been made and these definitions share a general notion of what moral injury entails, one must not ignore the variances as well. I seek to navigate and even reconcile these differences to an extent here. What one calls a moral injury and another a "soul wound," though similar, does not refer precisely to the same thing and their differences warrant articulation in a study like this. Many of these definitions and descriptions also hail from clinical perspectives and are generally written for other clinicians. I argue, however, that such clinical models cannot be inherited indiscriminately into a pastoral theological framework.

The unique contribution of this chapter is to explore moral injury from a pastoral theological perspective at the outset. This, I will later argue, begins with articulating a *telos* for pastoral care that is different than that of the clinical world. While some other pastoral theologians have addressed moral injury, the need remains for a sustained treatment on the nature of moral injury itself from a theological perspective that is in direct conversation with a broad swath of clinical and theological research on the subject. In addition, this study takes a unique direction by seeking to understand the phenomenon of moral injury with a view towards seeing how ritual in particular satisfies a spiritual need inherent in this unique form of trauma.

Section two of this chapter paints the backdrop for this study. By providing a summary of issues endemic to the veteran population, as well as the societal impact of trauma in general and moral injury in particular, I present a case for why these matters are pastoral concerns that deserve greater attention. In a way, these statistics serve as the impetus for this study. The focus of this section will be primarily at the societal level. Even as I later calibrate my focus more narrowly on moral injury proper, it is important to be reminded that MI is not just a matter of an individual and her guilt or simply one's relationship with God, but it manifests in ways that has broader implications for the community of faith, beginning with the veteran's family and ending no sooner than with society as a whole. The purpose of this section is not solely to emphasize the profound impact moral injury can have on the whole of society, but to provide a springboard for understanding the communal nature of illness and sin, as well as their healing—a point that will be elaborated further in subsequent chapters.

Section three offers a review of definitions of MI. Moral injury is a relatively new construct involving a phenomenon that easily evades visible detection and resists simple circumscription. As such, even though researchers look in the same general direction, there is yet to be a full consensus as to what this condition is. In this section I compile and analyze the various proposed definitions for moral injury by clinicians and theologians alike. Rather than being a simple summary of ideas, this review will highlight some of the problems inherent in previous definitions, particularly for use within the realm of pastoral theology in general and ritual care in particular.

Section four is an extension of the task of section one. Here I will explain how PTSD (and combat trauma in general) is related to moral injury. Once again, I will present varied views on this matter. Part of what has made moral injury so elusive as a recognizable condition in veterans is because its "symptoms," so to speak, are often subsumed or hidden within the larger phenomenon of Post Traumatic Stress Disorder (PTSD). Yet researchers and theorizers of moral injury disagree on the extent to which moral injury is in fact a part of PTSD or something different altogether. Therefore, just as important as arriving at a positive definition for moral injury is clarifying what it is not. What this section seeks to maintain, however, is that trauma is nevertheless an undeniable component of moral injury. This is an essential point to make here as I will later argue that it is because of the way that trauma forecloses rationality and appeals uniquely to the senses that moral injury necessitates something like ritual to address it.

Section five proffers a working definition of "moral injury" that will be the implied understanding of the phrase for the remainder of this study. With this definition I provide a detailed exposition of my lexical choices, which draw from and intentionally stand against aspects of prior definitions. More than anything, the definition is intended to stand apart as an understanding of MI that is grounded theologically from its foundation. By finally establishing MI as a pastoral theological construct, the study commences to explore ways in which this unique form of trauma can be addressed pastorally.

VETERANS' ISSUES AND TRAUMA AS SIGNIFICANT PASTORAL CONCERNS

Formulating a pastoral perspective on veteran care, moral injury, and trauma requires some background regarding the impact each of these matters have within the community. This section is dedicated first to establishing why each of these matters, which this study brings to the fore, are or should be significant pastoral concerns for the church community. As I set the stage for this study, I will move a bit beyond my primary focus of veterans suffering from moral injury, which I consider a form of trauma. One reason for broadening my scope here is that, to date, there have been no comprehensive sociological studies exclusively on the morally injured. In any case, without a general consensus regarding the very nature of moral injury, data regarding the numbers of such veterans and the effects of moral injury would be difficult to come by. On the other hand, considerable research has been conducted in recent years regarding Post Traumatic Stress Disorder (PTSD).[1] PTSD as a form of trauma cannot always be easily untangled from moral injury and, at times, MI is even subsumed within the category of PTSD. As a result, PTSD research can be illuminating for those investigating MI and its effects.

I also broaden my scope here by providing statistics regarding other social issues plaguing veterans as it is unrealistic to separate specific social issues, such as addiction, from phenomena like moral injury or PTSD, as trauma is a predictor of problems like substance abuse. These problems in turn lead to a constellation of other issues and the number of individuals affected in a secondary manner by the initial trauma only increases. For trauma is rarely just an individual psychological problem, but a bio-psycho-social, financial, and legal concern for the communities that bear them. Finally, I find it worthwhile to share some statistics regarding trauma in general, including among non-veteran populations, to draw attention to the fact that trauma may be a more common pastoral concern in life than clergy often recognize. Such data is not entirely unconnected to our focus on veterans too, as traumatized veterans can in turn be sources of trauma for non-veterans as well, whether within their families or in the wider community. In the end, my approach to ritual care will have implications for people even beyond the limits of those

14   *Chapter 1*

suffering from combat exposure. The information detailed here intends to illustrate a more holistic picture of the challenges faced within the veteran's world and the kind of impact trauma can have on the wider community. In short, this section should present a compelling case for why veteran care, moral injury, and trauma should be considered significant concerns requiring pastoral attention today.

Veterans in the US

Currently, there are about 16 million veterans in the United States, making about 6 percent of the adult population.[2] The veteran community, especially combat veterans, exhibits a number of significant social concerns that affect a broad span of elements related to personal health and welfare. For instance, statistics show that nearly 13 percent of the homeless adult population in the US are veterans.[3] Veterans, both who have deployed and those who have never deployed, have a suicide rate 1.5 times higher than that of the general population, resulting in about 17 suicide deaths per day.[4] A study at Brigham Young University also found that the first marriage of a combat veteran is 62 percent more likely to end in divorce or separation than the rest of the population.[5] Roughly one in three veterans report having been arrested at least once in their lives compared to fewer than one fifth of non-veterans.[6] These problems are compounded for certain veterans from minority populations and lower socioeconomic backgrounds who are already disproportionately represented in these statistical areas. Of course, none of these issues exists in isolation but each is interconnected with other problems, such as financial insolvency, that further perpetuate a plethora of other issues in a veteran's life.

PTSD and Moral Injury

The correlation between combat experience and social problems can be explained partly through the trauma these veterans sustain in battle. Research by the National Center for PTSD has demonstrated that PTSD continues to be a significant problem for veterans serving during times of war. Table 1.1 summarizes the Center's statistics regarding the instances of PTSD in each of the most recent wars/campaigns.

As one might expect, PTSD can be one of the precipitating factors that leads to each of the problems mentioned above. This demonstrates the complexity of veterans' issues. It is not simply that the symptoms of PTSD affect an individual's quality of life, but that they can lead to behaviors that result in grave ramifications and wider societal impact. A 2010 study funded by the Marine Corps and conducted by the Naval Health Research Center in San Diego surveyed 1,543 Marines with at least one combat tour and found

Moral Injury as a Pastoral Theological Construct

Table 1.1

Service Era	PTSD in the Past Year	PTSD at Some Point in Life
Operations Iraqi Freedom (OIF) and Enduring Freedom (OEF)	15 out of 100 (15%)	29 out of 100 (29%)
Persian Gulf War (Desert Storm)	14 out of 100 (14%)	21 out of 100 (21%)
Vietnam War	5 out of 100 (5%)	10 out of 100 (10%)
World War II (WWII) and Korean War	2 out of 100 (2%)	3 out of 100 (3%)

that Marines who had reported PTSD symptoms were more than six times as likely to engage in antisocial and aggressive behaviors than those who did not report PTSD symptoms. A similar study published in 1984 in the *Archives of General Psychiatry* found a "significant association between combat exposure and subsequent arrests and convictions that persisted when preservice background factors were controlled [for]."[7] As Shay explains, "Readiness to react instantly and violently when surprised, a learned skill in training and combat, often comes to haunt and impair veterans in civilian life."[8]

The consequences of such acts are not simply legal ones. A veteran may have to live with a profound sense of shame if his actions happen to hurt a family member or friend. Thus, moral injury, though precipitated by military training and war-time service, can actually occur off the battlefield as well. The National Center for PTSD reports significant connections between PTSD and substance abuse, specifically that more than 20 percent of veterans with PTSD also suffer from an addiction or dependence on drugs or alcohol.[9] Problems like substance abuse and aggressive behavior do not exist in a vacuum, but frequently lead to financial, relational, and legal issues.

Though no separate set of statistics has been produced regarding moral injury alone, in 2011, a survey was conducted of health and religious professionals familiar with moral injury and who have worked with active duty personnel and veterans. One of the questions included in the study was, "What are the signs and symptoms of moral injury?"[10] Among the responses, the most prevalent (70 percent) was "social problems."[11] This included social withdrawal, sociopathy, problems fitting in, legal and disciplinary problems, and parental alienation from their child. The second most common response category was "psychological and social functioning problems," which includes "occupational dysfunction."[12] Like PTSD, moral injury brings its own set of social and relational concerns that can affect the community at large.

Brett Litz—who defines moral injury as "perpetrating, failing to prevent, bearing witness to, or learning about acts that transgress deeply held moral beliefs and expectations"[13]—has attempted to sharpen the picture of this

16 *Chapter 1*

morally injured population by sifting through existing surveys about specific experiences veterans have had in war. He identified statistical data regarding the type of combat scenarios that generally fit the criteria for a morally injurious situation. Here, we garner a greater sense of the percentage of combat veterans exposed to circumstances with the potential for causing moral injury during Operations Iraqi Freedom and Enduring Freedom:

> In 2003, 52% of soldiers and Marines surveyed reported shooting or directing fire at the enemy, and 32% reported being directly responsible for the death of an enemy combatant (Hoge et al., 2004). Additionally . . . 60% reported having seen ill/wounded women and children who they were unable to help. The rates of exposure to violence and its aftermath remained high in a survey of soldiers in 2007 (Mental Health Advisory Team [MHAT-V], 2008) . . . Not surprisingly, a select field survey in theatre revealed that 27% of soldiers faced ethical situations during deployment in which they did not know how to respond (MHAT-V, 2008) . . . [I]n 2003, 20% of soldiers and Marines surveyed endorsed responsibility for the death of a non-combatant (Hoge, et al., 2004), arguably due to the ambiguity of the enemy . . . Also, using a similar methodology, in 2007, 31% indicated they had insulted or cursed at civilians, 5% indicated mistreating civilians, and 11% reported damaging property unnecessarily (MHAT-V, 2008).[14]

Killing someone seems to have a particularly significant impact on the well-being of the combat veteran. A recent study has further solidified the connection between killing-related exposure[15] to morbid thoughts and suicidal ideation (MTSI).[16] Killing-related exposure approximately doubles the risk of MTSI, and also increases the MTSI risk associated with other suicide vulnerability factors like depression, alcohol dependence, and readjustment stress. One of the conclusions of the study was that greater attention needed to be placed on the "morally injurious" experiences of combat veterans.[17]

Trauma

As we discuss the role of ritual in the care of veterans suffering from MI, we are, broadly speaking, inviting pastoral attention to the realm of trauma in human life. Many of the reasons for which ritual presents a faithful response to the problem of moral injury—as posited by this study—apply to the general category of trauma as well. Unfortunately, the military is also rife with trauma not tied directly to combat, among them Military Sexual Trauma (MST). According to the National Center for PTSD:

> MST includes any sexual activity during military service where a Veteran was involved against their will. They may have been:
>
> • Pressured into sexual activities

Moral Injury as a Pastoral Theological Construct

- Unable to consent to sexual activities
- Physically forced into sexual activities

Other experiences that fall into the category of MST include:

- Unwanted sexual touching or grabbing, including during "hazing" experiences
- Offensive remarks about a person's body or sexual activities that they found threatening
- Unwelcome sexual advances a person found threatening[18]

National data reveal that about 1 in 3 women and 1 in 50 men have experienced MST.[19] Though the rate is higher amongst women, the total numbers of men and women who report having MST are fairly balanced due to the prevalence of men in the armed forces. It is important to note that these statistics only reflect the reports of those who have received care from the VA and that it is possible the numbers are higher across the board.

Trauma is not primarily the domain of military life and neither is PTSD. Seventy percent of US adults have experienced at least one traumatic event in their lives.[20] Trauma, however, does not necessarily result in PTSD. About 6 out of every 100 people will have PTSD at some point in their lives. In 2020, about 13 million Americans had PTSD. Women are more likely to develop PTSD than men. About 8 of every 100 women develop PTSD some time in their lives compared with about 4 of every 100 men.[21] Sexual assault, violence and substance abuse are significant sources of trauma for the general population as well. Bessel Van der Kolk states that an alarming twelve million women in the United States have been victims of rape and more than half of all rapes occur in girls below age fifteen.[22] It seems that children are particularly vulnerable to traumatic experiences. Each year about three million children in the United States are reported as victims of child abuse and neglect.[23] The Centers for Disease Control and Prevention reports that one in five Americans is sexually molested as a child; one in four is beaten by a parent to the point of a mark being left on their body; and one in three couples engages in physical violence.[24] A quarter of the population grows up with alcoholic relatives, and one out of eight has witnessed their mother being beaten or hit.[25] The way that Van der Kolk frames the plight of children is that, "for every soldier who serves in a war zone abroad, there are ten children who are endangered in their own homes."[26] Some of these children grow up to be veterans and it has been shown that those with prior PTSD are at a much higher risk for developing PTSD from subsequent traumas, such as participation in war.[27]

Trauma in general, therefore, is a real yet often hidden pastoral concern in the life of the church. Trauma affects young and old, men and women, veteran and non-veteran. Combat veterans, however, seem to be especially susceptible to complex trauma and its effects. Moreover, combat trauma may be more common now in our communities than in any previous era. The benefits of improved body armor and medical interventions means fewer deaths on the field, but it also means more wounded coming home struggling with readjustment. These men and women return saddled with the grief over the loss of comrades, physical and mental capabilities, and even their sense of self.[28] Yet the burden of trauma is not borne solely by returning veterans. What Grossman states regarding the long-term legacy of the Vietnam War upon American society is true of other wars as well. He writes, "[It] is not just hundreds of thousands of troubled veterans, it is also hundreds of thousands of troubled marriages impacting women, children, and future generations. For we know that children of broken families are more likely to be physically and sexually abused, and that children of divorce are more likely to become divorced as adults, and that victims of child abuse are more likely to become child-abusing adults."[29] As Shay puts it, "Unhealed combat trauma blights not only the life of the veteran but the life of the family and community. In some instances, such as in the Weimar Republic in Germany after World War I, it can substantially weaken the society as a whole."[30]

Unhealed trauma also incurs a *literal* cost on society. "When violence against others results in injury," Shay writes, "society incurs the costs of medical care and lost productivity of the victims of this violence."[31] Considering that one out of every three veterans has been arrested at least once in their lifetimes, it is worth noting that the average court costs for someone arrested in 2015 was $13,607.[32] The government also shoulders a significant financial burden to mitigate the effects of trauma in veterans' lives. Between 2007 and 2010, the Department of Defense spent more than $2.7 billion for the treatment of and research on PTSD in combat veterans, while in fiscal year 2009 alone the Department of Veterans Affairs spent $24.5 million on in-house PTSD research.[33] One can add to this the $4.5 billion the Departments of Defense and Veterans Affairs spent on antidepressants, antipsychotics, and antianxiety drugs in one decade alone.[34]

Despite the resources poured into the study and treatment of trauma, efforts to alleviate conditions like PTSD and moral injury through traditional medical and psychotherapeutic means have not yielded optimum results. For instance, a 2010 report revealed that of the 49,425 veterans with newly diagnosed PTSD from the Iraq and Afghanistan wars who sought care from the VA, fewer than one out of ten actually completed the recommended treatment.[35] Even in my own encounters with veterans, it is apparent that while some of the most debilitating symptoms of PTSD might be reined in after months or even years of treatment, many will continue to struggle with issues like persistent anxiety and sleeplessness, and a pronounced absence of joy and sense of purpose. And if it is not their PTSD symptoms they are fighting against, it is the side effects of the medications for PTSD they are taking that they are struggling to manage. Many will opt out of these standard treatments, willing to live with a heightened level of anxiety rather than suffer from the flattening effect anxiolytics can have upon one's mood. As alluded to earlier, there seems to be even less recourse for those suffering from moral injury. Often mistaken for PTSD, these less-than-optimal treatment modalities for PTSD would be applied to moral injury with even less success.

All this is not simply to say that veterans require greater pastoral attention because a disproportionate number of them suffer from moral injury. The statistics I have presented here highlight two points that serve as the backdrop for this study. First, trauma in general is a significant issue that leaves no segment of society untouched and leads to deleterious effects upon communities. Second, the veteran population is a vulnerable one, not only because of moral injury, but because of a panoply of issues that reside disproportionately in this community. Moral injury, however, may be one of the more complicated issues that regularly surfaces amongst veterans, and it is one that pastors are particularly well-positioned to address. It is to this issue that I now direct my focus.

MORAL INJURY: A REVIEW OF DEFINITIONS

What specifically do I mean by "moral injury"? Despite the growing awareness of this concept among veteran care providers, a consensus definition has eluded this community. Most chaplains and mental health providers to veterans will have heard of the term, but one cannot assume that any two people will mean precisely the same thing when they use it. Not being a tangible condition observable by the eye, like a laceration or even cancer cells under a microscope, moral injury is recognized or defined most often by the circumstances that can cause it (which are various), or the symptoms that manifest from having such an injury (which are also various). Moral injury is also difficult to detect because the very nature of it is such that it wishes not to be revealed, like shame. As the moral injury hides within the depths of the soul, the individual bearing this burden may evade any discussion of it or even recuse herself from participation in wider society as a whole—a sort of self-imposed excommunication—in order to avoid its detection. And when signs of moral injury do manifest before the eyes of clinicians or caregivers of veterans, these "symptoms" are frequently secreted under the larger umbrella of PTSD and treated as such. Given these realities, this section will offer a review of various descriptions and definitions proposed for this elusive condition.

20 *Chapter 1*

I will first consider those definitions and descriptions that identify moral injury and its synonyms as a unique form of combat trauma. Next, I will highlight the observations of those authors who may not recognize moral injury by name, but nevertheless describe phenomena with relation to veterans consonant with most descriptions of moral injury. As part of this survey, I will discuss some of the problems of these proposed definitions, particularly for use from a pastoral theological perspective.

Definitions by Those Who Recognize Moral Injury as a Distinct Condition

The name, "moral injury," itself is an appropriate place to begin. It is true that not everyone who recognizes this phenomenon amongst combat veterans necessarily uses or prefers to use the phrase "moral injury." Nevertheless, this phrase has enough currency within this community of caregivers and researchers that they recognize to what type of phenomenon one is referring. The majority of the alternative names proposed for this condition over the years have been in fact conscious alternatives or offshoots to the usage of "moral injury," further underlining this term's ubiquity and perhaps its early provenance in the history of these studies. I thus include under this subheading any researcher who recognizes moral injury by that term or any variation of it. The key is that those in this category recognize this as a distinct condition. That does not mean, as I will present here, that every person defines moral injury or its variants in precisely the same way. Yet there is enough parity and mutual discourse to warrant this grouping. I will begin with those who explicitly use the term "moral injury," and then move to those who seem to pull away from that term.

Psychologist Brett Litz and his team have meticulously outlined the shape of moral injury and proposed treatment plans to address the needs of those suffering from this condition. Through his extensive research, Litz contends that "An act of serious transgression that leads to serious inner conflict because the experience is at odds with core ethical and moral beliefs is called moral injury. More specifically, moral injury has been defined as 'perpetrating, failing to prevent, bearing witness to, or learning about acts that transgress deeply held moral beliefs and expectations' (Litz et al., 2009)."[36] There are several distinguishing marks of this definition. For one, moral injury is presented fundamentally as an *act*. Herein lies some of the difficulty of defining what seems to be predominantly an internal state—whether it be emotional, psychological, or spiritual—as an "injury." Injuries are most often conceived as the *results* of harmful actions upon a person. For instance, if I were to run a sharp knife over my skin, my injury would be the resulting laceration, not the "act" of cutting myself. If I were to show my injury to a doctor, I would show the doctor the bleeding gash and not the slicing motion of the knife, though informing the doctor about the act would give some clues as to the nature of the injury. But if Litz's words are to be taken literally, the transgressive act is the injury itself. As a result, there is something inherently elliptical about such a definition. Litz's *act* is also described as being that of transgressing certain beliefs. This is a common refrain in Litz's work. Throughout his discussions of moral injury, one will find that for him this injury is ultimately grounded on beliefs. Hence, the primary symptom of moral injury is that of "serious inner conflict" arising from the dissonance between one's actions and beliefs.[37] This to an extent makes moral injury relative to each individual and/or her own milieu. The assumption then is that there are some acts that could be considered deeply transgressive to one person, resulting in moral injury, while of little consequence to another. This once again sets moral injury apart from, say, a flesh wound, further complicating the conventional notion of "injury." How one's arm responds to a bullet is not entirely relative to each person's constitution, as injury from a gunshot will result one hundred percent of the time. Finally, salient to Litz's conception of moral injury is a matter of degree. What this condition entails is a "*serious* transgression," "*serious* inner conflict," and the transgression of "*deeply* held moral beliefs."[38] For Litz, minor transgressions of beliefs held with only modest conviction therefore do not equate with or result in moral injury.

As far as definitions go, that of Warren Kinghorn, a medical doctor of psychiatry with a doctorate in theology, is more or less in line with Litz's. He describes moral injury as "the experience of having acted (or consented to others acting) incommensurably with one's most deeply held moral conceptions."[39] Citing Litz's 2009 study, Kinghorn acknowledges that this may involve "participating in or witnessing inhumane or cruel actions, failing to prevent the immoral acts of others, as well as engaging in subtle acts or experiencing reactions that, upon reflection, transgress a moral code, [or] bearing witness to the aftermath of violence and human carnage."[40] Kinghorn, however, cautions against Litz's tendency to view moral injury as primarily a psychological construct. Kinghorn's main concern, as will be discussed in more detail later in this chapter, is taking what is a moral-theological matter and treating it like a medical one. Kinghorn highlights the limitation of situating moral injury within medical models when it comes to identification:

> Psychological and moral injuries resemble flesh-and-blood injuries not univocally but, at best, by family resemblance. In each case there is indeed traumatic disruption followed by attempts at self-repair and, if all goes well, healing. In each case, the care of others may be necessary to facilitate this healing. But visible wounds to the body, however they might affect the experiencing self, can be formally identified without specific consideration of the soldier's response

22 *Chapter 1*

to them. A soldier may be relatively unfazed by a bodily wound, or may be psychologically devastated; but the wound can be considered apart from, and in some sense prior to, its effect on the experiencing self. In the case of psychological and moral injury, on the other hand, the wound is known only through the soldier's psychological and moral response to the experience of combat; epistemologically, it is that response.[41]

This recognition is reflected in his definition of moral injury. Whereas for Litz moral injury is located in an act, for Kinghorn moral injury is the response to an act. As he words it, moral injury is *the experience of having acted* incommensurably."[42] To invoke my analogy yet again, the injury for Kinghorn is not located in the act of cutting one's arm (as in Litz) or the gash itself, but the experience, presumably the resulting pain, that emanates from the act of cutting. As he notes, in moral injury no wound can be formally identified; it is known only by the experiencing self.

Rita Nakashima Brock and Gabriella Lettini's *Soul Repair* was the first pastoral theological text to address moral injury directly. At the same time, of all the works addressed here that explicitly mention the phrase, "moral injury," Brock and Lettini's definition may be the most elusive. For one, the theologians never quite arrive at one. What they describe in detail is what may cause this condition or from what this "injury" may result. "Moral injury," they write, "is the *result* of reflection on memories of war or other extreme traumatic conditions. It comes from having transgressed one's basic moral identity and violated core moral beliefs."[43] This definition has more in common with Kinghorn's than Litz's. To use my macabre analogy, injury for Brock and Lettini is what happens after having reflected on the memory of cutting oneself; it is not the act itself (as according to Litz). Nonetheless, Brock and Lettini's notion of injury is removed one step further from the precipitating trauma than Kinghorn's. Whereas Kinghorn's injury *is* the *experience* of *having acted*, Brock and Lettini's injury (whatever it is) occurs *following reflection* on these transgressive acts. Observe also the differences in terminology. Brock and Lettini's terminology is far more cognitive than Kinghorn's—note their usage of the word "reflection" rather than the word "experience."[44] They also use Litz's words, "moral *beliefs*,"[45] rather than Kinghorn's "moral *conceptions*."[46] The theologians go on to explain that "Moral injury results when soldiers violate their core moral beliefs, and in evaluating their behavior negatively, they feel they no longer live in a reliable, meaningful world and can no longer be regarded as decent human beings."[47] Brock and Lettini's moral injury comes as a result of a largely rational assessment of one's self and world based on past behavior.

Clinical psychologist Kent Drescher, in a team that included Brett Litz, conducted a study that explored "the viability and usefulness of the construct of moral injury in war veterans."[48] This study is particularly useful to our discussion as the researchers not only proposed a working definition of moral injury, but they sought out health and religious professionals who have worked with veterans to glean their thoughts regarding this proposed construct. Drescher's proposed definition of moral injury is as follows: "Disruption in an individual's confidence and expectations about one's own or others' motivation or capacity to behave in a just and ethical manner. This injury is brought about by bearing witness to perceived immoral acts, failure to stop such actions, or perpetration of immoral acts, in particular actions that are inhumane, cruel, depraved, or violent, bringing about pain, suffering, or death of others."[49]

"Disruption" may be the term so far most compatible with the conceptual framework of "injury." What is a flesh wound if not a *rupturing* of the skin? It is not the *act* of cutting, or the *experience* of having cut, or the *result* of a *reflection* on the memory of having cut oneself. In a sense, one may say that with Drescher's definition, moral injury has finally made contact with the point of trauma. Drescher also indicates the location of the disruption, noting that moral injury is the rupturing of an *individual's confidence* and *expectations*[50]—the very fabric of one's "morals" perhaps, the skin upon which the injurious knife is dealt. One must wonder, however, whether moral injury is contingent upon the status of an individual's confidence and expectations, and whether their disruption will always result anytime anyone bears witness to immoral acts, fails to stop such actions, or perpetrates such acts. And if moral injury does not occur every time, one would have to ask what the difference is in the constitution of one who experiences moral injury and one who does not.

The name most often associated with "moral injury," at least within VA and military circles, is that of psychiatrist Jonathan Shay. Ironically, the books he is known for, *Achilles in Vietnam* and *Odysseus in America*, do not rely so much on technical phrases like "moral injury" as describe ruined,[51] injured,[52] or damaged[53] *character*. Shay nevertheless accepts and has used the phrase "moral injury" in his multiple speaking engagements with military and VA personnel. In one webinar he even offered his own comprehensive definition of the term, which he broke into three parts, as follows:

1. Betrayal of what's right [that's in the culture's code of what's praiseworthy and blameworthy]
2. By someone holding legitimate authority [that's in the social system]
3. In a high stakes situation [in the mind of the person being injured—often poignantly love for a comrade][54]

24   *Chapter 1*

In this webinar, Shay distinguishes his own definition from that of Nash, Litz, and Maguen, who he sees breaking down moral injury in the following way:

1. Betrayal of what's right
2. By the self ["I did it"]
3. In a high stakes situation[55]

The difference between the two is particularly clear in the second step, where Shay sees the betrayal as being that of someone in authority, whereas most others situate the betrayal in the self, as a betrayal of one's moral standards. Yet Shay does not seek to absolve the acting agent in war of all responsibility. His differing conception of moral injury may lie more in his anthropology. One can see in his definition a view of the combatant that is unavoidably situated in and substantiated by his context. His very notion of what is right, that is violated, is given to him by his culture. The soldier's actions and inactions in war are not entirely driven by an isolated will. For example, in his webinar, Shay describes a hypothetical, but quite realistic situation, in which a sergeant commands a GI not to stay behind to save a fellow soldier so as not to compromise the rest of the squad.[56] Elsewhere, Shay gives the example of armed personnel being commanded to fire on civilians or disarmed, unresisting prisoners.[57] In both cases the combatant under orders has a choice, but is nevertheless compelled by a superior to act in a certain way. These elements thus create the high stakes situations, which he describes as often being created by love for a comrade—once again, only possible as a person-in-context. He writes, "We are just one writer: brain/body, mind, social actor, and culture inhabitant at every instant. None of these has ontological priority."[58] Another reason for Shay's emphasis on what he calls "leadership malpractice"[59] is due to his activist posture. Much of the impetus for his work as an author, academic, and public speaker is to drive policy changes relating to the way military personnel are trained and deployed. For him the someone-holding-legitimate-authority[60] is not just one's immediate superior, but the broader military culture reinforced by the chain of command. Shay does not reject the notion of injury by self-betrayal, but instead recognizes that his conception of moral injury can lead to the kind of moral injury espoused by Litz.

As far as pinpointing the essence of moral injury goes, Shay's definition thus far is about as elusive as Brock and Lettini's. Shay is more precise in defining moral injury in an article written for *Daedalus*, where he states that "*Moral injury is present when* (1) there has been a betrayal of what's right (2) by someone who holds legitimate authority (3) in a high-stakes situation."[61] Like Brock, Shay describes the conditions during which moral injury occurs without actually describing what moral injury is. Yet in this same article the psychiatrist makes a compelling note that moral injury is one category of psychological injury.[62] On this point Shay seems to deviate from Brock's view that "Veterans with moral injury have souls in anguish, not a psychological disorder."[63]

For various reasons, there are those within the community of veteran care who do not prefer the phrase "moral injury" and so refer to this phenomenon by another name. This is not always about semantics alone, as certain theorizers believe that the term "moral injury" represents a misconception of what is truly at the heart of a combat veteran's suffering. The most prominent clinician who deals directly with these matters, albeit by a different name, is psychotherapist Edward Tick. Tick has proposed the phrase "soul wound"[64] in lieu of the usual nomenclature. The word "soul" comes from Tick's belief that every person has a "warrior soul," which he describes as "that part of us that wishes to serve with high honor for moral purpose."[65] Tick explains regarding this warrior soul that, "when trained or used in illegitimate, abusive, disproportionate, or immoral ways, it is wounded. When used in moral ways for immoral ends, it is in anguish. When alone and unseen in its willingness to sacrifice life, when its pain is neglected, it falls into despair."[66] Tick thus eschews using the ambiguous word "moral" when naming this phenomenon. Indeed, it is actually never quite clear what is meant by the word "moral" in "moral injury." Is it used in the sense of the inverse of a "moral victory," which says less about the person and more about the circumstances of an event, or does moral refer to an aspect that exists within human nature? Tick sidesteps this conundrum by naming the very aspect of the human that he sees receiving harm under such traumatic circumstances, the soul. The word, "soul," however, is undoubtedly a complex word with various meanings in various traditions. In this case Tick seems to identify the soul with that ethical component of the human that can be nourished by honorable actions or wounded by *im*-morality.

Tick is also very deliberate in the use of the word "wound" as opposed to "injury." His reasoning is as follows:

> We commonly say that a person was "injured in an accident" but "wounded in battle." Injury comes from the Latin in juris, meaning not fair or right. It connotes damage or harm done to us as victims of circumstances or others' actions. A wound, on the other hand, connotes violence done by or to the sufferer. War causes moral wounding, moral trauma, as well as "injury" because it results not from happenstance but from the violence that human beings do. When we refer to a wound, visible or not, we recognize that warriors have survived violent exchanges with others, suffer for it, and are forever different. . . . Patients are ill. Victims are injured. Society is disordered. Warriors are wounded.[67]

Tick's concern is that the word encapsulates the feature commonly understood in moral injury, which recognizes that the sufferer may have been the perpetrator of violence, not just the recipient of it. This will be one of the main elements that distinguishes moral injury from PTSD, a matter discussed in the following section.

Tick is not the only stakeholder in the care of veterans who has proposed a different title to that of moral injury. Drescher's study, referenced above, involved asking a group of clinicians and chaplains whether the label was adequate. Some offered alternatives to the word "moral" preferring *spiritual* injury, *emotional* injury, *personal values* injury, and *life values* injury.[68] Alternatives to the word injury resulted in the suggested names of moral *trauma*, moral *wounds*, and moral *disruption*.[69] The real revolution of Tick's "soul wound" is doing away with the word "moral." By doing so, Tick simplifies the analogy between a "moral" injury and a physical one. The locus of harm is clearly identified. Tick ventures beyond the lexical restraints of the clinical world that seems to stifle others when it comes to trying to circumscribe what he believes are matters related to the soul. Though "soul" may still be an ambiguous term—and notably a term that Tick does not explicitly define—at the very least it seems to correspond to a concrete dimension and not an epiphenomenon of the human being.

Descriptions by Those Who Recognize the Phenomenon without Naming the Condition

Even though many clinicians, pastors, and theologians today are still unaware of the term "moral injury," one would be mistaken to assume these caregivers are completely agnostic to the moral and spiritual complications that can arise from combat trauma. Since the advent of the "Global War on Terrorism," several books have been published that recognize such phenomena amongst returning veterans without actually using the particular phrase "moral injury." I will briefly summarize their insights in this section. What I have looked for in each book is the author's presentation of at least these two elements of moral injury most often recognized by those who theorize regarding this condition: (1) the perpetration of martial acts that (2) results in some form of "moral" or spiritual turmoil. While specialists in the field often claim that there is more to moral injury than this, this dual aspect is what most uniquely sets apart this condition from other forms of trauma, particularly PTSD. I am especially interested in the way these authors conceptualize the nature of the injury, that most elusive aspect of this condition.

Psychologist Aphrodite Matsakis in her text *Back from the Front* seems as though she would follow Shay by locating moral injury in the psyche. She writes, "Just as the body can be traumatized, so can the psyche. On the psychological level, trauma refers to the wounding of your emotions, your spirit, your will to live, your beliefs about yourself and the world, your dignity, and your sense of security."[70] While Matsakis uses the ambiguous language of "wounding" such things as one's "emotions" and "your beliefs about yourself and the world" (somewhat reminiscent of Drescher's "disruption" of "confidence and expectations"),[71] it is notable that for her the psyche involves such things as one's "spirit."[72] The author, unfortunately, does not elaborate on what she means by "spirit." Matsakis also recognizes a number of the acts in war that are often said to lead to moral injury, such as dehumanizing the enemy, viewing corpses, not living up to the image of the ideal self, violation of religious or spiritual beliefs,[73] killing in ambiguous war situations, witnessing or participating in atrocities,[74] and engaging in sexual improprieties.[75] All of this she frames under the general terminology of trauma that can be either bodily or psychological.

As far as morally injurious experiences go, Chaplain John Sippola in his book, *Welcome Them Home—Help Them Heal*, only talks briefly about the difficulty coping with killing another person as it may conflict with one's upbringing and lifelong directive, "You shalt not kill."[76] Sippola does not make any distinction between "legitimate" killings from "illegitimate" killings in war, as some authors might. To kill at all, he seems to say, can create dissonance for anyone raised with particular religious beliefs prohibiting such acts. In fact, this points toward one of the main thrusts of Dave Grossman's book, *On Killing*. The counselor and Army veteran argues that for most people—the primary exception being sociopaths—there is an inherent resistance to killing. Therefore, anyone who has ever had to kill an enemy will have experienced conflict during and after this act. He describes the basic response stages to killing in combat as follows: concern about killing, the actual kill, exhilaration, remorse, and rationalization and acceptance.[77] The stages are generally sequential, he notes, but not necessarily universal, as some persons may skip or blend certain stages. With regards to the stage of remorse, however, he writes, "Whether the killer denies his remorse, deals with it, or is overwhelmed by it, it is nevertheless almost always there. The killer's remorse is real, it is common, it is intense, and it is something that he must deal with for the rest of his life."[78] It seems there is something particularly powerful about this stage that grabs hold of the individual. Especially when killing at close range, when one is able to view the fallen target, the brief feeling of euphoria is almost instantly overwhelmed with a sense of guilt.[79] This guilt is so strong that there are multiple documented accounts of veterans sharing that they felt such a sense of physical revulsion that they vomited after the kill. This remorse complicates the subsequent stage of attempting to rationalize and accept what one has done. Grossman writes, "This process may never truly be completed. The killer never completely leaves all remorse

28   *Chapter 1*

and guilt behind, but he can usually come to accept that what he has done was necessary and right."[80] Note that here, like Sippola, Grossman is addressing killing in general and is not focusing on the committing of atrocities in war.

On the other hand, in their discussion of the guilt brought on by participation in war, social worker Darlene Wetterstrom, along with chaplain-counselor David Thompson, relays the harrowing real-life example of a Vietnam veteran who drunkenly plowed through refugees with his vehicle in an act of self-preservation in war. In their book, *Beyond the Yellow Ribbon*, they write, "Many veterans who have done things they are not proud of in war struggle spiritually later in life because they feel guilty and unworthy of forgiveness for sins in their youth."[81] They point to ensuing "spiritual" problems and later mention a need for the "ministry of absolution,"[82] placing the resolution of the matter squarely within the domain of the church. Psychiatrists Matthew Friedman and Laurie Slone take a decidedly less religious or spiritual perspective on such matters in their book *After the War Zone*. They generally view such experiences as matters of guilt or remorse over actions done or not done in war. "Guilt," they write, "results when people act against their moral values, doing things that are contrary to their beliefs."[83] In a direct address to any of their combat veteran readers, they take a much more sympathetic and positive tone regarding what may have transpired while in battle. For instance, they highlight the experience of fear in battle as a potential source of guilt for combat personnel.[84] However, unlike Wetterstrom and Thompson they do not discuss the possibility that a soldier may be guilt-stricken over having committed atrocities against civilians or the unarmed. Friedman and Slone's way of talking through the guilt is having the combatants recognize that they are trained to follow orders and that they are placed in situations resulting in outcomes they may not have been able to prevent. Friedman and Slone reason that these combat veterans had little choice or control over these morally injurious situations. Whether this is a sufficient response to the morally injured will be dealt with later in this book.

This section offered a review of definitions for moral injury as well as descriptions for similar phenomena as understood by veteran care providers. Such a review would not be complete without addressing how these professionals understand the relationship between moral injury and PTSD. Again, there are a variety of opinions on this matter and these views contribute further insight into what MI is by also stating what it is not. I summarize the thoughts of MI specialists on this relationship in the following section.

THE RELATIONSHIP BETWEEN
PTSD AND MORAL INJURY

Just as there are varied definitions of moral injury that hover over the same general conceptual geography but do not all touch on the exact same points; similarly, the views on how MI relates to PTSD agree on certain points but do not align entirely. There are two main schools of thought regarding the relationship between MI and PTSD: First, that MI is an extension of PTSD, and second, that MI is a distinct but overlapping condition with PTSD. It is essential for the purpose of this study to note that in either case, the psychological understanding of trauma plays a significant role in moral injury.

Moral Injury as an Extension of PTSD

Jonathan Shay is the main proponent of the notion that moral injury is or should be viewed as an extension of PTSD. Shay once lamented that "The public, press, congress use PTSD as an umbrella word for everything bad that happens in the mind and spirit as a result of going to war."[85] Yet Shay's complaint did not seem to be primarily that PTSD was over-diagnosed by the general public, but that perhaps they missed the mark when it counted most. Shay's issue has long been that the official definition of PTSD was too narrow, that it did not include such conditions as moral injury. He, like others, points out that PTSD is fear-based, that it involves the persistence of valid adaptations that the mind and body make to danger even once the threat is gone.[86] This is what Shay terms "simple PTSD."[87] He goes even further to clarify that this is actually not a *disorder*, but an *injury*, as PTSD "is probably rooted in an array of changes in the physiology and anatomy of the central nervous system—and may be irreversible. . . . As with any injury, the symptoms can range from mild to devastating, depending on the severity of the wound, the robustness of health at the time of the injury, and the conditions—especially nutrition—under which recovery occurred. In the case of a physical wound what counts is physical nutrition; in the case of a psychological injury what counts is *social* nutrition."[88]

What Shay identifies as moral injury then would be "complex PTSD,"[89] that is, when this aforementioned post-traumatic stress injury invades character, "and the capacity for social trust is destroyed, all possibility of flourishing human life is lost."[90] To develop a treatment program focused on the fear-based aspect of trauma is grossly inadequate as Shay argues that the essential injuries in combat PTSD are *moral* and *social*, and consequently require treatment that is morally and socially based.[91] Tick seems to say as much when he argues that "PTSD is primarily a moral, spiritual, and aesthetic

30   *Chapter 1*

disorder—in effect, not a *psychological* but a *soul* disorder."[92] Grossman's
work supports this view, disputing the claim that most trauma in war is the
fear of death and injury—the classic description of PTSD. According to him,
clinical studies that attempt to demonstrate the dominance of fear in war
trauma have been consistently unsuccessful.[93] Instead, what Grossman deems
to be the main sources of trauma are the more intimate, personal threats to
one's life (as opposed to accidental threats, or indiscriminate bombing), and
the responsibility to kill.[94] Therefore, what Grossman and all these other
clinicians have in common is that they believe that PTSD, as it is currently
defined, does not adequately encapsulate the traumatic experiences of veterans in war. They all see missing within this diagnosis the mention of that
common phenomena of injury to character and the soul, due not to experiences of fear, but something closer to moral failure. Moral injury for them is
not a separate and distinct condition, but an oft unrecognized and fundamental aspect of PTSD.

Moral Injury as Separate from PTSD

In stark contrast, the theologians Brock and Lettini are direct in their assertion that "Moral Injury is not PTSD."[95] As they have noted, "Veterans with
moral injury have souls in anguish, not a psychological disorder."[96] Drescher
and Litz may agree that MI is not PTSD, but it is not evident that they would
be willing to withdraw MI from the domain of psychopathology. Everyone
recognizes that PTSD manifests from traumatic victimization or life-threat
trauma, hence Shay's fear-based characterization of "simple PTSD."[97] The
clinicians and pastors who separate MI from PTSD, however, contrast the two
by emphasizing that those suffering from MI may be perpetrators, not solely
victims. In other words, the suffering from moral injury is often that of guilt
or shame from having acted (or not acted) in a certain manner, as opposed to
the persistent unwelcome adaptations to fear. Shay stops short of including
the perpetration of trauma in his definition of MI, though he will say that MI
damages character.[98] In addition to separating the life-threat trauma of PTSD
from the MI of perpetrating trauma, Drescher and Litz also distinguish the
two based on some of the diverging symptoms of these conditions. Drescher
summarizes a list of common symptoms reported among combat veterans
with PTSD that are *not included* as PTSD diagnostic criteria, but which he
argues might be related to moral injury (which in this case includes both
the committing of atrocities and the participation in sanctioned war-zone
killings):

> (a) Negative changes in ethical attitudes and behavior (Mental Health Advisory
> Team, 2006); (b) change in, or loss of spirituality (Drescher & Foy, 1995;

Fontana & Rosenheck, 2004), including negative attributions about God (Witvliet, Phipps, Feldman, & Beckham, 2004); (c) guilt, shame, and forgiveness problems (Kubany, Abueg, Kilauano, Manke, & Kaplan, 1997; Witvliet et al., 2004); (d) anhedonia and dysphoria (Kashdan, Elhai, & Frueh, 2006, 2007); (e) reduced trust in others and in social/ cultural contracts (Kubany, Gino, Denny, & Torigoe, 1994); (f) aggressive behaviors (Begic & Jokic-Begic, 2001); and (g) poor self-care (Schnurr & Spiro, 1999) or self-harm (Bras et al., 2007; Lyons, 1991; Pitman, 1990; Sher, 2009). These are problems not included as criterion symptoms leading to a PTSD diagnosis (though some are listed as associated symptoms) but are frequently reported by combat veterans under clinical care.[99]

This survey was conducted prior to the release of the DSM-V. The newer edition of the DSM shows a slight shift in the way in which PTSD is presented. The DSM-V introduces a new symptom cluster under PTSD described as "Negative alterations in cognitions and mood associated with the traumatic event(s), beginning or worsening after the traumatic event(s) occurred."[100] This symptom cluster may manifest in such ways as "Persistent and exaggerated negative beliefs or expectations about oneself, others, or the world," "Persistent, distorted cognitions about the cause of consequences of the traumatic event(s) that lead the individual to blame himself/herself or others," "Persistent negative emotional state (e.g., fear, horror, anger, guilt, or shame), and "Persistent inability to experience positive emotions," among other symptoms.[101] These new criteria touch upon some of the symptoms presented for MI, but still stop short of approximating any definition of MI proposed above.[102]

Regardless of the extent to which clinicians or pastors distinguish PTSD from MI, there is universal agreement on three fronts: First, they believe that a fear-based understanding of combat trauma alone does not sufficiently account for why veterans are traumatized by war; second, they see that there is often a moral component to trauma that is overlooked in current diagnostic criteria; third, they seem to agree that the very recognition of the existence of moral injuries and its difference from PTSD, as it is currently defined, is important in providing proper care to veterans. This final point is a significant one. Drescher,[103] Maguen, and Litz[104] consider current PTSD treatments as not adequately dealing with the effects of moral injury. Indeed, reason would suggest that fundamentally different injuries would require different responses.[105] This distinction is particularly salient if one is moving from the domain of the mind, a psychological injury, to that of the whole human, inclusive of body, soul, and spirit, as I will outline in my definition of moral injury that follows.

32   *Chapter 1*

ARRIVING AT A PASTORAL
THEOLOGICAL DEFINITION

Based upon these reflections concerning moral injury (whether recognized by name or not), I seek to arrive here at my own definition of moral injury that will henceforth be the implied understanding of the phrase throughout this study. While I have my qualms about the term "moral injury" itself, this study will not be proposing any alternative titles for this condition, except to add the qualifying words "combat-related," as will be seen below. I refrain from engaging in the activity of renaming largely for two reasons: (1) While some names may be more accurate than others, no name will encapsulate fully and precisely something that is so complex; and (2) by retaining the name "moral injury" this study intends to remain conversant with those researchers in the majority who use this term. In this section I will propose my working definition for MI and then follow up with my rationale for my choices.

My definition of moral injury proper is as follows: *A disruption in the body, soul, and spirit, resulting from encountering or participating in sin.* To be clear, understanding moral injury theologically in this manner does not preclude recognizing that moral injury can still be a "trauma" in the clinical sense. Combat-related moral injury, which will be the focus of this study, refers specifically to those traumatic moral injuries received through participation in war, injuries resulting especially from the trauma of committing, witnessing, hearing about, or failing to prevent atrocities in war.[106] I will explain below the choices made in formulating this definition.

Moral Injury as Resulting from "Sin"

One of the most distinguishing aspects of this proposed definition of moral injury is that it invokes the language of sin. The word "sin" seems to be a natural choice in moving from a largely clinical definition of *moral* injury to a pastoral theological one. As Paul D. Fritts contends, "moral injury is a psychologically descriptive label for the normative problem of sin."[107] One cannot help but think that the elusive and often circuitous definitions of MI typically provided by these clinicians have come about because of their avoidance of such terms as "soul" and "sin." Such terminology comes with its own challenges, however, as not all theologians construe sin in the same manner. For this reason, I will offer below my definition of sin, describe how it was derived, and note my justifications for favoring this particular definition.

I define sin as *failing in the human vocation to worship God.* The phraseology is inspired in part by language used by biblical scholar N. T. Wright,[108] and it is grounded both in Wright's particular reading of the Bible, as well as

Moral Injury as a Pastoral Theological Construct

Alexander Schmemann's theological anthropology. Commenting on Romans 2:17–20, Wright observes:

> As we shall see presently, Paul is very much aware that the word Jew in the original Hebrew of the patriarch Judah's name means "praise": the point of being a Jew, then, is to call forth from the nations a song of praise for Israel's God. And because the worship of the true creator God is the primary human vocation, as opposed to the idolatry that produces all kinds of dehumanized behavior (1:18–32), if "the Jew" can enable humans to praise the true and living God instead of turning away to abominations, will that not solve the problem set out in 1:18–2:16?[109]

Note that Wright is addressing the relationship of Jews to the wider world. It is not just the vocation of Jews to worship God; that is the vocation of all humans. Israel has been entrusted with a special commission, however, to bring all peoples to the fulfillment of their human vocation. In light of Israel's faithlessness to this commission, the Messiah was sent to fulfill God's promises to rescue the world through Israel.[110] Following Christ, the church now continues to carry out this call to be a light to the world[111] and, as stated above, "to call forth from the nations a song of praise for Israel's God."[112] Wright's particular interpretation emerges from the "New Perspective on Paul" (and now *post*-New Perspective) school of thought. It is Wright's contention that this particular understanding of Romans 2 provides greater coherence between this chapter and those that follow it.[113]

Alexander Schmemann takes the more anthropological route, hinted at in Wright, seeing worship as fundamental to human nature. He repeatedly refers to "man" as a "worshipping being," or *homo adorans*.[114] For Schmemann, this too results in a vocation with global implications. He writes, "Man was created priest of the world, the one who offers the world to God in a sacrifice of love and praise and who, through this eternal eucharist, bestows the divine love upon the world."[115] The language is far more liturgical here. The model of the worshipping being is the priest. The means by which the nations offer their praise (to use Wright's terms) is by *becoming a Eucharist*, "a sacrifice of love and praise."[116]

A failure of human vocation then is a failure to worship. "'Sin,' for Paul," Wright explains, "is therefore not simply the breaking of moral codes, though it can be recognized in that way. It is, far more deeply, the missing of the mark of genuine humanness through the failure of worship or rather through worshipping idols rather than the true God."[117] He continues, "That action, to say it again, hands over to lifeless 'forces' or 'powers' the authority that should have belonged to the humans in the first place. The problem is not just that humans have misbehaved and need punishing. The problem is that their

34 *Chapter 1*

idolatry, coming to expression in sin, has resulted in slavery for themselves and for the whole creation."[118] If worship is the "mark of genuine humanness" it is no wonder that the Apostle Paul presents idolatry as one of the paradigmatic sins.[119]

Notably, Schmemann does not speak explicitly about "sin" in relation to human vocation. Schmemann does speak to the "negation of worship," however, which he calls "secularism."[120] Secularism, he clarifies, is not a denial of God's existence so much as the negation of the human as *homo adorans*, or worshipping being.[121] For Schmemann, this would include a denial of the sacramental character of the world. The world, he writes, "is an epiphany of God, a means of His revelation, presence, and power."[122] To be "sacrament" is the world's true nature and vocation, which is revealed in worship.

Wright, a New Testament scholar, and Schmemann, a liturgical theologian, may not be the expected sources for theological disquisitions on the nature of sin. There are multiple reasons, however, that their insights are especially fitting for this present study. Most importantly, both presume an anthropology that is grounded in worship, whether it is humanity's God-given vocation or a fundamental component of human nature. For a study centered on moral injury and ritual, the association between sin and worship is a compelling one. My later chapters will explore how worship, found in the Eucharistic liturgy, serves as an appropriate pastoral response to moral injury. This understanding of sin provides one theological grounding for this assertion.

This definition of sin makes possible another important claim that will resurface in chapter 4. As worship, understood by Wright and Schmemann, is communal, so too are failures to live out this vocation. One's transgression is not confined to the individual, but it is a failure of the whole human project. The early church is replete with examples of a communal understanding of sin, such that one's individual failing is conceived of as the burden and the responsibility of the community.[123] The conceit here then is that rehabilitation from moral injury requires nothing short of a reorientation of one's entire being, as well as of one's community, towards the very purpose for human existence, which is inherently liturgical in nature. Merely addressing one's guilt feelings would fall grossly short of remedying the damage done by MI.

Moreover, it is this communal aspect that makes moral injury possible even when *encountering or participating in sin*. This language actually follows Litz, Drescher, and Kinghorn, who recognize that moral injury can arise also from "failing to prevent, bearing witness to, or learning about acts that transgress deeply held moral beliefs and expectations,"[124] which can include simply bearing witness to the aftermath of violence and human carnage.[125] In each of these circumstances, the service member may, for all intents and purposes, be free from culpability in the atrocities committed, but will nevertheless exhibit the effects of moral injury. Chapter 4 will explore the notion of solidarity-in-sin within the Christian tradition, wherein one takes responsibility for the actions of another or is required to do penance even for "just" military actions. This discussion will be held in light of an ancient Christian penitential rite, the exposition of which will offer further theological explanation for why one might be stricken by sin even when not directly committing the transgressive act.

Finally, one of the reasons I included the controversial term "sin" was to draw attention to the fact that sin is unavoidably a pastoral theological matter. The matter of sin has largely been avoided in the field of pastoral theology, and the study of moral injury provides an opportunity to explore sin and its effects within this theoretical context. However, one of the challenges of broaching the topic of sin is that what one considers a failure of some ideal varies from person to person, resulting in quite pronounced disagreements today not only within the church, but also within society as a whole. This is certainly no less true when speaking of the legitimacy of war. To explore whether it is ever morally acceptable for a Christian to kill in war could exhaust the pages of an entire book itself. For this reason, and because it is not as important to this study that there be uniformity of opinion regarding the finer points of what constitutes sin, I largely avoid pursuing such a discussion. The theories, including the pastoral prescriptions, set forth here still stand regardless of these differences. This will be made clearer in chapter 4, where I make a further distinction between breaking a moral code, as in the sixth commandment, and falling short of the human vocation.

"Body, Soul, and Spirit" as the Site of Injury

Admittedly, I do not simplify the *site* of injury in my definition, but it is nonetheless more concrete and comprehensive compared to those identified by previous definitions. By naming "body, soul, and spirit," my definition intends to evoke a sense of moral injury's impact on the whole human.[126] Such a move is informed by early Christian theological anthropology, namely the ancient tripartite formula regarding the human being, which entails these three components. The Apostle Paul invokes this formula in 1 Thessalonians 5:23, which reads, "May the God of peace himself sanctify you entirely; and may your spirit and soul and body be kept sound and blameless at the coming of our Lord Jesus Christ."[127] This tripartite understanding of the human is carried through by the Church Fathers including Gregory of Nyssa who, in his treatise, *On the Making of Man*, explains that the body denotes the nutritive, the soul the sensitive, and the spirit the intellectual parts of the human.[128] In the same text Nyssa maps Paul's formula of body, soul, and spirit alongside Jesus's usage of the heart, soul, and mind in the gospels,[129] which for Nyssa represents the corporeal, the intermediate, and the higher natures

36   *Chapter 1*

(meaning the intellectual and mental faculty) respectively.[130] The nuances of each are not fully explored here; the important point is that as the passage in Thessalonians suggests, this tripartite formula connotes the *whole* person and nothing less. As theologian Jean-Claude Larchet states, "The Fathers often insist that the human being is neither body nor soul in isolation, but entirely and indissociably both."[131] The spirit, though not mentioned here, is implied, as it is understood to be the intellect (as in Nyssa's treatise), or the highest part of the soul. Larchet goes on to write, "The intimate connection of soul and body implies that they act simultaneously in every human activity and partake of the same emotions."[132]

This is a conception of the human not so different than those seen today within holistic care philosophies—models of treatment that are gaining ground currently in the mainstream medical world. Yet even so, the rigid compartmentalization of care pervasive within the industry tempts not just clinicians to divide the various faculties of the person into discrete domains. To this day, chaplains still may only claim their "clinical" specialty to be the care of *souls alone*, which in the ancient worldview may have seemed a metaphysical impossibility.[133] In the minds of the Fathers, the care of souls to an extent necessarily involves the care of bodies and vice versa.[134]

This indissoluble connection between body and soul is perhaps nowhere better illustrated than during moral injury. In Shay's aforementioned webinar on the topic, he states, "The human brain codes moral injury in the same way as it codes physical attack: The body responds massively in the same pattern as physical attack."[135] Is it any wonder then that many of Grossman's interviews with combat veterans reveal a pattern of vomiting after these men come to the full realization that they had just killed another human being? Consider: In these situations, of what underlying illness is this retching symptomatic? Is it based in the body or the soul? What kind of specialist would they need to see? One would be hard pressed to find anyone who disputes that MI lays claims to the mind. Few would argue against the notion that MI impacts the soul. By implicating the body in the suffering of moral injury, this study accomplishes the following: First, it draws greater attention to that physical component of the human being often overlooked in MI studies; second, this particular focus offers the opportunity to formulate a pastoral theological approach to the body, a vein of inquiry that also finds itself frequently underappreciated. Finally, this holistic approach to MI prepares the stage for understanding why ritual presents an appropriate response to various levels of trauma in general, and moral injury in particular.

Moral Injury as "Disruption"

In my definition I have sought to make as clear as possible not only the site, but also the *nature* of injury. In relation to the analogy of the knife wound, it seemed most helpful to identify the injury of MI closely with the actual laceration on one's flesh, not the act of cutting nor the ineffable result of one's reflection on the traumatic event. This approach presented here most closely approximates the notion of an injury and reduces ambiguity with regards to the nature of MI. Even still, incorporating the body into the domain of that which is affected by moral injury does not make the wound of MI any more visible. A holistic view of the person would have to concede that the effects of trauma are not localized, but commensurably holistic. Thus, I have borrowed the word "disruption" from Drescher to indicate that indeed some *things* have gone awry. Disruption is a helpful word as it denotes a form of disordering or breaking that is broad enough in meaning to apply collectively to all facets of the human being. In other words, there is a disruption not only in the mind and soul, but also in the body.[136] (This is in contrast to Drescher, who ultimately states that MI is a "disruption" of "an individual's confidence and expectations.")[137]

Theologically, the disruption may be understood to be that of the image of God reflected in humanity, like the effect of a stone tossed into the glass-like surface of a still pond. Yet in this analogy, the pond is not the individual but humanity as a whole. Proximity with the point of impact results in heavier distortions, whereas reflections further away will be less affected, but nevertheless be touched. Part of humanity's vocation to "worship" is reflecting this image of God to the world. The body, soul, and spirit are intended for this purpose. To fail in this vocation has deleterious effects on one's being as it does for anything in this world that is used for something other than its purpose. Thus, the psychological or physical "symptoms" that result from moral injury can be seen as a product of this misuse of one's humanity. However, these symptoms do not make the entirety of the disruption that is MI in the person and in the world. From the theological perspective, the harmful effects are not on one's life alone, as humanity's vocation is ultimately for creation as a whole, not just for the self. When a chainsaw is used as a plow, the unfortunate result is not just a broken chainsaw, but an insufficiently plowed earth. The failure of the human vocation results in a miscarriage of God's redemptive plan for all creation.

Not Simply Transgressing Beliefs

Another way my definition diverges from those of other theorizers of MI is that I do not present MI as being contingent upon an individual's own "deeply

38   *Chapter 1*

held moral beliefs."[138] One of my concerns is that this can be at best an overly simplistic, and at worst a misleading way to describe certain morally injurious acts in war. For instance: Would it be most fitting to describe following orders to fire on unarmed civilians (to use Shay's hypothetical scenario) or plowing through refugees in an act of self-preservation (to use Wetterstrom and Thompson's account) as fundamentally transgressing one's deeply held beliefs? In the first case it seems that the deeper belief of following orders supersedes the belief that one should not fire on unarmed civilians; while in the second case, the belief in the preeminent value of protecting one's own life outweighs the belief that one ought not to run over pedestrians indiscriminately. In other words, yes, a deeply held moral belief may have been violated, but it was done so in order to preserve what at the time seemed to be an even stronger belief. Thus, the issue at stake is more a matter of military personnel having to uphold certain strong moral convictions (e.g. following orders, protecting oneself) at the expense of other strong moral convictions (e.g. don't kill civilians). In other words, the resulting distress caused by such a choice is not so much the transgressing of some deeply held belief on a whim, but the product of one having to face the unexpected incompatibility of *two deeply held beliefs*: First, that "Thou shalt not kill," and, second, I should preserve my life at all costs.[139]

I contend with the notion of MI as a matter of transgressing deeply held moral beliefs for another reason. This is a point to which I alluded above when discussing Sippola and Grossman. The typical narrative regarding moral injury is that because people are schooled from a young age in some variation of the sixth commandment, killing on the battlefield is experienced as a terribly transgressive event. Yet when informally surveying the veterans with whom I regularly meet at the VA, all said that when they enlisted, they believed that it was morally acceptable to kill in war.[140] One would expect as much of anyone choosing to join the military. In fact, it is a requirement today that one not be a conscientious objector, should one wish to enlist or even be commissioned as a non-combatant officer such as a chaplain. For it does not necessarily follow that to believe "Thou shalt not kill" means one would consider this a prohibition of armed conflict in war. Many persons, service members included, interpret the commandment as prohibiting willful murder, as opposed to other forms of killing, such as those that take place when nations engage in war. In a sense, then, there should be no compromising of any beliefs when it comes to taking a life in war.[141] Why then the distress when killing in war, even when the target was another armed combatant? Grossman's contention is that every one of these veterans would be troubled by the act of killing, regardless of their beliefs entering the military. There seems to be a discrepancy between what one believes one can morally accept upon entering military service and what one actually experiences when faced

Moral Injury as a Pastoral Theological Construct 39

with the reality of taking a life. As S.L.A. Marshall puts it, the warrior may find that she is a conscientious objector after all when finding the enemy in her sights or, after to taking another's life, she may reassess her beliefs.[142] My own experience, thus far, has been that every veteran who has admitted to me that he or she has taken a life in war has struggled with it.

Consequently, the proposed definition here avoids this language that MI is relative to how one *thinks* or *feels* about a particular act or event. Instead, "disruption" is contingent upon the presence of sin itself.[143] In other words, one can presume the presence of moral injury by the presence of sinful actions. Something is fundamentally altered in the human when a person encounters or participates in sin, whether that person feels anguish or conflict over it or not. Sin, as presented in the *Catechism of the Catholic Church*, comes close to this understanding of moral injury, stating that sin "wounds man's nature and injures human solidarity."[144] These "wounds" will not always be readily apparent.

The focus of this study, however, is *combat-related* moral injury, the serious nature of which will almost always be made known through overt symptoms, such as inconsolable guilt, as detailed above by clinicians. On the other hand, Grossman argues that two percent of the population may not exhibit the usual symptoms when engaged in acts like killing, because such people are aggressive psychopaths or sociopaths.[145] Because this study understands moral injury as based ultimately on sin and not on one's inner turmoil, the absence of guilt amongst this population is not indicative of an absence of moral injury. In a way, if the rare person does not express any remorse over harming another human being and is able to go on with her own life, this may be indicative of an even more serious condition or "injury."[146] Such people may not fall within the parameters of those requiring medical help, but they would be in no less need of pastoral attention than those suffering from moral injury.

Not Contingent upon Severity

Finally, the matter of *degree* often expressed or implied in most definitions of MI is largely absent in my definition. As caregivers invested in the notion of moral injury uniformly have combat veterans in mind, they imagine their clients to be sufferers who have either witnessed or committed atrocities in war. Because MI is meant to encapsulate the unique experiences of a traumatized war veteran, moral injury commonly is described as occurring after *serious* transgressions of *core* or *deeply* held beliefs in *high stakes* or *extreme* traumatic conditions. Most definitions of MI refer to these extremes not so much because serious transgressions in themselves are concerns, but because serious transgressions in war are what send veterans to hospitals.

The definition thus caters to this specific population, even though the concept of a moral injury, as typically presented, would seem to carry much broader theological implications. Once again, the predominant view of MI largely exhibits a clinical perspective. Remember too that MI was not a construct before traumatized veterans began presenting themselves to professionals for help. In comparison, one may notice that while a considerable percentage of the population likely cheats on their taxes, no one ever thought to create a concept like MI to apply to them, partly because these people do not crowd the waiting rooms of psychiatrists' offices.

I am interested also in the usefulness of moral injury as a general construct for pastoral theology. If the moral injury of soldiers in war is a pastoral theological issue, why shouldn't also the apathy of the man who cheats on his taxes be a pastoral theological issue? The words, "Thou shalt not steal," are as deeply ingrained in most people as is "Thou shalt not kill." In fact, the prohibition against stealing may be even more universal than the prohibition against killing. Therefore, to steal is also to engage in an act of violating a "deeply held moral belief"; however, neither psychologists like Maguen and Litz, nor theologians Brock and Lettini, apparently felt compelled to develop a construct for this age-old human issue. If one is to theorize about moral injury—whether about sin or the transgressing of one's core values—from a pastoral theological perspective, one cannot limit the scope of this theory to just those cases that result in the most overt suffering. Any pastoral theological answer to the moral injury of a veteran should have some relevance for the moral injury of the petty thief, though the cause and the experience of each may be vastly different.[147] Because these differences are not insignificant, it may be more helpful to think of different *types* of moral injury if it is to be used as a construct for pastoral theology. That is the reason why my foundational definition of moral injury proper does not include any qualifying words that presuppose any of the extreme conditions seen in war. I intend to use this understanding of moral injury as a basis to advocate viewing sin as a pastoral theological concern in the final chapter of this text. The study of moral injury in combat veterans is an essential step to arrive at that point. Therefore, in the interim, any mention of "moral injury" in this study should be understood as referring to combat-related moral injury, as denoted above.

One of the most dramatic differences between this definition and those before it may be one that is implicit. To ground the definition of moral injury in pastoral theology, specifically in the language of sin and the whole human, is to imply a fundamentally different problem at stake. Consequently, a different problem will require a different means of remediation. In general, the clinicians above may be particularly concerned with quelling the most damaging symptoms of MI—such as inconsolable guilt—that conspire to depreciate one's quality of life. However, if moral injury is a matter of participating in or encountering sin, then one can surmise that that sin will at some point have to be addressed. Moreover, if that sin is a failure of the human vocation to worship that results in a disruption in one's very being, then restoration from moral injury will require a return to this fundamentally human vocation. In contradistinction to medical definitions, the pastoral theological understanding of healing advanced in this study is *the restoration of one's humanity, whose fundamental vocation is the worship of God.* Nothing in this view of healing necessarily establishes the reduction of suffering as its aim. That is not to say that a pastoral theological approach is unconcerned with existential pain or that the restoration of one's human vocation is irrelevant to that. These matters will be discussed further in chapter 4. For now, it is enough to say that such definitions of moral injury, healing, and sin as posited by this study present these complex phenomena as liturgical concerns as much as anything else. The following chapter addresses how rituals can play a role in addressing the complexities of this form of trauma.

NOTES

1. Jonathan Shay once described PTSD for veterans as "the valid adaptations in the mind and body to the real situation of other people trying to kill you (and doing a [damned] good job of it), when those adaptations persist into life *after* danger." (Jonathan Shay, "Moral Injury." Webinar transcript, 2016.)

2. "What Are the Basics on Veterans?" USA Facts, accessed October 3, 2023, https://usafacts.org/topics/veterans/.

3. "Veteran Homelessness," National Coalition for Homeless Veterans, accessed October 3, 2023, https://nchv.org/veteran-homelessness.

4. Charles R. Hooper, "Suicide among Veterans," American Addiction Centers, accessed October 3, 2023, https://americanaddictioncenters.org/veterans/suicide-among-veterans.

5. William Ruger et al., "Warfare and Welfare: Military Service, Combat, and Marital Dissolution," *Armed Forces & Society* 29, no. 1 (2002): 85–107.

6. "From Service through Reentry: A Preliminary Assessment of Veterans in the Criminal Justice System," Council on Criminal Justice, August 9, 2022, https://counciloncj.org/vjc-preliminary-assessment/.

7. David J. Morris, "War Is Hell, and the Hell Rubs Off," *Slate Magazine*, April 17, 2014, accessed March 16, 2018, http://www.slate.com/articles/health_and_science/medical_examiner/2014/04/ptsd_and_violence_by_veterans_increased_murder_rates_related_to_war_experience.html.

8. Jonathan Shay, *Achilles in Vietnam: Combat Trauma and the Undoing of Character* (New York: Scribner, 2003), 178.

9. "PTSD and Substance Abuse in Veterans," PTSD: National Center for PTSD, accessed October 3, 2023, https://www.ptsd.va.gov/understand/related/substance_abuse_vet.asp.

42 *Chapter 1*

10. Kent Drescher et al., "An Exploration of the Viability and Usefulness of the Construct of Moral Injury in War Veterans," *Traumatology* 17, no. 1 (2011): 11.

11. Ibid.

12. Ibid.

13. Shira Maguen and Brett Litz, "Moral Injury in Veterans of War," *PTSD Research Quarterly* 23, no. 1 (2012): 1.

14. Brett Litz, Nathan Stein, Eileen Delaney, Leslie Lebowitz, William P. Nash, Caroline Silva, and Shira Maguen, "Moral Injury and Moral Repair in War Veterans: A Preliminary Model and Intervention Strategy," *Clinical Psychology Review* 29, no. 8 (2009): 696.

15. Killing-related exposure includes intentional and unintentional killing of both combatants and non-combatants.

16. Anna Kline et al., "Morbid Thoughts and Suicidal Ideation in Iraq War Veterans: The Role of Direct and Indirect Killing in Combat," *Depression and Anxiety* 33, no. 6 (2016).

17. Ibid., 473.

18. "Military Sexual Trauma," PTSD: National Center for PTSD, accessed October 3, 2023, https://www.ptsd.va.gov/understand/types/violence/sexual-trauma-military. asp.

19. Ibid.

20. "How to Manage Trauma," National Council for Mental Wellbeing, accessed October 3, 2023, https://www.thenationalcouncil.org/wp-content/uploads/2022/08/ Trauma-infographic.pdf.

21. "How Common Is PTSD?" PTSD: National Center for PTSD, accessed October 3, 2023, https://www.ptsd.va.gov/understand/common/common_adults.asp.

22. Bessel Van der Kolk, *The Body Keeps the Score: Brain, Mind and Body in the Healing of Trauma* (New York: Penguin Books, 2015), 20.

23. Ibid.

24. Ibid., 1.

25. Ibid.

26. Ibid., 21.

27. Naomi Breslau et al., "A Second Look at Prior Trauma and the Posttraumatic Stress Disorder Effects of Subsequent Trauma," *Archives of General Psychiatry* 65, no. 4 (2008): 431–37.

28. David A. Thompson and Darlene F. Wetterstrom, *Beyond the Yellow Ribbon: Ministering to Returning Combat Veterans* (Nashville, TN: Abingdon Press, 2009), 76–77.

29. David Grossman, *On Killing: The Psychological Cost of Learning to Kill in War and Society* (Boston: Little, Brown, 1996), 291.

30. Shay, *Achilles in Vietnam*, 195.

31. Ibid.

32. Tara O'Neill Hayes, "The Economic Costs of the U.S. Criminal Justice System," American Action Forum, July 16, 2020, https://www.americanactionforum.org /research/the-economic-costs-of-the-u-s-criminal-justice-system/.

33. Van der Kolk, *The Body Keeps the Score*, 156.

34. Ibid., 224.

35. Ibid., 222.

36. Maguen and Litz, "Moral Injury in Veterans of War," 1.

37. Ibid.

38. Ibid. Italics mine.

39. Warren Kinghorn, "Combat Trauma and Moral Fragmentation: A Theological Account of Moral Injury," *Journal of the Society of Christian Ethics* 32, no. 2 (Fall/Winter 2012): 57.

40. Kinghorn, "Combat Trauma and Moral Fragmentation" 61, paraphrasing Brett Litz, et al., "Moral Injury and Moral Repair in War Veterans: A Preliminary Model and Intervention Strategy," *Clinical Psychology Review* 29, no. 8 (2009): 700.

41. Kinghorn, "Combat Trauma and Moral Fragmentation," 64.

42. Ibid., 57.

43. Rita Nakashima Brock and Gabriella Lettini, *Soul Repair: Recovering from Moral Injury after War* (Boston, MA: Beacon Press, 2013), xiv, italics mine.

44. Brock and Lettini, *Soul Repair*, xiv.

45. Maguen and Litz, "Moral Injury in Veterans of War," 1.

46. Kinghorn, "Combat Trauma and Moral Fragmentation," 57.

47. Brock and Lettini, *Soul Repair*, xv.

48. Kent Drescher et al., "An Exploration of the Viability and Usefulness of the Construct of Moral Veterans," *Traumatology* 17, no. 1 (2011).

49. Ibid., 9.

50. Ibid.

51. Jonathan Shay, *Achilles in Vietnam*, 188.

52. Shay, *Odysseus in America*, 150.

53. Shay, *Achilles in Vietnam*, 191.

54. Jonathan Shay, "Moral Injury." Webinar transcript, 2016.

55. Ibid.

56. Ibid.

57. Jonathan Shay, "Casualties," *Daedalus* 140, no. 3 (2011): 183.

58. Shay, "Casualties," 186.

59. Ibid., 182.

60. Jonathan Shay, "Moral Injury." Webinar transcript, 2016.

61. Shay, "Casualties," 183, italics mine.

62. Ibid., 182.

63. Brock and Lettini, *Soul Repair*, 51.

64. David Kupfer, "Like Wandering Ghosts," *The Sun Magazine*, June 2008, accessed April 04, 2018, https://www.thesunmagazine.org/issues/390/like-wandering -ghosts.

65. Edward Tick, *Warrior's Return: Restoring the Soul after War* (Louisville, CO: Sounds True, 2014), 14.

66. Ibid.

67. Ibid., 145.

68. Drescher et al., "An Exploration of the Viability and Usefulness of the Construct of Moral Injury in War Veterans," 11.

44 Chapter 1

69. Ibid.

70. Aphrodite Matsakis, *Back from the Front: Combat Trauma, Love, and the Family* (Baltimore, MD: Sidran Institute Press, 2007), 23.

71. Drescher et al., "An Exploration of the Viability and Usefulness of the Construct of Injury in War Veterans," 9.

72. Ibid.

73. Matsakis, *Back from the Front*, 30–32.

74. Ibid., 46.

75. Ibid., 47.

76. John Sippola, et al., *Welcome Them Home—Help Them Heal: Pastoral Care and Ministry with Service Members Returning from War* (Duluth, MN: Whole Person Associates, 2009), 20.

77. Grossman, *On Killing*, 231.

78. Ibid., 237.

79. Ibid., 115.

80. Ibid., 237.

81. Thompson and Wetterstrom, *Beyond the Yellow Ribbon*, 26.

82. Ibid.

83. Matthew J. Friedman and Laurie B. Slone, *After the War Zone: A Practical Guide for Returning Troops and Their Families* (Cambridge, MA: Da Capo Lifelong, 2008), 97.

84. Ibid., 96.

85. Shay, "Moral Injury."

86. Shay, *Odysseus in America*, 149.

87. Ibid., 4.

88. Ibid., 149–50.

89. Ibid., 4.

90. Ibid., 150–51.

91. Shay, *Achilles in Vietnam*, 187.

92. Edward Tick, *War and the Soul: Healing Our Nation's Veterans from Post-Traumatic Stress Disorder* (Wheaton, IL: Quest Books, 2005), 108.

93. Grossman, *On Killing*, 52.

94. Ibid., 57–58.

95. Brock and Lettini, *Soul Repair*, xiii.

96. Brock and Lettini, *Soul Repair*, 51.

97. Shay, *Odysseus in America*, 149–50.

98. Ibid., 156ff.

99. Drescher et al., "An Exploration of the Viability and Usefulness of the Construct of Moral Injury in War Veterans," 9.

100. "Posttraumatic Stress Disorder," *Diagnostic and Statistical Manual of Mental Disorders: DSM-5* (Washington, DC: American Psychiatric Association, 2013), https://dsm-psychiatryonline-org.proxy.library.emory.edu/doi/full/10.1176/appi.books.9780890425596.dsm07 (accessed 3/17/2018).

101. Ibid.

Moral Injury as a Pastoral Theological Construct 45

102. Interestingly, the DSM-III was the first to include PTSD and in this first iteration, "guilt about surviving while others have not or about behavior required for survival " was included as a symptom of PTSD. Litz suggests that PTSD was framed in this manner with Vietnam veterans in mind and that clinicians in VA settings had been encountering patients with instances of moral conflict and guilt. This same attention to moral conflict has since been remarkably absent. (Liz et al., "Moral Injury and Moral Repair in War Veterans," 696.)

103. Drescher et al., "An Exploration of the Viability and Usefulness of the Construct of Moral Injury in War Veterans," 9.

104. Maguen and Litz, "Moral Injury in Veterans of War," 1.

105. Recent research suggests that current PTSD treatment for PTSD has also been less than successful. Van der Kolk writes, "A 2010 report on 49,425 veterans with newly diagnosed PTSD from the Iraq and Afghanistan wars who sought care from the VA showed that fewer than one out of ten actually completed the recommended treatment. As in Pitman's Vietnam veterans, exposure treatment, as currently practiced, rarely works for them. We can only 'process' horrendous experiences if they do not overwhelm us. And that means that other approaches are necessary." See Bessel van der Kolk, *The Body Keeps the Score: Brain, Mind and Body in the Healing of Trauma* (New York: Penguin Books, 2015), 222–23. This leads this author to believe that either the current recommended treatment for PTSD is ineffective, or that a number of the veterans being treated for PTSD could be suffering from something else like moral injury that requires a decidedly different treatment approach.

106. By "atrocities" I do not necessarily mean in an official sense violations of the Geneva Convention as often understood by the public. Even legal actions, such as killing an enemy combatant, can be morally injurious.

107. Paul D. Fritts, *Adaptive Disclosure: Critique of a Descriptive Intervention Modified for the Normative Problem of Moral Injury in Combat Veterans*. Seminar paper. Yale Divinity School (April 29, 2013), 1.

108. N. T. Wright, *The Day the Revolution Began: Reconsidering the Meaning of Jesus's Crucifixion* (San Francisco: HarperOne, 2016), 84.

109. N. T. Wright, "Romans 2:17–3:9: A Hidden Clue to the Meaning of Romans?" *Journal for the Study of Paul and His Letters* 1, no. 2 (2011): 13.

110. Wright, "Romans 2:17–3:9," 3, 22.

111. Ibid., 20.

112. Ibid., 13.

113. Ibid., 1.

114. Alexander Schmemann, *For the Life of the World: Sacraments and Orthodoxy* (Yonkers, NY: St. Vladimir's Seminary Press, 1973), 118, 120, 125.

115. Schmemann, *For the Life of the World*, 92.

116. Ibid.

117. Wright, *The Day the Revolution Began*, 86.

118. Ibid.

119. Paula Fredriksen, *Sin: The Early History of an Idea* (Princeton: Princeton University Press, 2014), 26, 50.

120. Schmemann, *For the Life of the World*, 118.

46   *Chapter 1*

121. Ibid.

122. Ibid., 120.

123. See Appendix A.

124. Maguen and Litz, "Moral Injury in Veterans of War," 1.

125. Kinghorn, "Combat Trauma and Moral Fragmentation," 61, paraphrasing Litz et al., "Moral Injury and Moral Repair in War Veterans," 700.

126. In one VA presentation, Litz seems to move in this direction with the working definition of moral injury he presented: "The lasting psychological, biological, spiritual, behavioral, and social impact of perpetrating, failing to prevent, or bearing witness to acts that transgress deeply held moral beliefs and expectations." (Brett Litz, *The Viability and Usefulness of the Construct of Moral Injury in War Veterans*, 2014.) PowerPoint slides.

127. All scripture citations will be taken from the NRSV unless otherwise noted.

128. Gregory of Nyssa, *On the Making of Man*, 8.5.

129. Mt 22:37, Mark 12:30, Luke 10:27.

130. Gregory of Nyssa, *On the Making of Man*, 8.5.

131. Jean-Claude Larchet, *Mental Disorders & Spiritual Healing: Teachings from the Early Christian East* (Hillsdale, NY: Sophia Perennis, 2005), 16.

132. Larchet, *Mental Disorders and Spiritual Healing*, 20.

133. Warren Reich, "History of the Notion of Care" (1995) retrieved March 14, 2018, from http://care.georgetown.edu/Classic%20Article.html. Article originally from *Encyclopedia of Bioethics*. Revised edition. Edited by Warren Thomas Reich. 5 Volumes (New York: Simon & Schuster Macmillan, 1995), 319–31.

134. Even the influential second-century physician and philosopher, Galen, who was not a Christian, wrote about this connection between body and soul.

135. Shay, "Moral Injury."

136. Later chapters, and chapter 2 in particular, will detail how trauma lays claim to bodies as well.

137. Drescher et al., "An Exploration of the Viability and Usefulness of the Construct of Moral Injury in War Veterans," 9.

138. Maguen and Litz, "Moral Injury in Veterans of War," 1.

139. Hauerwas neatly resolves this conflict through a "Christological pacifism" that assumes "it is better to die than to kill." See Stanley Hauerwas, *War and the American Difference: Theological Reflections on Violence and National Identity* (Grand Rapids, MI: Baker Academic, 2011), 80.

140. One veteran stated he was not religious at the time of his military service. Save for one Jew, all other veterans surveyed were raised in a Christian environment.

141. I would only qualify this statement to acknowledge that some enlistees may make exceptions for what they believe to be unjust wars or commands to engage in atrocities.

142. This squares with social-functionalist accounts of moral emotions that argue from an evolutionary perspective that experiential morality preceded verbal morality. In other words, it's not that beliefs about the wrongness of killing first emerged that then led to guilty feelings when the act was done. It's that people first killed and then felt guilty about it, which led to the belief that there must be something wrong

with this act. [Jason Nieuwsma et al., "Possibilities within Acceptance and Commitment Therapy for Approaching Moral Injury," *Current Psychiatry Reviews* 11, no. 3 (2015): 199.]

143. In this sense, I share with Litz the importance of the transgressive act in determining the presence of moral injury, but I would not go so far as to say that the act itself is the injury.

144. *Catechism of the Catholic Church*, paragraph 1872.

145. Grossman, *On Killing*, 50.

146. Augustine, commenting on war, even so-called "just" wars, writes, "And so everyone who reflects with sorrow on such grievous evils, in all their horror and cruelty, must acknowledge the misery of them. And yet a man who experiences such evils, or even thinks about them, without heartfelt grief, is assuredly in a far more pitiable condition, if he thinks himself happy simply because he has lost all human feeling." (*City of God* 19.7)

147. The Catholic distinction between mortal and venial sins may be the closest theological corollary to what I am discussing here. According to the *Catechism of the Catholic Church* 3.1.1.1855: *Mortal sin* destroys charity in the heart of man by a grave violation of God's law; it turns man away from God, who is his ultimate end and his beatitude, by preferring an inferior good to him. *Venial sin* allows charity to subsist, even though it offends and wounds it.

Chapter 2

Ritual and the Problem of Moral Injury

Chapter 1 focused primarily on understanding moral injury itself and defining it in the context of pastoral theology. Having understood moral injury as a pastoral issue, this current chapter turns to the problems moral injury poses for conventional pastoral care and the means by which ritual care might provide one answer. Posited here is an argument about why ritual is especially suited to address some of the unique challenges of moral injury in the context of pastoral care. Yet the purpose of this section is not only to satisfy this curiosity as to why rituals "work" for morally injured vets. An understanding of the *why* will help to determine *how* to incorporate ritual into the practice of pastoral care, as well as *which* rituals would be most appropriate. Currently, we have examples from a range of psychiatrists, chaplains, and pastors who care for combat veterans utilizing a variety of liturgies and rituals in equally various settings. For example, there is a parachurch ministry—known as a "Biblical Response to Post Traumatic Stress Injury"—dedicated to providing ritual cleansing to a traumatized veteran population.[1] Another practice is a sweat lodge purification ritual run by a Native American veteran for Native American veterans.[2] And again, as mentioned above, one psychiatrist has "prescribed" to a veteran a visitation to his parish priest for confession as an addendum to the clinical care received.[3]

A better understanding of why ritual is an appropriate response to moral injury will suggest how to integrate ritual and liturgy into the practice of pastoral care in a more thoughtful, theologically astute, and ritually honest manner. The following section draws upon the work of some ritual scholars to establish the understanding of ritual deployed throughout this text. This is not intended to be an exhaustive survey of definitions, but a conversation with relevant theories, including a justification for the choices made for the definition and approach used in this work. Any discussion of rituals and its effects must be prefaced with a definition regarding to what "ritual" refers.

50   *Chapter 2*

I will thereafter outline the unique challenges that moral injury poses for pastoral care, specifically because of its unique etiology and complex symptoms. The three main challenges moral injury presents for the practice of pastoral care are its basis in sin, its situation in the body, and its ineffability. This section addresses each facet of this challenge in detail.

The final section of this chapter will examine how ritual provides an answer for each of the particular challenges that moral injury poses for the practice of pastoral care. I will demonstrate that rituals directly address sin, engage the body, and provide a vehicle for communicating and containing the ineffable.

DEFINING RITUAL FOR RITUAL CARE

This project's exploration of ritual studies is restricted to the purpose of illuminating the role and significance of *Christian rituals and liturgies in the formation of people*. One of the limitations, however, of conversing with the field of ritual studies in a project like this is that the field often investigates rituals as a general phenomenon rather than the particularities of any one ritual tradition. This broader focus on rituals and ritual-like behaviors is still an important one, and this study will examine ritual's role in forming beliefs, attitudes, and behaviors. At the same time, attention to particularities is a significant part of the present theological task as far as assessing *Christian* rituals go and is necessary for achieving a thoughtful pastoral theology of ritual care. Consequently, a balance between scholarship in ritual studies and liturgical theology informs my approach to ritual. This section will present my chosen definition of ritual, drawn from Elaine Ramshaw's work, followed by justifications for why her particular understanding of ritual is fitting for this theological investigation. In my justifications, I will use Catherine Bell's exposition of rituals as a foil to highlight the distinctives of Ramshaw's definition that make hers a better fit for this study. This section will close with a note on my use and understandings of the words *ritual*, *liturgy*, and *worship*, as they are invoked throughout this study.

While there are many definitions of ritual from which to choose, this project will employ that of Elaine Ramshaw, who is not a ritual scholar per se but a theorist of ritual and pastoral care. She writes, "A ritual proper is a relatively formalized, corporate, symbolic act of ritualization. Ritualization is a much wider phenomenon, including all the aspects of our biosocial behavior that are planned, repetitive, [and] conventionalized."[4]

While Catherine Bell's exposition on rituals—which has a prominent standing in ritual scholarship—informs Ramshaw's definition of ritual and ritualization, this project sides with Ramshaw for a number of reasons: First, given her shared interest in the intersection of ritual and pastoral care, particularly from the Christian tradition, Ramshaw's work seemed an appropriate starting point. Remaining conversant with Ramshaw serves the interest of remaining conversant within a shared field of common interests and seeking to contribute knowledge to that field.

Second, she does not mark *religious* rituals as the paradigmatic form of ritual. Though political rites are included in Catherine Bell's six genres of ritual activity,[5] they are greatly overshadowed by the strong association between rituals and practices rooted in beliefs in divine beings. This is not only a feature of Bell's work, but arguably common within the imagination of the general public. One point to which this study will allude is the prominence of "secular" rituals in the shaping of human life. Ramshaw's conception of ritual more freely allows for this association.

Third, while Bell distinguishes between rituals and ritual-like activities,[6] there appears to be less of a gap between Ramshaw's understanding of ritual and ritualization. For Ramshaw, ritualization is about the "ordering of experience" and ritual is a form of that ritualization.[7] Therefore, what Ramshaw implies is that there is a human impulse that, when made formal, symbolic, and corporate, manifests in this activity called ritual. In Ramshaw's definition, there is a fluidity in which ritual emerges from a natural feature of human existence, which, again, does not necessarily involve religion (an ambiguous category in itself) or a belief in a divine being. This understanding of ritual suitably frames the theories posited in this study.

To be fair, Bell may not disagree with Ramshaw's definition (or my interpretation of it). Bell's taxonomic approach, however, does not suit the methods and aims of this study as well as Ramshaw's does. Ramshaw's definition better illustrates the multitudinous ways in which humans engage in ritualization that often unconsciously conspire to shape their identities, dispositions, wills, and very constitutions for both good and ill. One conceit of this study is that pastoral care providers must actively engage this process of ritualization to provide a more faithful response to the problem of moral injury for the restoration of afflicted veterans.

The specific ritual in question for this study is that of the Christian Eucharistic liturgy, a particular form of ritual. Understanding that there are varieties of Eucharistic liturgies, one should not assume that this study refers to any one version to the exclusion of others. Instead, "Eucharistic liturgy" here should be understood to include those collections of liturgies—typically Roman Catholic, Eastern Orthodox, or Anglican—that are patterned after traditional Christian orders in which the communal partaking of the Eucharist, understood in some way to be the presence of Christ, is central. For this project, such matters as how exactly Christ is present in the bread and wine and which creeds are to be recited are ancillary to the central feature

52 *Chapter 2*

of a community gathering regularly to worship and receive communion and encounter Christ. Though this present chapter speaks to rituals in general, as understood by the definition above, the focus on the Christian Eucharistic liturgy will become more apparent in subsequent chapters.

Finally, I will be invoking the term "worship" as well, which I define as *the orientation of a subject towards the primary object of its desire*. Worship can manifest in any manner of ways in one's life as the primary object of one's desire can be virtually anything. This study presumes the Eucharistic liturgy to be the paradigmatic form of true worship. What makes a Eucharistic liturgy the paradigmatic form of true worship is the presence or the presumptive presence of the Eucharist itself. Chapter 3 will elaborate upon what this means and how this understanding of worship is significant for pastoral care. For now, this chapter turns first to the challenges that moral injury poses to the conventional practice of pastoral care, and then to the ways in which rituals can meet those challenges.

CHALLENGES THAT MORAL INJURY POSES FOR PASTORAL CARE

Moral injury poses particular challenges to conventional modes of pastoral care. The discipline of pastoral care is founded on the notion of the "care of souls," and so it would seem like a fitting recourse to a construct such as MI, which appeals to matters of character, morality, and the spiritual dimension of the person. However, much of modern pastoral care, though well suited to address a vast array of life's challenges, is not prepared to address the complex problems posed by moral injury. Here, I will outline three facets of MI that present difficulties for conventional models of pastoral care.

The Problem of Sin

Having argued that moral injury is a pastoral theological matter grounded in *sin*, one of the first challenges MI poses for the discipline of pastoral care is a need to address that sin. The influence of modern psychotherapeutic theories and practices on the development of pastoral care may have led to the movement away from viewing sin as a primary concern for pastoral care. To the extent that contemporary pastoral theology deals with sin, its primary focus has been victims of individual acts of sin, such as survivors of sexual sin, or those disenfranchised and marginalized by systemic sin, including the poor, persons of color, or other marginalized groups. Pastoral theologians have not significantly addressed the needs of those who are perpetrators of sin. To the extent that they do address perpetrators of sin, theologians' focus has tended to be on psychotherapeutic approaches that offer support for alleviating the guilt feelings resulting from sinful acts, not the avenues for making redress for those transgressions.[8] It is the latter, however, that is most needed by the morally injured, and often the former cannot occur without it. This is the conundrum illustrated in this section.

Rather than elaborating on the lack of attention to sin in pastoral theology, I will use James Newton Poling's work as an illustration of how psychotherapeutically-based pastoral care can come close, but ultimately falls short of offering the redress to sin needed in cases of moral injury. Poling is a pastoral theologian distinctive for his work with perpetrators, particularly of sexual abuse, and not only victims of "transgressive" acts. Poling's work in this area revolves around his role as a therapist for a child sexual abuse treatment agency. The offenders he meets are mandated by the court to receive treatment and Poling provides his clients with psychoanalytically-oriented psychotherapy. While reflecting on the nature of the human self in the context of child sex abuse, Poling does not speak directly about sin, but does raise the matter of "evil" (his term), which he defines as "the injury to the human self caused by disruption of bonding."[9] Poling asserts that the evil of child sex abuse is almost universally caused by molestation or abuse—a form of "disruption in bonding"—in the life of the perpetrator as a child. Child sexual abuse is thus a "symptom" of an injury in the life of Poling's clients.[10] Conceived in this fashion, the evil of child sex abuse is addressed by preventing further injury to the client's self and others by setting non-hostile limits on the client's behavior, while providing a therapeutic relationship, which includes validation and empathic mirroring.[11] "Evil" is thus addressed by keeping it from being perpetrated any further and healing the disruption in bonding that is its cause.

Though from the start Poling seems to diverge from this present study by the use of the word "evil" in lieu of sin, his work bears some deep resonances with my own interests as far as moral injury goes. For one, evil for him is an injury.[12] Though I would not refer to sin as an injury, I have stated that sin leads to a disruption in the person that can be called a "moral" injury. This may seem like an insignificant detail, but this notion of injury is an important concept when speaking of perpetrators. Victims alone are not injured. A perpetrator cannot commit a transgressive act and be unscathed, whether prior to the act or because of it. Even more, the word injury implies a need for a process of healing. Perpetrators too require restoration and a rehabilitation of sorts.

Second, Poling highlights the importance of community in the matrix of evil and its aftermath. Poling cites the responsibility of communities to protect the vulnerable and set limits on the destructive in their midst.[13] The presence of evil is ultimately the failure of a community.[14] This resonates

54 *Chapter 2*

with my own communal conception of both human vocation and sin. Poling also notes the power community has in the formation of personal identities. Communities that lack firm identities can create scapegoats as "objects of public rage" to detract from their own insecurities and failures.[15] This brings to mind America's labeling of Vietnam veterans as "baby killers" and how this denotation led to further victimization of a largely morally injured population.[16]

Finally, Poling narrates instances in which perpetrators with whom he has worked have begun to seek healthier relationships with their prior victims.[17] This may indicate that making amends has been a part of the therapeutic process for some of his clients. For veterans suffering from MI, seeking forgiveness and making reparation is undoubtedly a central, if elusive, step towards restoration.

As close as Poling comes to formulating a pastoral theological response to moral injury, his psychotherapeutic aims and context ultimately set him on a different path than what this current study is seeking. For instance, evil for Poling is caused by a disruption in bonding. Therefore, one prevents evil within a community through ensuring "empathic bonding with other selves."[18] Evil is construed through the lens of attachment theory and has a commensurately psychotherapeutic response. In contrast, the theological anthropology assumed in this study understands sin, and evil for that matter, as affecting body, soul, and spirit. This is nowhere more explicitly the case than in morally injured combat veterans.[19] Any response to these phenomena that comes short of fully and intentionally addressing every component of the human would be insufficient.

Poling's clinical context also informs his methods. Despite Poling's assertion about the importance of community, he deems it not necessary that the offender be restored to a community following treatment, nor that a community participates in his rehabilitation. This is not unusual for conventional individual therapy and much of pastoral counseling. My proposed understanding of sin and the human person cannot conceive of restoration in the absence of a community. This is particularly important for the healing process of morally injured veterans, who to their detriment isolate themselves from family, friends, and faith communities.

Moreover, it is evident that Poling's ultimate aim with his clients is not to make redress for sin and restore their vocation in worship of God. This again is partly informed by his context. One can infer that the court mandated therapy for his clients is to ensure that these offenders are no longer a threat to society. Poling appears to assume this as his goal. In their treatment of veterans, my VA colleagues largely share this form of pragmatism. Yet I argue that though a veteran can be stabilized to the point that she is no longer a threat to herself and others and even be sufficiently free from anxiety or

The Problem of the Body

depression, that veteran can still suffer from the failure of humanity's vocation. My conception of sin is such that the redress of sin would require more than the restraint of destructive tendencies.

While Poling's work is distinctive in the literature for his focus on perpetrators, he remains squarely within the norm in his reliance on psychotherapeutic modalities in pastoral care. In this way Poling's work illustrates why conventional approaches to pastoral care struggle to address some of the complexities inherent in moral injury, including offering a sufficient response to sin.

The Problem of the Body

The deep connection between moral injury and the body also poses problems for most common approaches to pastoral care in dealing effectively with those suffering from MI. Though post-traumatic stress is commonly perceived as a psychiatric matter, careful attention to the symptoms of traumas, like MI, reveal that they are grounded in and manifest through an interlocking of body, mind, and emotions. A focus only on the thoughts, beliefs, and emotions of a traumatized person at the expense of the body, or vice versa, is once again to overlook the integrated nature of the human being. At the same time, pastoral theologies like that of Poling, that are based on psychotherapeutic principles do not consciously attend to the body, which bears a significant portion of the weight of moral injury. This section is dedicated to illustrating the ways in which trauma in general and moral injury in particular lay claim to the body in various ways that the pastoral caregiver must not ignore.

There are several ways the material body is affected by and contributes to the experience of trauma. To begin, there is the intimate connection between body and soul, such that injury to the body in war increases the likelihood of a veteran subsequently suffering from PTSD. Shay writes, "Psychiatric and physical battle casualties rise and fall together. The more war wounds in the body, the more mind wounds,"[20] and "The rates of physical wounds and psychological casualties track each other very closely: what spills blood spills spirit."[21] In other words, listening to the history of the body is as important as documenting the story of the conscious experiencing self in order to understand the very nature of one's trauma.[22] Remarkably, recent studies show that the inverse is just as true. The "psychological" experience of trauma can also result in physiological change and disruption to the body. Trauma has shown to cause actual physical alterations to the brain and has the potential to inhibit the proper functioning of one's immune system.[23] Somatization is a further illustration of this principle. Somatization describes the phenomenon of intense emotions, such as anger or grief, manifesting in real bodily pain.[24] Therefore, to see a physician for bodily complaints without reference to one's spiritual and psychological distress, or to see a counselor without

56   *Chapter 2*

attending to the distresses of the body, is to seek care with only an incomplete picture of the problem. The lesson of this research is that no component of the human person ever operates in complete isolation and treatment should consequently respond to that reality.

One can assume then that a form of trauma like moral injury leaves lasting impressions not only on the mind, but also on the body. When Kinghorn writes that "In the case of psychological and moral injury . . . the wound is known only through the soldier's psychological and moral response to the experience of combat,"[25] he neglects to mention the significant physiological responses to MI. As Shay writes, "The body codes moral injury as physical attack and reacts with the same massive mobilization. . . . We are just one critter: brain/body, mind, social actor, and culture inhabitant at every instant. None of these has ontological priority."[26]

The physical coding of moral injury is manifest when traumatized individuals undergo what is termed the "re-experiencing" of traumatic events. Re-experiencing can take the form of intrusive memories, nightmares, and flashbacks. These experiences can be triggered by sights, smells, sounds, and even the sensations of objects or temperatures[27] associated with past traumatic events.[28] On two occasions I have witnessed these triggers affect veterans. In one instance I saw as a veteran friend of mine freeze and his affect turn deadly serious as fireworks went off near my apartment. He had just returned from Iraq and I (to his dismay) had just moved next to Disneyland, where the explosion of fireworks is a nightly occurrence. In the other instance I was walking a veteran into a VA chapel to talk just as a Muslim prayer service was about to begin. As soon as the veteran saw the prayer rugs on the floor his body tensed and twisted in his wheelchair, looking as if it was seizing. He insisted on leaving the room immediately. In some cases, these triggers cause veterans, quite literally, to relive past traumatic events. The DSM-V explains that "Such events occur on a continuum from brief visual or other sensory intrusions about part of the traumatic event without loss of reality orientation, to complete loss of awareness of present surroundings."[29]

Whereas in the two cases above triggers can cause momentary discomfort, Slone and Friedman describe the latter end of the continuum as "like being in a horrible time machine where you actually believe you're back in the war zone surrounded by the enemy, witnessing death all around you, or watching helplessly as innocent children are caught in a crossfire."[30] Thus, flashbacks cannot be said to be purely cognitive. Flashbacks can be olfactory, in which veterans smell odors associated with battle, or somatic, in which the body re-experiences some or all of the physical sensations related to past combat, as in significant pain or hunger endured on the battlefield.[31] One veteran in my clinic was not sure at first why his flashbacks seemed to get worse in the summers, but then he began to think that it might be because the heat and

Ritual and the Problem of Moral Injury

stickiness of the season reminded him of Iraq, where he spent two summers of his deployment. It is for reasons like this that traumatized veterans make efforts not only to avoid thoughts and memories related to traumatic experiences, but also activities, objects, situations, and people that might arouse recollections of them.[32] Hence, the massive use of medication, drugs, and alcohol amongst veterans serves not only to calm the mind but to numb the physical sensations of re-experienced trauma.

When one considers the phenomena of olfactory or somatic flashbacks, it is helpful to envision the body as having traumatic "memories" of its own. This is vividly illustrated in Act 5 Scene 1 of *Macbeth*. In this famed scene, Lady Macbeth is found sleepwalking, as she has become wont to do, reliving the night she and her husband murdered King Duncan in cold blood. In her somnambulistic state she upbraids her husband for his ill-timed display of conscience, but soon her own seems to get the best of her as she tries desperately to clean her hands of Duncan's blood. As the following excerpts of dialogue show, this proves to be a much more difficult task than expected:

> Out, damned spot! out, I say! . . . who would have thought the
> old man to have had so much blood in him. . . .
> What, will these hands ne'er be clean? . . .
> Here's the smell of the blood still: all the
> perfumes of Arabia will not sweeten this little
> hand. Oh, oh, oh![33]

What Lady Macbeth experiences while slumbering, veterans likewise experience in both sleeping and waking hours. The body continually revisits the sights, sounds, smells, and feelings of trauma.[34] In the case of Lady Macbeth and the morally injured, it is the trauma of having caused or allowed harm to come to another. What Lady Macbeth and the morally injured also share is a dissonance at times between the mind's determinations and those of the senses. The mind has assessed that a course of action is or was most expedient at the time, and yet the body seems to be less forgiving. Notice how Lady Macbeth cannot help but continue to "see" and "smell" the blood.

I have spoken with a number of veterans who, like Lady Macbeth, feel that they did what they had to do in combat, but "smell the blood still" (though few may say so in those words). It is not uncommon for these veterans to qualify or preface their stories of moral injury with immediate justifications for their actions in war. "I did what I had to do" or "I was following orders" are common sentiments. In that moment, it is clear there was no more sensible decision to make at the time and few would hold them guilty of any crime or misconduct. For all intents and purposes, the matter has been settled rationally. Yet as I stand over their hospital beds or sit by their sides in rehab

58 *Chapter 2*

units, listening about their inability to sleep or be in public due to the things they continue to "see" and "hear," it is evident that their bodies, their senses, betray a different message.[35] Moreover, when the veterans dare to disclose these incidents, it is interesting to note the sensually descriptive details on which they seem to linger in telling. One veteran recalled: "The Iraqi just bled out in front of me as his family stood there watching," "I thought it interesting how human brains actually look like cauliflower," "And the smell . . ." This one vet could rationalize the decisions he made in combat, but he could not anymore cleanse his senses of them than Lady Macbeth could the blood from her hands.

During a holistic pain management group at the VA, one psychologist stated that, technically, *all pain is in your head*, as pain arises from your nervous system. It does not matter that you have the proof of where the stone struck your arm. The phrase "it's all in your head" cannot be used then to dismiss one person's phantom pain as being any less real than the person with a visible gash to prove hers. This highlights the difficulty of categorizing pain as a matter of the mind or the body, as the two are so closely linked. Similarly, moral injury may all be *in the head*, so to speak, but it no less implicates the body. Moral injury manifests in what one *really* sees, hears, smells, tastes and feels, as these senses all point to the very faculties in the human that are tainted and injured. The experience of killing a Vietnamese boy can cause a soldier emotional distress, but it also can lead to permanent groin pain and a change in taste for foods like scrambled eggs, as it has for one veteran I met. Moreover, moral injury does not begin any more in the mind than it does in the finger that pulled the trigger or the eyes that saw the unfurled brains of a Vietnamese child. Counseling alone, pastoral or otherwise, seems like a grossly inadequate and disproportionate answer to the kind of multi-sensory experience that precipitates MI.

The Problem of Ambiguity and Ineffability

The third challenge moral injury poses for pastoral care is the ineffability of the traumatic experience. Conventional pastoral care methods, as well as those of psychotherapy, rely heavily on language and one's ability to accurately recall experiences and reflect inner states. Because of the way traumatic memory is encoded in the brain, asking people like veterans who have experienced severe trauma to recall painful events in a coherent narrative will be a challenging task. This section will explore that unique feature of trauma—its tendency to inhibit one's ability and willingness to recall traumatic experiences.

Those readers who know current and former military personnel may already recognize in them a general reluctance to talk about the experiences

Ritual and the Problem of Moral Injury 59

of war. Yet when one considers a veteran population suffering from moral injury, one could only expect more resistance than usual. There are a variety of reasons for this. For one, veterans do not want to recall severely traumatic experiences simply because they do not want to relive them. As discussed in the previous section, reliving combat trauma can lead to painful flashbacks of events that vets would rather avoid. In certain cases, this could even be deleterious to a veteran's sense of well-being. Sharing about the pains of war undoubtedly can have salubrious effects for many veterans; for others, sharing the pains of war has led to an increase in symptoms or depression.[36] My own experiences as a VA chaplain have validated this point. Veterans have shared intensely personal and traumatic experiences with me they have not shared with their own spouses and, as difficult as it was, they said they felt relieved by doing so. I have also met more than one veteran who has gone through the VA Prolonged Exposure Therapy program for PTSD and stated their nightmares and anxieties have only gotten worse as a result. Given this consideration, one should not be surprised to find that traumatized veterans are especially tight-lipped after having suffered such effects of sharing their memories with others.

Second, a veteran's reluctance to share about her combat experiences may come from another type of fear. A veteran may not want others to know about their actions in combat or the atrocities they had seen, for fear of receiving condemnation or hurting others with their knowledge. Withholding their experiences may be a way of protecting themselves in the eyes of society, as well as protecting loved ones from having to experience and know the kind of atrocities the veteran has come to see exists in the world. This is particularly an issue for veterans suffering from moral injury, as one can imagine, when the veteran sees the source of great evil within himself. For instance, how can a married soldier with children ever disclose that he gunned down women or children in war?

Finally, veterans may resist speaking to someone about their experiences in war because of an acquired mistrust of words. Engaging with a pastoral caregiver or mental health provider assumes an exchange: a disclosure of information by the veteran in exchange for guidance, advice, and other help. As Shay explains, however, words have little currency for some veterans:

> It is not enough to talk about trust and tell patients verbally what they need to do. Vietnam combat veterans, like veterans of many other wars and other traumatized populations have great suspicion of words. They were deceived by words as part of their trauma. Our patients were told many idealistic things about war service, but were not told of its sorrows and suffering or that the personal cost could be so high. They were told about codes of conduct, but they then saw that the rules did not apply. They were told the enemy was weak and

60   *Chapter 2*

ill equipped, but then they saw how skillful the enemy's tactics and how well suited their weapons were. They were told in many voices that it was noble to be a warrior and that they would come home as heroes, but then they learned they were not wanted.[37]

Given such skepticism, veterans may never even consider darkening the doorway of a church or doctor's office in the first place, let alone accepting offers to receive counseling and share their experiences.

More difficult than overcoming a veteran's reluctance to speak is finding a way around her *inability* to speak. The inability is a product of two circumstances. The first is that combat veterans suffering from moral injury often have found themselves in situations of such moral and situational ambiguity that they are unable to put words to their inner and outer experiences of a traumatic event. As Litz suggests, morally questionable and ethically ambiguous situations are not new to war, but they may be more prevalent in recent wars than those past.[38] This is especially true in situations involving counterinsurgency and guerrilla warfare in urban contexts. Unmarked enemies, civilian threats, and IEDs contribute to environments of greater uncertainty and increase the chances of armed personnel harming non-combatants. One select field survey published in 2008 revealed that an alarming 27 percent of soldiers faced ethical situations during deployment in which they did not know how to respond.[39] More than one veteran has shared that he arrived in the field having been told he had one mission only to find that it was something else. Such conditions produce "[s]oldiers who kill in ambiguous circumstances [that] are often to themselves neither guilty nor innocent, neither victims nor perpetrators, neither heroes nor villains, but some complex amalgam of them all that is not well captured in the sound-bite conversation with which the American public has to date discussed our current wars."[40] As a result, pastoral caregivers may find themselves with veterans who are clearly suffering, but confused, not able to articulate the source of their suffering and without any idea of how they want to relate with their past.

A second reason veterans may not be able to relay their traumatic experiences is because of the way such events are processed by the brain. Studies show that in moments of extreme trauma, the left hemisphere of the brain—or the rational brain—is deactivated, while the right hemisphere—the emotional brain—remains alert. Van der Kolk was able to observe on brain scans what happens when a person re-experiences a traumatic event:

> When memory traces of the original sounds, images, and sensations are reactivated, the frontal lobe shuts down, including, as we've seen, the region necessary to put feelings into words, the region that creates our sense of location in time, and the thalamus, which integrates the raw data of incoming sensations.

Ritual and the Problem of Moral Injury

> At this point the emotional brain, which is not under conscious control and cannot communicate in words, takes over. The emotional brain (the limbic area and the brain stem) expresses its altered activation through changes in emotional arousal, body physiology, and muscular action. Under ordinary conditions these two memory systems—rational and emotional—collaborate to produce an integrated response. But high arousal not only changes the balance between them but also disconnects other brain areas necessary for the proper storage and integration of incoming information, such as the hippocampus and the thalamus. As a result, the imprints of traumatic experiences are organized not as coherent logical narratives but in fragmented sensory and emotional traces: images, sounds, and physical sensations.[41]

Shay puts it this way, "Traumatic memory is not narrative. Rather, it is experience that reoccurs, either as full sensory replay of traumatic events in dreams or flashbacks, with all things seen, heard, smelled, and felt intact, or as disconnected fragments."[42] Severe traumatic experiences are thus ineffable. They are mired in the domain of human experience not ordered by time. The fullness of the event cannot be recollected, but only re-lived, not as something that happened way back when, but something that is in the now—hence, the exceptional frightfulness of having a flashback.

When the re-experiencing of the trauma renders the rational brain impotent, a veteran cannot be talked out of the reality that is the offending event and back into the present world. And the experience, while real and vivid for the veteran, may only be processed as a chaotic mishmash of sensory experiences and feelings. As Shay writes, "These fragments may be inexplicable rage, terror, uncontrollable crying, or disconnected body states and sensations, such as the sensation of suffocating in a Viet Cong tunnel or being tumbled over and over by a rushing river—but with no memory of either tunnel or river."[43] This may be the only "memory" a veteran has of a morally injurious event. The soul and body nevertheless continue to suffer, the body perhaps knowing at times more than the mind does.

For these reasons, traditional talk therapy, the model for much of pastoral care, may be frustrated in its efforts to address moral injury fully. In particularly severe cases, morally injurious experiences cannot be recalled, let alone understood or reasoned with. Yet rather than abandoning traditional pastoral counseling and psychotherapy in response, my experience is that it is better joined with other means for meeting the particular challenges of moral injury, and perhaps of all trauma.

RITUAL'S ANSWER TO MORAL INJURY'S CHALLENGES

Having outlined the three unique challenges moral injury poses for the practice of pastoral care, here I will argue that ritual, as defined in section one, can provide an answer to the issues of sin, the body, and ambiguity that moral injury presents.

An Answer to Sin

The problem sin poses for modern pastoral care is that its conventional methods—often influenced by the psychotherapeutic realm—are not concerned with offering remediation for sin. Ritual, on the other hand, is one of the widely recognized, transcultural, and historical means by which sin, or some culturally or religiously understood transgressive act, has been and continues to be addressed. Paul Pruyser names placation or restitution as one of four motivational reasons that determines the nature of people's worship or liturgical acts.[44] If what Wittgenstein states is true, that a "ritual instinct lies at the bottom of all rites," and that "one could almost say that man is a ceremonial animal," then it is unsurprising that some form of ritual would be a normative human response to sin.[45] This section will illustrate how this is particularly the case when it comes to military service. Below I will provide examples of ritual responses to the communal and personal disruption caused by participation in war, spanning various cultures and ages.

When looking for postwar rituals, Shay and Tick both reference the ancient Greco-Roman world. Shay's research reveals that Athenian tragic theater was one composed *of* combat veterans primarily *for* combat veterans.[46] This contention places the cathartic nature of dramatic tragedy into perspective. Relevant to this discussion are the three meanings of catharsis that circulated in Aristotle's time: (1) religious purification of a ritual taint and expiation of a religious sin; (2) medicinal purgation of something unhealthy, poisonous, or impure; and (3) mental clarification, removing obstacles to understanding, the psychological equivalent of producing clear water from muddy.[47] Shay saw tragic theater as part of a public endeavor to provide the purification, healing, and reintegration of returning soldiers into the community. By enacting and being a spectator to tragic drama, these soldiers experienced a form of ritual purgation. Early Roman society also bears evidence of a ceremony of purification. Though not of a dramatic nature as in the Athenian practice, it was also for returning armies. Among other things, the ancient Roman purification rite involved passing under a beam erected over a street with one's head covered.[48]

Additional examples of purification rituals following participation in warfare can be found in Native American cultures. Notably, included in Tick's "Necessary Steps" of a "Warrior's Return"[49] is the stage of "purification and cleansing." Among the examples he provides are those of Native American participation in vision quests and sweat lodges, a practice still used by some Native American service members today.[50] Brock and Lettini provide the example of the Navajo people of the Southwest who engage in a ceremonial process called 'Anaa 'ji, or "the Enemy Way."[51] This is a ritual that is used to cure the sickness that comes from contact with "a deceased non-Navajo, participation in war, fatal accidents, and other encounters with death, such as corpses and graves."[52] It is a form of ritual purification and rehabilitation required of soldiers seeking re-entry into their ordinary lives following war.[53]

Cultures outside the West also have their share of postwar rituals. For instance, there are a variety of ways in which African tribes purge their warriors from the toxins accumulated in combat. One such ritual involves burying a warrior up to his neck in earth to allow for the "poisons" to leach out.[54] Looking further east, one Hmong man shared with me at a clergy training event that in his culture shamans conduct rituals for service members going off to war as well as when they return in order to ensure that they not lose their souls.

The Hebrew Bible even relates its own version of the postwar cleansing ritual. In the post-exilic era, sin was addressed on the Day of Atonement and through offerings made at the temple. John Gunstone surmises that this may have included confession to priests and some type of satisfaction for injuries made.[55] In the book of Numbers, Moses gives specific prescriptions to Israelite officers returning from war: "Camp outside the camp seven days; whoever of you has killed any person or touched a corpse, purify yourself and your captives on the third and on the seventh day. You shall purify every garment, every article of skin, everything made of goats' hair, and every article of wood."[56] It is notable that Moses's own command to "execute the LORD's vengeance on Midian"[57] does not preclude the need for purification following the Israelites' encounter with death in war.

Of course, Christianity is not without its rituals, both in ancient and contemporary practice, for addressing sin. One of the oft-cited Christian rituals within moral injury literature is that of the ancient and medieval practice of assigning forms of penance to Christian soldiers, particularly that of abstaining from the Eucharist for a period of time.[58] I will offer a more detailed treatment of this rite in chapter 4.

Comparative practices of cleansing following battle are numerous and far-reaching and so it may be fitting to close with the—perhaps, overzealous—claim of late journalist and veteran Arthur Hadley, who, according to Grossman, conducted an extensive study on major warrior societies around

64 *Chapter 2*

the world and concluded that "all warrior societies, tribes, and nations incorporate some form of purification ritual for their returning soldiers, and this ritual appears to be essential to the health of both the returning warrior and the society as a whole."[59] This is similar to the claim of Richard A. Gabriel, who writes:

> Societies have always recognized that war changes men, that they are not the same after they return. That is why primitive societies often required soldiers to perform purification rites before allowing them to rejoin their communities. These rites often involved washing or other forms of ritual cleansing. Psychologically, these rituals provided soldiers with a way of ridding themselves of stress and the terrible guilt that always accompanies the sane after war. It was also a way of treating guilt by providing a mechanism through which fighting men could decompress and relive the terror without feeling weak or exposed. Finally, it was a way of telling the soldier that what he did was right and that the community for which he fought was grateful and that, above all, his community of sane and normal men welcomed him back.[60]

Gabriel goes on to add that "When soldiers are denied these rituals they often tend to become emotionally disturbed."[61] Despite the difficulty of corroborating Hadley's sweeping claim that "*all* warrior societies" did this and Gabriel's claim regarding what rituals "tell" soldiers,[62] such accounts nevertheless point to the ubiquity of such rites.

What this survey demonstrates is that there is a seemingly universal human need to address the stain of war, even for participation in so-called "just" wars. While not all the traditions presented speak to "sin" in a specifically Christian manner, there is a prevailing sense that battle sullies the warrior in some way and creates the need for purification. The evidence shows that communal, cultural, and religious rites are one of the primary means by which the stain of battle has been addressed by various cultures throughout history. That the modern western world is largely absent of such rites appears to be the anomaly when viewed from the vast witness of history. At a time when the medical community is still struggling to manage the traumatic fallout of our recent wars, greater attention to the importance of ritual for addressing sin may prove to be beneficial for individuals and societies.

An Answer to the Body

I have established that the implication of the body, along with the soul and spirit, in trauma and the problem this poses for pastoral care. The question then is, How does one address those punishing self-conceptions that arise not from the intellect but the traumatic memories embedded in the body? Drawing upon medical science, theology, and ritual theory, I will demonstrate how perhaps ritual provides one of the means by which a pastoral care provider can accomplish this.

Trauma psychiatrist Bessel Van der Kolk offers a physiological model for how the body can serve as an avenue for shaping the mind. The basis for the psychiatrist's model is the polyvagal theory. The theory is named for the vagus nerve that connects the brain with many internal organs. As Van der Kolk notes, about 80 percent of the nerve fibers are afferent, meaning that they carry nerve impulses *from* sensory receptors in the *body to* the *brain*.[63] The implication of this—which has been observed through Van der Kolk's own work with patients—is that "we can directly train our arousal system by the way we breathe, chant, and move, a principle that has been utilized since time immemorial in places like China and India, and in every religious practice that I know of, but that is suspiciously eyed as 'alternative' in mainstream culture."[64] Van der Kolk explains that such practices "rely on interpersonal rhythms, visceral awareness, and vocal and facial communication, which help shift people out of fight/flight states, reorganize their perception of danger, and increase their capacity to manage relationships."[65] The trauma psychiatrist refers collectively to these kinds of activities as "self-management," which he holds in contrast to a "Western reliance on drug and verbal therapies."[66]

Over on a different end of the theoretical landscape, James K. A. Smith makes a theological, yet similar claim regarding the nature of humanity, stating, "we are the sorts of animals whose orientation to the world is shaped from the body up more than from the head down."[67] Rather than pointing to breathing exercises (pranayama), chanting, qigong, drumming, group singing and dancing, as Van der Kolk does for training the arousal system,[68] Smith specifically has in mind liturgies, which, like Van der Kolk's practices, evoke "interpersonal rhythms, visceral awareness, and vocal and facial communication." Smith goes on to explain:

> Being a disciple of Jesus is not primarily a matter of getting the right ideas and doctrines and beliefs into your head in order to guarantee proper behavior; rather, it's a matter of being the kind of person who loves rightly—who loves God and neighbor and is oriented to the world by the primacy of that love. We are made to be such people by our immersion in the material practices of Christian worship through affective impact, over time, of sights and smell in water and wine.
>
> The liturgy is a "hearts and minds" strategy, a pedagogy that trains us as disciples precisely by putting our bodies through a regimen of repeated practices that get hold of our heart and "aim" our love toward the kingdom of God.[69]

66   *Chapter 2*

Smith here continues to provide somewhat of a theological mirror to Van der Kolk's clinical theory, by stating that the bodily practices of the liturgy actually train the mind (and heart, for that matter) in some fashion. Even while focusing primarily on "loves," Smith similarly considers the unexpected connection between sensory stimuli through communal practices and the shaping of the mind.

Finally, Barry Stephenson provides a perspective from the field of ritual studies on the role that ritual plays in cognition. The key feature of his position is his explanation of "embodiment" within the context of ritual. He writes, "In ritual studies, the notion of embodiment has a couple of distinct connotations. The term can refer, in a rather suspicious fashion, to the ways in which ideas and values are inscribed into the body through ritual practice. Second, the language of embodiment highlights the fact that ritual is one of the ways people go about making sense of their world. Like reason, ritual is a way of knowing."[70] While Stephenson describes these two connotations as distinct, both share a common resonance with the medical and theological perspectives above. For Smith, ritual through embodiment can inscribe in one's body the preeminent values of the love of God and neighbor. For Van der Kolk, ritual can aid in shifting one's arousal system from seeing the world as a place of unremitting danger to one as a potential for peace. If we shift our focus more acutely to the morally injured, ritual embodiment could mean inscribing into the body the notion of one's forgiveness, a concept readily accepted in one's mind but heretofore unknown in the body. This could also mean that through ritual the morally injured could change one's perspective of the world as a place of condemnation to one holding the potential for acceptance.

As trauma is inscribed not only in the minds of veterans, but also their bodies, ritual provides a means by which competing ideas and values can be embedded in the body in turn. Ritual and liturgical practices can be particularly helpful when the mind is forfeit or unable to make sense of traumatic circumstances. By appealing to the language of the body, rituals speak to people in a way that circumvents the rational and the discursive, yet they are no less meaningful or formative. It is not only because of their embodied nature that rituals can better address the ambiguities of life, however. Rituals in their very form provide space for containing the ambiguous and the ineffable. It is to this matter that the following section turns.

An Answer for Ambiguity and Ineffability

One of the abiding frustrations of those with severe trauma and moral injury is that words prove too inadequate when it comes to describing, making sense of, and treating these phenomena. I have heretofore given various reasons for why this is the case, not the least of which is that the experience of trauma is often ineffable.[71] So what does one do when a therapist or pastoral counselor has limited recourse to the use of speech and reasoning in the face of the complex problems presented by MI, problems that are both psychological and encoded in the body? Here, I will present the reasons for which ritual may be a more suitable response, or container, for the ambiguity, confusion, and pain that leaves morally injured veterans speechless.

To understand the suitability of the ritual response for moral injury, one must explore further trauma's tendency to foreclose on rational engagement. It may simply be the case that the encoding of trauma on the person occurs at a prereflective level, outside the plane of reason and cognition. Thus, there is the difficulty of rationalizing away the persistent fear that a veteran may hold of Emperor Hirohito hiding around every corner of a North Carolina nursing home. This may also contribute to the inability to feel forgiven by God for a moment of bloodshed in a war long past that is all but a faded memory, whose only proof of existence is an unabated sense of guilt.[72] In both cases the mind can reason that the fear or guilt is entirely unnecessary given the circumstances, but it struggles to alleviate those feelings (or, perhaps, the *knowledge*) of danger or guilt imprinted on the body and soul.

Thus, one of the reasons why some care providers find that religious rites assist in the restoration of veterans from moral injury may be that rituals too work on a precognitive level. This is an observation made by theologians, liturgists, and ritual scholars alike, among them James K. A. Smith, who sees implicit in liturgies an understanding of the world that is "pretheoretical, that is on a different register than ideas."[73] Liturgies provide a sort of noncognitive training that trains the heart through the body. He continues, "The senses are portals to the heart, and thus the body is a channel to our core dispositions and identity."[74] Susan Smith similarly describes ritual as "Working below the level of conscious awareness," noting that it "does not explain but enacts the real."[75] We can add to this Quack's statement that Wittgenstein's notion of the "ritual instinct"—seen parallel to Bourdieu's "practical sense"—is "a very basic, *prereflective* aspect of human beings."[76]

Morally injurious experiences could be said to function similarly by circumventing rational thought to impress its own vision of the world upon the body and soul of the veteran—a world where no one, including the veteran herself, can be trusted. The effects of such prereflective training have all the more impact given Smith's belief, again, that "we are the sorts of animals whose orientation to the world is shaped from the body up more than from the head down."[77] This is a new visceral understanding of the world that cannot be expressed or unseated by propositional discourse. As Smith puts it, practices (which in this case can be liturgies or participation in war atrocities) "carry their own understanding that is implicit within them . . . and that understanding can be absorbed and imbibed in our imaginations without having to kick into a mode of cerebral reflection."[78] To be clear, Smith has in mind the training of human desires for the Kingdom, a model of Christian pedagogical practice. Yet any practice that could realign one's "disposition and identity" seems eminently relevant to the treatment of moral injury. Smith's conceit is that if one's disposition and identity can be shaped for ill through bodily practices, one can also be oriented towards the good through the same means. Perhaps in the same way the morally injured veteran's vision of herself and the world can be recalibrated through the quiet and unassuming pedagogy of the Christian liturgy. As Smith writes, "The senses are the portals to the heart . . ."[79] A veteran may know cognitively that she should be forgiven by God, but her body and soul may be noncommittal. Perhaps if she were not simply to know with her mind, but also taste, hear, smell, and touch forgiveness through the rhythms of a weekly liturgy, she would come to encounter the fullness of forgiveness.

Further frustrating the articulation of moral injury and combat trauma is the ambiguity of war. Combat is all the more jarring for military personnel as the time spent in the hierarchical structure of the military accustoms one to a world without ambiguity, "where the aims are clear and everyone knows what needs to be done."[80] Some veterans unfortunately leave the field confused as to the true nature of their mission, whether they had done right or wrong, who the enemy was, and who they are now as a person. This ambiguity is brought back to the home front, and, without a container, it often spills out onto the civilian world around them destroying relationships, jobs, property, and the self.

One of the benefits of ritual, not only for the traumatized veteran but for society as a whole is that it provides a space for addressing the ambiguities of human existence. This feature of ritual is characterized in multiple ways by various scholars of ritual. In addition to allowing for "a recognition of the ambiguous nature of empirical reality,"[81] ritual "renegotiates boundaries, living with their instability and labile nature,"[82] that is, both positing boundaries and allowing the move between boundaries.[83] Erik Erikson suspects that "in man the overcoming of ambivalence as well as of ambiguity is one of the prime functions of ritualization."[84] Seligman contends, however, that ritual is less about *overcoming* ambivalence and ambiguity, and more a matter of "*expressing* the ambivalence/ambiguity and allowing for the participants to manage the uncertainties and contradictions."[85] Seligman later concludes, "We are thus arguing that the ritual mode has a built-in ability to abide with the inevitable ambiguities of life, even within an equally inevitable impulse toward an even delayed—yet also never abandoned—desire for wholeness and totality."[86]

The question, however, remains: What are the ambiguities, boundaries, and contradictions that rituals address? The answers provided range across the various theoretical landscapes, but they are not necessarily mutually exclusive. Moreover, they all seem pointedly relevant for the veteran whose world has been upturned by moral injury. For one, Susan Smith sees rituals as creating room for contrasting tones or a multiplicity of contradictory meanings.[87] Anderson and Foley similarly argue that rituals should honor ambiguity, which to them may be experienced as "a baffling array of feelings and thoughts."[88] For the morally injured veteran, the competing thoughts may be with regards to "paradoxes of selfhood,"[89] such as one's identity as both hero and murderer.

On a macro level, some scholars view rituals as holding together disparate and even contending *worlds*. Schmemann, writing as a liturgical theologian from an Eastern Orthodox perspective, states, "In the [early Church], sacrament was not only 'open' to, it truly 'held together' the three dimensions or levels of the Christian vision of reality: those of the Church, the world, and the Kingdom. And 'holding' them together it made them known—in the deepest patristic sense of the word knowledge—as both understanding and participation."[90] What the early church saw in the sacrament as the "holding together" of three dimensions of reality, Jonathan Z. Smith sees as a more dichotomous tension. He writes, "Ritual is a means of performing the way things ought to be in conscious tension of the way things are in such a way that this ritualized perfection is recollected in the ordinary, uncontrolled, course of things."[91] In both conceptions of ritual, there is the coexistence of the present world and a type of ideal. This may be the space where the veteran comes to grips with both the messiness of a world at war and the ambiguity-free world of pre-combat military life.[92]

One of the final benefits of ritual in the face of a mum cadre of veterans is that participation does not require a penchant for speaking. There may be some morally injured vets for whom trauma is a coherent experience, but one simply too painful to relay. It is to the veteran's benefit that she is not alone or singled out in the liturgy but engaging communally in a shared practice where all come to receive forgiveness for their sins. In many of these liturgies participants are given a script and rubrics to follow, thus alleviating that pressure to express oneself. Instead, self-expression is traded for synchronization with a wider community oriented towards a common good.

The ritual-liturgical model presented here stands in stark contrast to the clinical encounter where a veteran sits face to face with a doctor or psychologist in an examination room or small office. While the latter is necessary to treat a whole host of ailments, moral injury to the body, soul, and spirit, of a veteran may be better met by a sense of community in a sensually rich space that can abide with ambiguity, not an isolating encounter in a sterile

70 *Chapter 2*

environment scrutinized under the cold precision of some diagnostic criteria. Of the many times I hear of veterans storming out of doctors' offices in the VA, most are not due to any lack of sincerity on the part of the provider to heal, but more often the frustration of communication and the dehumanizing experience of the clinical encounter altogether. Also, I have come to recognize a persistent addiction of veterans, not only to the medications distributed at these clinics, but to the seeming promises of healing from a panoply of conditions that often leave these vets frustrated and disappointed. One of the drawbacks of the growing optimism and promise of medical science is that it makes us further immune to notions of a world where ambiguity, ambivalence, and contradictions ultimately prevail. The wisdom of the liturgy is not that we overcome this aspect of existence but that we live with it.

This chapter is not intended to portray ritual as a sort of panacea for curing all of moral injury, nor is ritual to be viewed as a replacement for conventional psychotherapeutically-based pastoral care. Rather, the chapter highlights how the intentional use of rituals may provide new avenues for pastoral care providers to address the unique challenges presented by traumas like moral injury. Beginning with chapter 3 I turn my attention more pointedly towards interfacing ritual as a form of pastoral care with the problem of MI. This next chapter will explore, draw from, and converse with two fields of inquiry that will serve as a springboard for the synthesis I provide in chapter 4.

NOTES

1. The Warrior Wash ministry founded by David L. Bachelor.
2. Rick Emert, "Lodge Offers Traditional Ceremonies," www.army.mil, August 5, 2010, https://www.army.mil/article/43370/lodge_offers_traditional_ceremonies (accessed March 16, 2018).
3. Shay, *Achilles in Vietnam*, 153.
4. Elaine Ramshaw, *Ritual and Pastoral Care* (Philadelphia: Fortress Press, 1987), 23.
5. Catherine Bell, *Ritual: Perspectives and Dimensions* (Oxford: Oxford University Press, 2009), 220ff.
6. Ibid., 235ff.
7. Ramshaw, *Ritual and Pastoral Care*, 23.
8. As Ramshaw cautions, "A distinction must be made, however, between the sense of sin and the presence of sin, between guilt feelings and guilt. The confusion can go both ways in our culture. People may go to a therapist to handle their 'guilt feelings' when their guilt is real, and what they need to do is apologize or make reparation. . . ." [Ramshaw, *Ritual and Pastoral Care*, 62.]
9. James N. Poling, "Child Sexual Abuse: A Rich Context for Thinking about God, Community, and Ministry," *The Journal of Pastoral Care* 42, no. 1 (Spring 1988): 58.

10. James N. Poling, "Issues in the Psychotherapy of Child Molesters," *The Journal of Pastoral Care* 43, no. 1 (Spring 1989): 25.

11. Poling, "Issues in the Psychotherapy of Child Molesters," 27–28.

12. Poling, "Child Sexual Abuse," 58.

13. Ibid., 59–60.

14. Ibid., 58–59.

15. Ibid., 60.

16. Though Poling does not address this, I wonder if the hyper-valorization of a subgroup, like veterans today, does not also betray a certain measure of insecurity.

17. Poling, "Issues in the Psychotherapy of Child Molesters," 28–29.

18. Poling, "Child Sexual Abuse," 58.

19. I should add too that a "disruption in bonding" has little to do with armed personnel killing in war. One need not be disturbed in this way to be trained to take someone's life. In the case of MI, one need only take orders and serve their country in war.

20. Jonathan Shay, *Odysseus in America: Combat Trauma and the Trials of Homecoming* (New York: Scribner, 2010), 205.

21. Shay, *Odysseus in America*, 209.

22. Notably, studies have also demonstrated that somatic impulses influence moral judgement and decision making. [Jason Nieuwsma, Robyn Walser, Jacob Farnsworth, Kent Drescher, Keith Meador, and William Nash, "Possibilities within Acceptance and Commitment Therapy for Approaching Moral Injury," *Current Psychiatry Reviews* 11, no. 3 (2015): 199.] In a way, the foundation of one's morality can be found in the body.

23. Bessel Van der Kolk, *The Body Keeps the Score: Brain, Mind and Body in the Healing of Trauma* (New York: Penguin Books, 2015), 1–3.

24. Aphrodite Matsakis, *Back from the Front: Combat Trauma, Love, and the Family* (Baltimore, MD: Sidran Institute Press, 2007), 102–3.

25. Warren Kinghorn, "Combat Trauma and Moral Fragmentation: A Theological Account of Moral Injury." *Journal of the Society of Christian Ethics* 32, no. 2 (Fall/Winter 2012): 64.

26. Jonathan Shay, "Casualties," *Daedalus* 140, no. 3 (2011): 186.

27. I have met with one veteran who states that warm temperature can trigger his flashbacks of being in combat as it reminds him somatically of the Middle Eastern sun. At times it is difficult for him to come out of the episode if he is sitting in a metal chair as the touch of the metal reminds him of his gun.

28. Matsakis, *Back from the Front*, 76.

29. "Posttraumatic Stress Disorder," *Diagnostic and Statistical Manual of Mental Disorders: DSM-5* (Washington, DC: American Psychiatric Association, 2013), https://dsm-psychiatryonline-org.proxy.library.emory.edu/doi/full/10.1176/appi.books.9780890425596.dsm07 (accessed 3/17/2018).

30. Matthew J. Friedman and Laurie B. Slone, *After the War Zone: A Practical Guide for Returning Troops and their Families* (Cambridge, MA: Da Capo Lifelong, 2008), 154.

31. Matsakis, *Back from the Front*, 90.

32. "Posttraumatic Stress Disorder," *Diagnostic and Statistical Manual of Mental Disorders: DSM-5* (Washington, DC: American Psychiatric Association, 2013), https://dsm-psychiatryonline-org.proxy.library.emory.edu/doi/full/10.1176/appi.books.9780890425596.dsm07 (accessed 3/17/2018).

33. William Shakespeare, *Macbeth* Act 5 Scene 1.

34. One veteran described to me his first kill in Vietnam—his most traumatic. He was commanded to sneak up on an unsuspecting Viet Cong and slit his throat, "quietly." As a result of this experience, the veteran developed a compulsion both to see blood on his hands as well as to clean his hands excessively. When the veteran returned to the States from war he would get into fights and ensure that he would cover his hands with the other man's blood, and he would find himself entranced as he stared at them. In Lady Macbeth fashion he also felt the need repeatedly to rub his hands together as though continually cleaning the blood off his hands. To this day when he is reminded of war, the anxiety can cause him to return to this compulsion.

35. The example here of a dissonance between the mind and body is not an assertion of a mind body dualism, but a reflection of the inner conflict commonly described as part of moral injury that I see as a battle waged throughout the different faculties (body, soul, spirit) of the morally injured person. It is not so simple as to say that the mind uniformly carries one belief while the body another. The bodily instincts may have contributed to the morally injurious action taken in war and the mind's eye may stir the body's re-experiencing of the traumatic event. In other words, the conflicts are multiple and exist not solely between distinct faculties of the human but within each faculty as well. As integrated as the body, soul, and spirit are it is difficult to even think of any action or phenomenon occurring solely in one "faculty." What I present here is simply one instance, albeit a common one, in which one's intellectually-oriented rationalizations conflict with the more sensually-oriented guilt that one experiences.

36. Matsakis, *Back from the Front*, 378.

37. Shay, *Odysseus in America*, 176.

38. Brett Litz, Nathan Stein, Eileen Delaney, Leslie Lebowitz, William P. Nash, Caroline Silva, and Shira Maguen, "Moral Injury and Moral Repair in War Veterans: A Preliminary Model and Intervention Strategy," *Clinical Psychology Review* 29, no. 8 (2009): 696.

39. Ibid.

40. Warren Kinghorn, "Combat Trauma and Moral Fragmentation: A Theological Account of Moral Injury," *Journal of the Society of Christian Ethics* 32, no. 2 (Fall/Winter 2012): 63.

41. Van der Kolk, *The Body Keeps the Score*, 176. As Van der Kolk states later on, "Confusion and mutism are routine in therapy offices" (245).

42. Shay, *Achilles in Vietnam*, 172.

43. Ibid.

44. Pruyser, *A Dynamic Psychology of Religion*, 337–39; cited in William H. Willimon, *Worship as Pastoral Care* (Nashville: Abingdon, 1979), 59.

45. Wittgenstein, *Remarks on Frazer's Golden Bough* (1993), 128; cited in Johannes Quack, "Bell, Bourdieu, and Wittgenstein on Ritual Sense," in *The Problem*

of Ritual Efficacy, edited by William Sturman Sax, Johannes Quack, and Jan Weinhold (Oxford: Oxford University Press, 2010), 179.

46. Shay, *Odysseus in America,* 152–53.

47. Ibid.

48. Ibid.

49. Edward Tick, *Warrior's Return: Restoring the Soul after War* (Louisville, CO: Sounds True, 2014), 206–15.

50. Emert, "Lodge Offers Traditional Ceremonies," army.mil, August 5, 2010.

51. Rita Nakashima Brock and Gabriella Lettini, *Soul Repair: Recovering from Moral Injury after War* (Boston, MA: Beacon Press, 2013), xvii.

52. Brock, *Soul Repair,* xvii.

53. Ibid.

54. Tick, *Warrior's Return,* 206–15.

55. John Thomas Arthur Gunstone, *The Liturgy of Penance* (New York: Morehouse-Barlow, 1966), 9–10.

56. Numbers 31:19–20.

57. Numbers 31:3.

58. See for instance Brock, *Soul Repair,* xviii, and Kinghorn, "Combat Trauma and Moral Fragmentation," 68.

59. Grossman, *On Killing,* 271–72.

60. Richard A. Gabriel, *No More Heroes: Madness & Psychiatry in War* (New York: Farrar, Straus and Giroux, 1988), 15–56.

61. Ibid., 156.

62. Gabriel's claim that these rites were a way of "telling the soldier that what he did was right and that the community for which he fought was grateful" poses difficulties on two levels. First, there is the implication that the symbolic weight of ritual lies in what it "tells" or points to other than itself. This is a common interpretation of what rituals "do" that is questioned by such theorists as Adam Seligman in *Ritual and Its Consequences* (2008). The second difficulty I have with this statement is that the postwar purification ritual is viewed as a means for informing the soldier that "what he did was right." The problem of moral injury posed in this study is that sometimes soldiers do things knowing full well that they are *not* "right."

63. As opposed to efferent nerve fibers which carry *from* the central nervous system *to* the body/organs.

64. Van der Kolk, *The Body Keeps the Score,* 207.

65. Ibid., 86.

66. Ibid., 207–8.

67. James K. A. Smith, *Desiring the Kingdom: Worship, Worldview, and Cultural Formation* (Grand Rapids, MI: Baker Academic, 2009), 25.

68. Van der Kolk, *The Body Keeps the Score,* 86.

69. Smith, *Desiring the Kingdom,* 32–33. As Hogue puts it, "We live in breathing bodies and in a world of things we can see, touch, smell, taste, and hear. Yet touchable, visible objects can also connect us to the spiritual and unseen realities of which we are not usually aware." See David Hogue, *Remembering the Future, Imagining the Past: Story, Ritual and the Human Brain* (Eugene, OR: Wipf & Stock, 2009), 131.

74   *Chapter 2*

70. Barry Stephenson, *Ritual: A Very Short Introduction* (Oxford: Oxford University Press, 2015), 93.

71. I once worked with a Vietnam veteran who was invited one day by his granddaughter to accompany her to a nail salon. He refused as he knew that the salon consisted of mostly Vietnamese employees. In the face of his granddaughter's protestations, suggesting that he was being ridiculous, the veteran explained that he has nothing personal against these Vietnamese workers, many of whom were not even born during the war. There is, however, something triggered in him when he sees someone of Vietnamese descent, a feeling of hatred and fear perhaps, that he knows has nothing to do with the actual person in front of him. The feeling is so unpleasant that he would rather avoid it at all costs. In cases where he is arranged to meet someone of ambiguous Asian descent, such as a medical provider, he becomes anxious until he is assured that the person is not Vietnamese. He recognizes that it is not rational to avoid Vietnamese people, particularly those of younger generations, but he says he cannot help it.

72. I am reminded of a veteran who has struggled with moral injury since the Korean War during which he was asked to execute a man for raping a girl. What was striking by his account was how little of the memory he actually remembered. Who asked him to execute the man? Whom did he execute? Who was the girl? These details seem to escape him, but what has been clear to him always is his profound sense of guilt.

73. Smith, *Desiring the Kingdom*, 25–26.

74. Ibid., 58–59.

75. Susan Marie Smith, *Caring Liturgies: The Pastoral Power of Christian Ritual* (Minneapolis, MN: Fortress Press, 2012), 138.

76. Quack, "Bell, Bourdieu, and Wittgenstein on Ritual Sense," *The Problem of Ritual Efficacy*, 181 (italics mine). Tobelmann states that "in any instance of habitus-informed practice, the action performed and its perception are structured on a level once removed from conscious interpretation." In "Excommunication in the Middle Ages," *The Problem of Ritual Efficacy*, ed. by Sax et al., 107.

77. Smith, *Desiring the Kingdom*, 25.

78. Ibid., 166–67.

79. Ibid., 58.

80. Friedman and Slone, *After the War Zone*, 77.

81. Catherine M. Bell, *Ritual Theory, Ritual Practice* (New York: Oxford University Press, 2010), 113.

82. Adam B. Seligman, *Ritual and Its Consequences: An Essay on the Limits of Sincerity* (Oxford: Oxford University Press, 2008), 11.

83. Ibid., 12.

84. E. H. Erikson, "Ontogeny of Ritualization," *Psychoanalysis: A General Psychology*, ed. by Rudolph Loewenstein (New York: International Universities Press, 1966), 605.

85. Seligman, *Ritual and Its Consequences*, 50, italics mine.

86. Ibid., 112.

87. Smith, *Caring Liturgies*, 94.

88. Herbert Anderson and Edward Foley, *Mighty Stories, Dangerous Rituals: Weaving Together the Human and the Divine* (San Francisco: Jossey-Bass, 2001), 130.

89. Seligman, *Ritual and Its Consequences*, 47, 59.

90. Schmemann, *For the Life of the World*, 144.

91. Jonathan Z. Smith, *Imagining Religion: From Babylon to Jonestown* (Chicago: University of Chicago Press, 2013), 63.

92. For the Christian veteran, the ritual space may also be one where the veteran seeks to reconcile living in a world in which the Church claims the Kingdom has been inaugurated while people continue to die in war.

Chapter 3

Contributions from Moral Injury and Ritual Care Literature for a Pastoral Theological Approach to Moral Injury

CLEOMENES
Sir, you have done enough, and have perform'd
A saint-like sorrow: no fault could you make,
Which you have not redeem'd; indeed, paid down
More penitence than done trespass: at the last,
Do as the heavens have done, forget your evil;
With them forgive yourself.

LEONTES
Whilst I remember
Her and her virtues, I cannot forget
My blemishes in them, and so still think of
The wrong I did myself; which was so much,
That heirless it hath made my kingdom and
Destroy'd the sweet'st companion that e'er man
Bred his hopes out of.

(William Shakespeare, *A Winter's Tale*, 5.1–12)

This excerpt from Shakespeare's *A Winter's Tale* is a seventeenth-century representation of a type of exchange probably shared by people of every generation. It presents one's well-intentioned, but ultimately feckless attempt to soothe a friend's guilty conscience. Why do we instinctively think it helpful to tell the guilt-ridden, as Cleomenes does, "you have done enough . . . forgive yourself"? And why does such a response perennially seem to fall short of its intended outcome?

78   *Chapter 3*

In chapter 2 I argued that a ritual response is the most appropriate pastoral response to moral injury. In advance of proposing a specific model of what that might look like, this chapter will offer a summary and analysis of two bodies of literature. Whereas chapter 1 offered a review of *definitions* of moral injury, the following section of this chapter will outline current treatment models for the care of veterans suffering from guilt and/or moral injury. Here we will see ways in which veteran care providers approach the challenge faced by Cleomenes, that of needing to palliate the guilt-stricken soul of another. Analysis of this literature will be done with a view toward contributions these studies can make toward a pastoral theological approach to moral injury.

Given that chapter 2 determined that some form of ritual care is the most fitting pastoral response to MI, the question that remains is: *Which* form of ritual care? The subsequent section will explore past models of ritual care found in literature that puts ritual, liturgy, and worship into conversation with the practice of pastoral care. Again, this investigation will seek to glean insights that can serve as a foundation for a pastoral theological response to moral injury.

Having investigated the contributions of moral injury and ritual care studies that have been conducted to date, this chapter will culminate in section four where I propose three main principles that should be foundational to a ritual approach to pastoral care. These principles will draw consciously from these past ritual care studies and have as a consideration complicated pastoral issues like moral injury.

MORAL INJURY TREATMENT LITERATURE

This section will summarize the strategies presented in veteran care literature for addressing guilt and moral injury. As noted in chapter 1, not all such literature recognizes the term or condition "moral injury" by name. As such, any recommendations found in this literature regarding the addressing of combat-related *guilt* are included here. There is enough of a connection between the two to assess them together here. For instance, one text defines guilt as, "a negative feeling state triggered by the idea that one should have acted, felt, or thought differently," further adding that, "The death, injury, or insult of another, as is common in war or any type of traumatic experience, is a breeding ground for guilt."[1] This definition bears many similarities to traditional definitions of moral injury. This presentation of intervention models will begin with the outlining of texts that do not speak to moral injury directly, but a veteran's "guilt," followed by those more recent works that directly address moral injury. An analysis of these largely clinically-based

Interventions for Combat-Related Guilt

The past couple of decades have produced a collection of literature addressing the needs of veterans returning from what was the longest war in US history. These texts are typically written by psychologists, counselors, and pastors/chaplains for a general audience largely agnostic to the unique experiences and needs of modern-day warriors. Though none of the books is wholly devoted to the topic of combat-related guilt, the majority make at least some mention of this common phenomenon amongst veterans. Below I focus on two texts in particular, summarizing their recommendations for how to address this guilt.

Matsakis's *Back from the Front* is the text alluded to above that furnishes the definition of guilt. The author asserts, "To feel guilty about a certain situation implies that one had some control over the outcome of that situation."[2] Therefore, if the warrior were to come to realize how little control she had in preventing an unfortunate outcome, she may in turn decrease her level of guilt feelings. For example, a soldier could have been in a combat situation where she lost a fellow soldier and friend to enemy gunfire. It would not be uncommon for the surviving warrior to experience guilt over her perceived failure to protect her friend. In such scenarios, Matsakis's recommendation is to help this soldier "feel the feelings" associated with the event and "reformulate" her experiences to see that she had little control in changing the outcome. The message is that she "did the best job in the situation that could have been done considering the circumstances and the resources available in the situation."[3]

Slone and Friedman's *After the War Zone* echoes much of the perspective presented in Matsakis's work. According to Slone and Friedman, "Guilt results when people act against their moral values, doing things that are contrary to their beliefs."[4] Again the big culprit behind guilt is the presumption of control over complex situations. They write, "Guilty thoughts may convince you that you're responsible for a bad outcome that you really never could have prevented in the first place. You may think that some actions that you took were not reasonable or justifiable. You may think that you should have known what was going to happen before it actually did, also known as hindsight bias. People sometimes blame themselves for not being able to predict the future, especially when bad things happen."[5] The authors appear concerned that these guilt-stricken veterans place an unreasonable standard upon themselves in light of situations gone wrong. The issue, perhaps, is a

80   *Chapter 3*

matter of perspective: "If you're in a critical situation and all options available to you are not good, the most moral and righteous thing you can do might still lead to a negative outcome, such as someone getting killed or having to leave a wounded civilian behind. However, just because the outcome was bad doesn't mean that your decision was bad. Your intentions were in the right place and you did the best you could."[6] Like Matsakis, these authors take a more cognitive therapeutic approach to addressing combat-related guilt. The aim is to reframe the veteran's experiences in such a way that the warrior can come to understand her limitations as a human being to control unpredictable circumstances. This process is a step towards self-forgiveness and ultimately minimizing the distress on the part of the veteran.[7]

What happens, however, if all evidence points to the veteran being genuinely responsible for an incident over which she is guilt-ridden? Such a consideration is not addressed in these texts and is a glaring lacuna in popular veteran literature. Recent moral injury literature, however, does take into account this grave reality of the warrior experience and will be summarized below.

Interventions for Moral Injury

The challenge that moral injury poses to attempts at reframing guilt-inducing combat situations is brought to the fore in MI literature. Litz has stated outright, "Cognitive models (e.g., cognitive-processing therapy; CPT; Resick et al., 2008) fail to provide sufficient specific strategies and heuristics to target moral injury, and cognitive therapy assumes that distorted beliefs about moral violation events cause misery, which may not be germane. In the case of morally injurious events, judgments and beliefs about the transgressions may be quite appropriate and accurate."[8] This is just one of many similar observations in moral injury studies. Even still, there is not as much of a consensus regarding a standard method for treating moral injury. MI is a relatively new phenomenon in the psychotherapeutic world and treatment models are in their incipient and evolutionary stages. The following is an outline of some of the current proposed models for treating MI.

First, Litz proposes a modified CBT treatment plan that involves the following steps:

> (1) A strong working alliance and trusting and caring relationship; (2) preparation and education about moral injury and its impact, as well as a collaborative plan for promoting change; (3) a hot-cognitive (e.g., Greenberg & Safran, 1989; Edwards, 1990), exposure-based processing (emotion-focused disclosure) of events surrounding the moral injury; (4) a subsequent careful, directive, and formative examination of the implication of the experience for the person in

terms of key self- and other schemas; (5) an imaginal dialogue with a benevolent moral authority (e.g., parent, grandparent, coach, clergy) about what happened and how it impacts the patient now and their plans for the future or a fellow service member who feels unredeemable about something they did (or failed to do) and how it impacts his or her current and future plans; (6) fostering reparation and self-forgiveness; (7) fostering reconnection with various communities (e.g., faith, family); and (8) an assessment of goals and values moving forward. Although these steps are presented in a sequential order, we realize that there will be substantial overlap in their application; some steps are intended to occur throughout the entire treatment.[9]

Much of the outline is self-explanatory and this is not the place to provide a detailed description of each step. Yet I will expound on a couple of the steps here that may require further explanation.

Step three (exposure-based processing) is meant to be completed in tandem with steps four and five. This form of processing entails a "focused emotional reliving" of the morally injurious event.[10] The purpose of revisiting the event is to unveil the thoughts, meanings, and attributions tied to it. By doing so, the veteran with the therapist can tackle any harmful beliefs that have emerged from the experience, which include such thoughts as "this event will define me forever" or "I am evil."[11] While using cognitive methods, the approach is not to convince the veteran that she is free from responsibility or guilt. This method allows for the veteran to accept her own shortcomings in the morally injurious event but seeks to protect the veteran from allowing the event to define her totally and indefinitely in a detrimental way. The goal is to lead the veteran towards growth and hope to become a person not circumscribed by the transgressive act or acts.[12]

As step six infers, this process explores avenues for making some form of reparation. As one can imagine, it is not easy for combat veterans to make actual amends with some of their victims in foreign lands. With this in mind, Litz envisions this stage in the process as committing to engage in "good deeds."[13] This may not right the wrong of the past but allows the veteran to reconnect to his or her values and move towards self-forgiveness.[14] The point is not to try to fix the past, but to circumscribe the morally injurious act in such a manner that it does not forever define the present and the future.

Shira Maguen, who co-authored the above proposed model, has gone on to develop the Impact of Killing (IOK) treatment plan. As the name suggests, this plan is geared primarily towards those veterans suffering from moral injury due to the experience of killing. Maguen breaks down the core stages of the program as such:

82   *Chapter 3*

- Education about the complex interplay of the biopsychosocial aspects of killing in war that may cause inner conflict and moral injury.
- Identification of meaning elements and cognitive attributions related to killing in war.
- Self-forgiveness (which entails cognitive therapy and for some the promotion of spirituality or faith-based religious practices).
- Making amends tailored to the individual (this may include writing forgiveness letters and an action plan to start the process of making amends).[15]

The program is undertaken in six to eight sessions of individual psychotherapy with each session lasting from 60 to 90 minutes. One of the prerequisites for participating is that the veteran must have already completed trauma-focused individual or group psychotherapy.[16] As can be seen, many of the basic components of Litz's proposed model are replicated here.

Adaptive Disclosure (AD) is another similar treatment model developed by Matt Gray with assistance from Litz. This particular model is comprised of six 90-minute weekly sessions, shorter than typical CBT programs to accommodate the time constraints of active duty personnel. Adaptive Disclosure is appropriate for fear-based traumatic experiences as well as moral injury. As soon as the type of trauma is recognized, the remaining steps of the program are shifted to address the particular need.

Adaptive Disclosure for moral injury features two main components. The first is an "imaginal exposure exercise . . . devoted to emotionally processing the war memory, unearthing various elements and associations, as well as helping veterans to articulate their raw uncensored beliefs about the meaning and implication of the experience."[17] The subsequent step for the morally injured veteran is to have a therapist-guided imagined dialogue with a "forgiving and compassionate moral authority."[18] As Gray explains, "The approach is designed to facilitate perspective taking and to shift beliefs from blameworthiness, which may be objectively true, to forgiveness and compassion and to accommodate the potential for living a moral and virtuous life going forward."[19] Again, this procedure closely resembles the model Litz proposed above, particularly in steps three through five.

One proposed method for treating moral injury that does not fall within the theoretical network of Litz is that of Nieuwsma. Nieuwsma in his 2015 study does not so much formulate a novel treatment plan for managing MI as explore the potential for using an established form of therapy, Acceptance and Commitment Therapy (ACT), to address the particular needs of morally injured veterans. This therapy distinguishes itself from other cognitive models in that its practitioners do not look at thoughts, feelings, and emotions as problems to be solved. It is the struggle to control negative emotions that is perceived to be part of the problem.[20] Thoughts are to be observed and felt mindfully, while viewed with compassion and accepted as "part of the normal human experience."[21] A person does not want to fuse with her thoughts, however. Practitioners lead patients to recognize that they *have* thoughts, but they are not literally the thoughts they have (e.g. "I am evil").[22] Such therapy creates ontological distance between thought and thinker.

Another aspect of ACT that sets it apart is that this treatment model does not view curing mental health problems or reducing suffering as its primary aim.[23] As Nieuwsma writes, "ACT presupposes that human suffering is inevitable and normal."[24] He continues, "the primary objective is to foster values-based living, helping the patient to be present to discomfort in the service of this goal."[25] In this way, ACT resonates with Litz's plan to counter the morally injured veteran's inclination to define herself by the traumatic event by guiding her into living out her values. While ACT does not intend to cure psychological maladies, research shows that this method does reduce symptoms of mental illness. Yet this is only a secondary effect of ACT and not its main goal.

Analysis

What these proposed care models for moral injury depict is something of an evolution of cognitive approaches for addressing combat-related guilt over time. Though it is hardly fair to compare popular veteran care literature to journal articles on moral injury, the latter clearly evinces greater sophistication and attentiveness to the reality of this phenomenon. One of the significant correctives the latter provides to the former is the recognition that one cannot simply rationalize away all the guilt of combat veterans or always expect to justify their actions. The suggestion that this would be sufficient for dealing with guilt is the greatest weakness of the interventions for combat-related guilt.

While the latter interventions for moral injury do exhibit a greater sophistication on the matter, there is yet to be a consensus as to what the best practices are for treating moral injury. One of the common features of the four MI treatment plans is the notion of being present to the traumatic experience and not shying away from it. For the first three, this involves exploring the meaning veterans attribute to these morally injurious events. The ACT plan would involve more simply *being present* to the emotional thoughts and feelings that these memories elicit. For all, there is an aim not to allow the personal associations attached to these events to have a totalizing effect on one's sense of self. All seek to point the veteran towards some commitment to live according to her values. Only two models (Litz's proposed model and Gray's AD) consist of an imagined dialogue with a sympathetic "moral authority." Finally,

84   *Chapter 3*

an interesting omission in the latter four plans is Litz's integration of a community into the rehabilitation of the morally injured veteran (step seven).

Only two of the above models—the IOK and AD—have been tested on morally injured patients, even if on a modest scale. Insofar as one views the goal of these treatments to be a reduction of the symptoms of mental illness, preliminary findings do reveal promising results. For instance, the IOK program patients exhibited fewer symptoms of PTSD, depression, and anxiety following treatment in comparison to the control group.[26] For the AD study, a pre- and post-test given to a group of active duty marines showed improvement in PTSD and depressive symptoms as well as in post-traumatic cognitions. Interestingly, there was significant improvement in all post-traumatic cognitions (for instance, beliefs about the self and world) except in the category of "self-blame."[27] In this instance there was only marginally significant improvement.

Strengths and Weaknesses in Pastoral Theological Application

There is much that is laudable in this literature from the perspective of pastoral care and the church, perhaps first and foremost that the secular-clinical world continues to recognize the power of guilt to ravage a person's life. Moreover, all the interventions above insist veterans be present to their experiences, whether it be through *feeling the feelings* of the traumatic event (Matsakis), *emotion-based disclosure* (Litz), or *observing mindfully one's thoughts* (Nieuwsma). This is an essential step toward restoration, as veterans may have a natural tendency not to want to face their moral injuries. Some may see in this very practice a sacramental component as well. For instance, Paul Fritts sees that in prompting veterans to recall and narrate their transgressions for therapeutic purposes, they are in some ways making confession.[28] For the morally injured, to tell the story of their pain necessarily involves confessing their offenses.

Another strength of this clinical work is that, with great attention and precision, these studies have detailed precisely how the "symptoms" of these conditions can manifest in the life of a warrior and how they can be reduced. Insofar as the church sees it as its mission, at least in part, to alleviate the sufferings of others, pastoral care providers do well to look at studies like these. As noted above, the IOK and AD models of care have thus far yielded some promising results.

Though pastoral care is known to borrow often from the psychotherapeutic world, there is much reason to tread carefully before wholeheartedly embracing the methods outlined above. For one, the limitations found in Poling's work (noted in chapter 2) are also found here for the most part. For instance, as in Poling's approach, MI is viewed narrowly as a psychological illness and is addressed primarily through cognitive and discursive means. To this, one can level the critiques of Kinghorn and Fritts who offer theological reasons for caution when countenancing these promising models of care. I will dedicate the remainder of this section to summarizing their thoughts on the matter.

As both a psychiatrist and trained theologian, Kinghorn has an exceptional standpoint from which to assess Litz's study. One problem he identifies is that "the medical model, once invoked, inducts postcombat suffering into the means-ends logic of technical rationality."[29] Kinghorn further expounds, "Christians can clearly affirm that it is good to ameliorate suffering—but is it always appropriate to do so by medical technique? And if so, what are the limits of this? At this point the clinical disciplines, so eager to relieve suffering, are left with little to say; the use of technique to relieve suffering seems to require no justification and seems to have no clear boundaries."[30] As noted above, Christians and the discipline of medicine may share, generally speaking, a common commitment to alleviate human suffering. Kinghorn sees a danger, however, when these traditions lose their "teleological frame" in pursuit of these commitments.[31] He supposes that there must be some greater end beyond seeking indiscriminately to relieve all suffering by any means necessary.[32] Without this sense of teleology as a caregiver, one is "unable to distinguish between suffering that aids in the realization of the good life and suffering that thwarts the achievement of these ends, such that all suffering, any suffering, becomes the appropriate object of technical modification: suffering becomes not a sign but a surd" [meaning irrational].[33] One might wish to reflect first, for instance, whether it is not appropriate that a veteran feel guilt for killing a child in war. Is such suffering necessarily bad? Moreover, if such guilt were to be addressed, should it be done through medical means?

Kinghorn's argument here for a teleological frame can apply not just to the nature of the veteran's suffering. The implication behind his word "technique" also casts a critical eye over the methods posited by the above clinicians. As a Christian, one would not take serious issue with the suggestion that one reconnect with a community or engage in good deeds. Yet it is one thing to participate in such activities because studies show they can alleviate stress or guilt; it is another thing if these actions are situated within a broader vision of one's vocation as a child of God and what it means to be a human made in God's image. If these were mere techniques in the former sense, one could imagine that the veteran would see it fitting that she no longer performs either of these activities once her symptoms of moral injury have subsided. The achievement of the end of alleviating suffering obviates the need for these means. Is this the realization of the good life for both medicine and for the church?

The one model that evades some of the pitfalls Kinghorn expresses is that of Nieuwsma's ACT plan. Nieuwsma makes clear that the objective of ACT is not to avoid or eliminate suffering. In fact, attempts to do so should be looked upon with skepticism. The *telos* beyond the mitigation of suffering is values-based living.[34] Nieuwsma writes, "Positive change is measured not by feeling better but by engagement in personal values and a renewed sense of vitality, by being able to flexibly respond to the current context in a healthy way."[35] Though this model still falls short of the form of ritual care that will be advanced in this study, it presents a potential bridge between the "means-end logic of technicist rationality"[36] maligned by Kinghorn and more sacramental models of ritual care. The next chapter expounds further upon this connection.

To Kinghorn's caution we could add one significant limitation Fritts sees in Litz and Gray's treatment plans. Fritts, a military chaplain, takes issue with their suggestion that the morally injured warrior has an *imagined* dialogue with a moral authority. Citing Anselm, Fritts asserts, "real is qualitatively superior to imaginary."[37] Fritts notes that the title and profession of chaplain has within it a certain weight and presumption of trust amongst soldiers.[38] Practically speaking, chaplains are experts on matters of morality and forgiveness and will be able to respond better than others to any theological questions that arise regarding one's transgressions.[39] All that is to say: Why not invite the veteran or service member to speak with an *actual* moral authority? Fritts feels, "inviting the morally injured Soldier to muse upon his own self-forgiveness is tantamount to asking a dental patient to pull his own tooth."[40] The suggestion that one *imagine* a conversation with a moral authority further highlights the rather solitary nature of the clinical processes presented above, only one of which suggests fostering "reconnection with various communities."[41]

Fritts's critique could potentially be applied to the last step in Maguen's IOK model as well. In the process of "making amends" the veteran is invited to write a letter to the enemy soldier or civilian killed by her hands.[42] This is referred to as the "forgiveness letter," and the veteran would presumably be using the letter as a means for asking forgiveness from her victim.[43] An insistence upon the *real* over the *imaginary* may appear to be less apt here as one cannot ask a nameless enemy in a foreign land (or a corpse for that matter) for forgiveness. However, one may invoke Fritts's principle to advocate for *real* practices for making amends that are grounded in tradition, socioculturally substantiated, and situated within a witnessing community, as opposed to ersatz ones aimed at therapeutic benefit. According to Maguen, writing forgiveness letters can be a very "powerful" experience for the veteran,[44] but no one is understood to make actual reparation or receive forgiveness by such a practice. The pastor has the benefit of a theological tradition that allows for the individual to make reparation with God and receive forgiveness (even in the absence of the injured party) and provides material practices for doing so. As the following chapter will demonstrate, this does not have to occur at the expense of therapeutic benefit.

The clinical and psychological world is the domain of MI research and with it comes many strengths. Cautions must be taken, however, before assuming wholeheartedly its theories into a pastoral theological context. As this study focuses on ritual care in particular, these clinical insights will be juxtaposed in the following section with a summary of ritual approaches to pastoral care. The considerations of these studies will be brought to the fore as I explore the possibilities of a ritual form of care for the problem of moral injury.

RITUAL CARE LITERATURE

This section presents an exploration of contemporary literature on the scholarly work done at the intersection of ritual and pastoral care. As this study has determined that a ritual response is an appropriate and fitting pastoral response to moral injury, this section will investigate various proposed ritual models for pastoral care. This summary of literature will be arranged in chronological order, followed by an analysis of this work. The section will end with comments regarding where I see my study in relation to this body of literature.

Chronological Summary of Ritual Care Works

One of the first books to explore the intersection of religious ritual and pastoral care is William Willimon's *Worship as Pastoral Care* (1982). Willimon's text is distinctive within this body of work in a number of ways. For one, Willimon's text does not use the more general term of "ritual," favoring instead the more specifically Christian terms of "worship" and "liturgy."[45] Willimon also recognizes the therapeutic benefits of worship as others essentially do, but he rigorously maintains that the main purpose of worship is to be in the presence of God[46] and respond to God[47] with glorification and enjoyment,[48] focusing primarily upon God and God's relationship to God's people.[49] While he views social action, human comfort, and education as worthy aims, worship directed towards these anthropocentric ends is an abuse of worship, he says.[50] Yet Willimon also endeavors to show that "the liturgy itself and a congregation's experience of divine worship already functions, even if in a secondary way, as pastoral care."[51] He adds, "The pastoral care that occurs as we are meeting and being met by God in worship is a significant by-product that we have too often overlooked."[52] One of the practical benefits of liturgy that Willimon highlights is its function "as a means of helping us cope with life's most difficult circumstances. It helps us get by."[53] The point is not to draw away from the pastoral aspects of worship but to attend to it more closely and place it in right relationship with worship's primary aim.

An influential and classic text is Elaine Ramshaw's *Ritual and Pastoral Care* (1987). Ramshaw's theory is founded on the belief that "the paradigmatic act of pastoral care is the act of presiding at the worship of the gathered community."[54] As a result, all other forms of pastoral care must be an extension of—or at least be viewed in relation to—this central feature of community life. In this text, Ramshaw makes a point of expounding the *relationship* between ritual and pastoral care.[55] This discussion leads Ramshaw to the concept of "ritual honesty,"[56] probably the most significant legacy she leaves to subsequent texts that explore the union of ritual and pastoral care. Ramshaw's notion of ritual honesty is more expansive in its meaning than it appears at first glance. Herbert Anderson and Richard Foley do their best to summarize this concept succinctly by describing rituals that achieve ritual honesty as "those in which the public, private, and official meanings converge."[57] Ramshaw is keen to protect the integrity of rituals passed down from tradition and makes it clear that the purpose of liturgy is first and foremost to glorify God and not to service human needs and wishes.[58] In this way, she is in agreement with Willimon. On the other hand, she writes that rigidity is also a sign of sickness,[59] hedging against a complete dismissal of human concerns in favor of the divine. Ramshaw's is a foundational early text on ritual care that provides a map and establishes boundaries for where pastoral care and ritual meet.

Anderson and Foley's distinctive contribution to the study of ritual and pastoral care is their joining of the two theoretically on the ground of narrative. In *Mighty Stories, Dangerous Rituals* (2001), the authors draw attention to the stories communities tell or ought to tell around key ritual moments. The book's usage of narrative is organized around John Dominic Crossan's understanding that all narration can be understood as existing someplace along a continuum between the binary points of myth and parable.[60] Whereas myths tend toward mediation, reconciliation, and stability, parables create contradiction and disruption.[61] The authors see that rituals too fall somewhere on this spectrum. Therefore, with careful reflection and orchestration, stories can work symbiotically with rituals to bring about reconciliation and stability when such is needed, or disruption when a situation demands greater instability.

David Hogue's text, *Remembering the Future, Imagining the Past* (2003), is something of an outlier on this list. The book's ambitious scope explores not only the intersection of ritual and pastoral care, but also includes theological expositions on neuroscience and narrative. In fact, the first half of the text is preoccupied by these latter two themes. As the author engages both ritual and pastoral care beginning with chapter 4, he highlights a number of similarities between ritual and the practice of pastoral counseling. For one, as Hogue sees it, both effect a break from the rhythms of everyday life.[62] The author is also keen to highlight the ritual nature of counseling itself. Hogue views public worship and pastoral counseling as sharing the common goal of "nurturing persons in their love of God and neighbor."[63] This understanding of ritual care is based on Arnold van Gennep's model of the three-stage structure of rites of passage.[64] Again, Hogue understands that counseling, like ritual, takes its participants through these same three stages: the preliminary, the liminal, and the postliminal phases.[65] The pastoral benefit of rituals he further explores by using Tom Driver's categorization of rituals in terms of shelter and pathway rituals.[66] Hogue's interest is not only in the analysis of rituals of care but also in their formulation. In his text, he provides advice on the creation of rituals to make them more "effective."[67]

If Willimon and Ramshaw seem at all beholden to tradition, one will find a distinct contrast in Susan Smith's *Caring Liturgies* (2012). Early on in her book Smith enumerates five reasons to "create caring liturgies."[68] There is a strong emphasis in the creative aspect of ritual formation in her text. Rather than straining all the pastoral possibilities out of those standard rituals that have existed within the church for centuries, she seeks to fill the liturgical gaps in between those rites to attend better to the diversity and complexity of life experiences in the modern world. The book guides the reader through the process of creating new rituals for those in-between and ambiguous moments that traditional orders of worship often overlook, providing examples and thoughtful considerations to ensure the impact and authenticity of each new liturgical experience. The impetus for Smith's text seems to be summed up in her first two reasons for creating caring liturgies: (1) *Rituals are needed to enable human growth and maturity,* (2) *Rituals are needed to help people through many and particular times of suffering and times of transition.*[69] These two reasons are particularly salient as she evaluates various case studies in the creation of caring liturgies. Whereas Willimon wants to ensure that the ultimate end of the ritual be directed towards God, Smith prefers to focus on individual human needs.

Analysis

While five texts spread over three decades do not constitute a significant pool of work in which to look for patterns, one cannot help but notice one particular trend: the gradual movement from a more theocentric view of ritual/liturgy/worship in earlier texts to a more anthropocentric view in the later. At one end, Willimon expresses skepticism towards people's attempts

90   *Chapter 3*

to alter traditional rites (of weddings and funerals, for instance) to cater to human whim. Smith at the other end of the spectrum is eager to produce new liturgies that attend more carefully to the vicissitudes of human existence. This is a tension frequently acknowledged in these works. Hogue for instance observes, "The very word 'ritual' evokes for many a sense of history and tradition. Some even argue that 'creating rituals' is an oxymoron. Rituals are received, either from God or from the accumulated wisdom of previous generations of the faithful who have worshiped God. Others contend that rituals are being constantly created. Even in the reenactment of ancient rituals, those rituals are being changed to meet the circumstances of the day. The only rituals that really work, they say, are those that we have discovered or created for ourselves."[70] As these later texts fall increasingly into Hogue's latter category, their creative bent is betrayed by a willingness to offer instruction and guidance on how to formulate new and effectively pastoral rituals. This is a tendency decidedly absent in Willimon.

Where one stands on this liturgical spectrum ranging from the traditional-theocentric to the creative-anthropocentric has implications for how one engages ritual as a source of care. In this, Ramshaw sees a related tension: "Liturgy without pastoral care is bad liturgy, and pastoral care dissociated from ritual and symbol is perhaps good psychotherapy, but certainly deficient pastoral care. . . . Even more common are those who try to practice both good liturgy and sensitive pastoral care, but who end up subordinating one concern to the other. On the one side are those who force their pastoral care into a ritual straitjacket. . . . On the other side are ministers who subordinate ritual to their understanding of pastoral care, seeing ritual as a 'pastoral hook' which must be used according to therapeutic norms."[71] One might then ask, At what point does the process of crafting rituals to meet human needs compromise ritual integrity? To what extent does slavish commitment to traditional liturgical forms neglect the human element so essential to ritual participation?

Antecedent to answering these questions is an understanding of how ritual relates to pastoral care. Again, the authors vary in their views. As Ramshaw suggests above, and as she has stated elsewhere, "ritual and pastoral care are not separate activities . . . they each involve the other necessarily."[72] For Willimon, liturgy functions in a secondary way as pastoral care; this care is a "significant by-product" of worship.[73] Anderson and Foley advocate for the increasing integration of worship and pastoral care, assuming perhaps a greater separation between the two than seen in Ramshaw and Willimon.[74] Hogue construes ritual and pastoral counseling as separate practices with a common goal and experiential effect.[75] Both Hogue's and Anderson and Foley's texts also conceive of ritual and pastoral care as connecting at the level of narrative, ritual being the means by which God's story and humanity's story come together.[76] Finally, Smith presents the creation of liturgies as one of the foundational tasks of the church to promote growth, maturity, life, and liberation.[77] In Smith's text there is not a strong articulation of ritual's role in the life of the church apart from these pastoral ends.

Ritual Care for Moral Injury

Collectively these texts offer much to this present exploration of ritual care in the context of moral injury, even iterating some of the points this current study wishes to build upon. For one, these authors make note of the bodily character of rituals and the interplay between the body and mind that occurs therein. Hogue for instance muses:

> Our conscious images also influence our bodies . . . This is a top-down process.
> So why do we pay so little attention to what worshipers will be experiencing in their bodies? Given that the brain records and takes its own cues from the body's movements, why do we not more carefully think through the forms of gesture, posture, and movement that can most likely help worshipers experience awe, reverence, and peace? . . .
> We sense, remember, and imagine through our bodies. Therefore posture, emotional state, and movement are central to our experiences of ritual.[78]

Already, the previous chapters have noted the significance of attending to the body when addressing trauma. Chapter 4 will follow in some ways the path that Hogue and Anderson and Foley take in drawing attention to the narrative aspect of rituals. Theoretically, this study will venture in a slightly different route as it will view elements of a liturgy in light of narrative *therapy* in particular. Finally, all the authors highlight to some extent the importance of community in ritual care, another point upon which the following chapter will expound. Even without explicitly considering combat trauma in their treatments of ritual care, these authors have highlighted a number of the unique features present in ritual that further reinforce liturgy as an appropriate locus for addressing moral injury within the context of the church.

The construct of "ritual honesty," invoked by a number of the authors beginning with Ramshaw, is also an important one this study will appropriate. I will employ a different definition of the term, however, than posited by Ramshaw and her followers. Concerned less with ritual in general and more with the integrity of Christian rites, I deem ritually honest those liturgies that place the worship of God as its sole aim. Here, I follow Willimon in his view that worship should not be directed towards pastoral or practical aims.[79] The pastoral benefits gleaned from liturgies should be viewed as secondary but significant by-products of worship. Willimon hints that there

92   *Chapter 3*

are ways to amplify these pastoral benefits without compromising ritual honesty. What the Methodist bishop says of funerals, this study accepts as true of all Christian liturgies: As they "become more explicitly and intentionally theological they will become more pastorally helpful."[80] This notion of ritual honesty should be understood to underlie my constructive pastoral theological work in ritual care.

This section illustrates a vast array of approaches to ritual care. This diversity is not finally grounded in a preference for different forms of ritual, but differences in understanding the purposes for which Christian liturgies exist. These underlying beliefs in turn anticipate the kinds of rituals these authors see as appropriate for various pastoral situations. As I have assessed these various approaches, I have already begun to hint where I stand within this spectrum. The following section will build upon this one as I outline in more definitive fashion three principles that I see as foundational for ritual care.

THREE PRINCIPLES OF RITUAL CARE

This section expounds three principles that I propose should undergird the task of ritual care. The principles are that:

1. Ritual care, understood as a form of worship, should aim first towards the worship of God.
2. The Eucharist should be central.
3. A greater balance of the task of ritual care should involve hermeneutics.

The three are necessarily linked, each subsequent principle building on the earlier one. The first point is one that has been introduced in the previous section, while the second is somewhat implied in the first. The majority of this section will be focused on expounding the third principle, the main thrust of this chapter.

These principles will serve as a basis for the pastoral theological commentary and analysis of a penitential rite for moral injury in chapter 4; however, the three principles should be understood as applying to ritual care in general, not only in addressing moral injury. Exposition of the third principle towards the end of this chapter will make this evident as these principles serve as the standard that separates theocentric liturgies as a whole from humanistic ones.

The Primacy of Worship in Ritual Care

In asserting that ritual care is to be first and foremost worship directed towards God, this project largely follows Willimon and Ramshaw's understandings of worship and ritual care. Willimon writes, "To be sure, the main purpose of Christian worship is the glorification and enjoyment of God,"[81] a point Ramshaw likewise endorses: "The normative aim of the liturgy is not human comfort but the glory of God."[82] This is the standard of ritual honesty and provides the "teleological frame" for ritual care. The previous section anticipates this first principle, but this present section endeavors to add a bit more clarity, noting what this principle does and does not imply.

What this principle posits is that any Christian liturgy directed towards anything less, even good humanistic ends, may be good therapy but an abuse of worship.[83] Another way of stating this is that the liturgy should not be a means to anything else. It is not mere technique. It is an end in itself.[84]

That is not to say that human needs are abandoned in worship. This is not theology at the expense of anthropology. No: theocentrism is the height of humanism. As St. Irenaeus states, "The glory of God is the human being fully alive."[85] In worshiping God, humanity is not being wrested from its natural proclivities, but is finding fulfillment in its true vocation.[86] While God does not need worship, humans need to worship God. As a result, ritual worship naturally satisfies in a secondary way certain psychological needs.[87] True Christian worship, however, must not aim first at psychologically therapeutic ends.

To be clear, making the worship of God the primary aim in ritual care is not to say that worship should be the only form of pastoral care. Moreover, this is not an argument that there is no place for the use of psychotherapeutic methods in pastoral care.[88] Even for Ramshaw, who believes that "the paradigmatic act of pastoral care is the act of presiding at the worship of the gathered community," also adds that, "this priority in no way contravenes the importance of the one-on-one, 'private,' counseling-oriented dimension of pastoral care or the psychological insights that today inform that dimension."[89] This first principle is merely a statement regarding the use of worship in pastoral care and not a diminishment of other forms of pastoral care.

The Centrality of the Eucharist

Tied to the first principle is the second, which is that central to ritual care should be the presence or the presumptive presence of the Eucharist. It is the Eucharist that makes worship about God.[90] In a sense, the problem is that humans, as "worshipping beings"[91] and "ceremonial animals,"[92] will still find objects to worship even when they do not worship God.[93] It is in their nature to engage in this fundamentally human act of devotion. St. Thomas Aquinas suggests for instance that wealth, honor, fame, glory, power, and pleasure are common competing substitutes for God.[94] As such, the liturgy calls people not simply to the task of worship, as they already do that, but to worship *God*.

94 *Chapter 3*

Earlier, chapter 2 defined worship as *the orientation of a subject towards the primary object of its desire*. Worship at the liturgy, however, is not simply a site where one's earnest feelings and beliefs are expressed.[95] The liturgy is also the place that desires are formed.[96] Atheists and Christians alike are engaged daily in rituals and processes of ritualization such as those of commerce, politics, and nationalism, each of these competing interests conspiring to shape the ultimate desires of its adherents.[97] The Eucharistic liturgy has a calibrating effect of redirecting humanity's desires towards its intended focus in the Eucharist. This is the importance of the human being's regular return to the Eucharist and the need for a ritual that places the Eucharist at the center.

This assertion that the Eucharist should be present in Christian rites does not strictly refer to that part of the mass or liturgy that is the *institution narrative* and *consecration*. Even in the absence of these, what makes Christian rites the worship of God is an underlying Eucharistic consciousness. In other words, the reality to which the Eucharistic Prayer refers must be the focus of every Christian rite even if its very words and the actual partaking of communion are not included in the rite, such as in many weddings or funerals. This is what I refer to as a *presumptive* presence. As the Eucharist makes particular claims about God, humanity, and the cosmos, funerals and weddings should make manifest how those claims come to bear on such occasions in human life. To make a Christian funeral ultimately about grieving and celebrating the life of the deceased, or a Christian wedding about the love between two joined in matrimony, is to make it no longer true worship.[98] It is by anchoring even these occasional liturgies in the Eucharist that they are oriented towards truth, are life-giving, and ultimately are more pastoral.

Pastoral Ritual Hermeneutics

The main thrust of this argument is that a greater portion of the pastor's task in ritual care should be a patiently hermeneutic one, wherein the Eucharist serves as the interpretive key. The primary constructive aspect of this process involves guiding a person to understand her life, her weaknesses, and her joys in relation to the Eucharist. This approach resists the trend of formulating ad hoc liturgies to address emergent pastoral situations. This section will explicate here a pastoral ritual hermeneutic approach to ritual care by contrasting it with what I will call a *humanistic* approach to ritual care. The exposition will begin by offering a critical analysis of a divorce ritual offered in this humanistic mode. The section closes by providing a contrasting model of addressing pastoral situations through a hermeneutic posture toward ritual care.

Humanistic Liturgy: The Divorce Ritual

Having reviewed multiple works on ritual care and liturgy, I have encountered descriptions of various examples of what I call *humanistic* liturgies. The phrase, "humanistic liturgies," refers to ad hoc liturgies designed to address emergent pastoral situations with the primary aim of providing some therapeutic or practical benefit for its central participants. The examples given have involved everything from driver's license procurement ceremonies to rituals for morgue visits. Of these, I have chosen to address Hogue's description of a divorce ritual. This particular humanistic liturgy is ideal for this present critical analysis for two reasons. First, more than one text has made mention of pastors creating divorce rituals, signaling the perceived need for such in the life of the church. Second, Hogue's presentation of the liturgy is the most detailed, offering not only descriptions of the rite itself, but a brief statement regarding his own rationale for the ceremony.

To begin, I have reproduced below the two relevant excerpts from Hogue's text that describe the ritual:[99]

> In a class at the seminary, a colleague and I asked two students to design a ritual for divorce. The service was carefully and sensitively done, acknowledging that the congregation was called together not to celebrate a divorce, but to celebrate the steadfast presence of God in all of life's pains and joys.
>
> The ritual was clearly a role-play—we all knew that. But that did not stop us from experiencing the pain as two actors declared their singleness and returned rings to each other in a silent act. We watched, as a temporary congregation, as two "parents" vowed in front of these witnesses to continue to love and care for each of their "children" in turn. We watched this divorcing couple as they gave gifts to each child, symbols of the relationship they hoped to have with them. And everyone there participated in the rituals of blessing these two people as they went their separate ways. The two students who wrote the ritual found themselves deeply touched during its enactment and looked to the two of us professors for some reassurance. We were too busy reaching for tissues.[100]

> Students in a recent class . . . wrote and enacted a ritual for divorce. A sand tray held small clay figures representing each member of the family, arranged in a circle. A particularly powerful moment came when the divorcing parents moved their own figures away from each other, breaking the circle.[101]

Like other humanistic liturgies, there is much that is commendable in this rite from a pastoral perspective. For one, it attends acutely to the situation at hand, a divorce, in a more obvious way that traditional rites would not. This to me is the greatest strength and appeal of liturgies in this mode. The ritual is also communal in a thoughtful and intentional way, involving "witnesses" and the participation of the divorcing couple's children. This decision recognizes the important fact that divorce, like many ruptures in life, is not merely a private matter between two people with no ramifications for the family and community at-large. Finally, the liturgy makes use of movement and tactile symbols in a creative way. As argued above, the bodily nature of rituals is one of its strengths in service of tending to the needs of people.

These strengths notwithstanding, this particular approach to ritual care exhibits a number of the shortcomings inherent in many humanistic liturgies. One of the weaknesses of the divorce ritual may be the very rationale for its existence. In other words, the absence of a divorce ritual, seen as a lacuna within the tradition by some, may be by design. Some sectors of the church that view marriage as a sacrament can question the propriety of formulating a ritual that effects the severing of a marriage relationship. From a humanistic perspective, one can understand utilizing liturgies to offer comfort in times of crises. The Christian funeral, for instance, is a ritual that can provide the comfort and stability needed to endure and move past the death of a loved one. Yet the funeral liturgy is not the vehicle through which the death of that loved one comes to pass. No life is ended by virtue of the funeral. This is a fundamental difference between a funeral and a divorce ritual.

If there is a basic equivalence between a marriage rite and that of a divorce, one would have to see the divorce rite as the church sanctioned means by which a marriage is severed (as much as the marriage rite is the means by which the two lives are joined). While Christians vary on the acceptability of divorce, one can see that at least from a sacramental perspective the very notion of a Christian divorce ritual is problematic. The introduction to *The Order for the Celebration of Holy Matrimony for Use by the Ordinariates* states, "Married Christians, in virtue of the sacrament of Holy Matrimony, signify and share in the mystery of that unity and fruitful love which exists between Christ and his Church. . . . In celebrating the sacrament of Holy Matrimony, Christians proclaim the communion of love between Christ and the Church and ask God's blessing on the new couple that their nuptial union might be the sacramental sign of this same love."

If a wedding proclaims the communion of love between Christ and the Church, a Christian divorce liturgy presents a ritual contradiction.[102] How can a Christian marriage, a proclamation of the communion of love between Christ and the Church, be followed with a divorce rite that ends with a blessing of the couple as they go their "separate ways?"[103] Its very existence threatens not only the significance and integrity of wedding rituals, but that of ritualization as a whole within the church. This lack of coherence with other sacraments in the church is a common shortcoming of humanistic rituals.[104]

Hogue circumvents this contradiction to a degree by stating that the congregation is called together "not to celebrate a divorce, but to celebrate the

Contributions from Moral Injury and Ritual Care Literature 97

steadfast presence of God in all of life's pains and joys."[105] From a pastoral perspective, this is an important sentiment to convey, particularly when faced with such heart-rending circumstances. If this is the primary purpose of the divorce ritual, however, there is still difficulty in justifying its existence. For one, the Eucharistic liturgy arguably conveys this very sentiment in a more theologically and pastorally rich manner.

Hogue perhaps finds justification for this particular liturgy in Tom Driver's understanding of shelter and pathway rituals. Hogue cites Driver and summarizes his ritual categorizations in this way: "Shelter rituals are those rituals that sustain us in times of distress or change. They underscore the continuity of life. Communion is a good example, as are our celebrations of the seasons and national historic remembrances like Independence Day. Pathway rituals help us move from one condition or status to another. They ease transitions that otherwise would be invisible or severely painful. Baptisms and funerals are good examples here."[106] Based on these descriptions, presumably Hogue understands the divorce liturgy as a pathway ritual. The liturgy allows for the couple to transition visibly from the status of a married couple to divorced individuals in the caring context of a supportive community. Again, the pastoral instinct to rally a faith community in support of an often alienating and trying process is a good one. Driver's categorizations, however, run the risk of instrumentalizing ritual towards some practical benefit. The liturgy again becomes not worship, but a therapeutic technique or method for easing people through difficult circumstances.[107] Note that Hogue does not say the divorce ritual is a *celebration of God* (period). But that it is a celebration of God's *steadfast presence in all of life's pains and joys*. An emphasis on the latter part of this statement seems to me to move a seeming theocentric statement towards anthropocentrism.

Finally, humanistic liturgies like this one have a greater tendency to be atomizing. Of the humanistic liturgies presented within ritual care literature, a good number of them are occasional, one-off liturgies, catered towards a specific situation for particular individuals. Hogue even asserts that "Some rituals may be developed and performed just once for a unique purpose."[108] Hogue also recommends involving ritual participants in the planning of rituals,[109] which presumably allows for further personalization and customization to meet individual needs and preferences. As anyone can observe, traditional rites of the church, such as the wedding, have tended increasingly in this direction.

What results is a community without a common, shared ritual infrastructure. Absent a Eucharistic consciousness to bind all rites together, people are not drawn towards a common vision of the world and the worship of God. These unique, occasional, and personalized liturgies of the church instead conspire with secular liturgies to assert human individuality and independence.

98   Chapter 3

One of the humanistic impulses tied to this pattern of personalization and atomization is the privatizing of ritual practices. Hogue writes, "Some rituals take place more privately. Some events that prompt us to ritual are too sensitive to share the intimate details much beyond our families or ourselves. When a couple promises again after the end of one partner's affair, they may wish to name the wrongs and seek forgiveness within a smaller circle. Ritualizing an abortion or miscarriage may best be limited to those directly involved."[110] The sensitive nature of divorces, as discussed here, likely presents an additional occasion for a more private ritual according to Hogue's views. Yet this movement towards privacy is not found only in these painful and delicate events. Weddings today are predominantly exclusive events involving invitations and carefully drafted guest lists (as mine was). If Christian ritual presumes an occasion for worship, however, these appeals to privacy are unwarranted. As Willimon writes:

> But, as with the funeral, the wedding is a service of worship. There is nothing "private" about this moment. Like the funeral, the wedding belongs to the whole church. Its intent is to do and say more than to merely express the whims and idiosyncrasies of any individual couple (or of any individual couple's parents, for that matter). The minister, at the very beginning of the service, proclaims that we are gathered "before God and these witnesses," thus affirming the public, corporate nature of the wedding.[111]

With a conception of ritual that involves the celebration of God's steadfast presence in life's pains and joys, Hogue gives no rationale for why "sensitive events" may be kept within a more private context. One may suspect that this provision for privacy is motivated at least in part by people's desires not to want to expose the most personal moments of their lives, particularly those most painful, with others. This is a desire which will find a great deal of sympathy in this present culture and age. A worship-centric approach to ritual, however, renders such appeals to privacy gratuitous. For if Christian rites are ultimately about the worship of God, then one's personal shame, shyness, or whims cannot be the reason for which people are excluded from that worship. One must consider that the very act of intentionally excluding oneself or others from a rite in itself carries (perhaps, unintended) ritual meaning and force.

To use Hogue's examples, What would a Christian rite of abortion or miscarriage convey, if the participants were "limited to those directly involved?"[112] While celebrating God's steadfast presence in life's pains, these rituals may also assert that shame is an insurmountable wedge between the suffering and the rest of the community. They reaffirm that pain is a private matter and need not (or cannot?) be shared with others. One can find the same conundrum in joyous occasions. What does a wedding convey when the attendees at a ritual proclamation of the communion of love between Christ and the Church is limited to a privileged guest list?

To his credit, Hogue himself senses a potential "danger" here and follows his statement regarding privacy with an addendum, stating, "North American individualism has so emphasized privacy and confidentiality that we lose the power and support of the communities to which we belong."[113] Hogue recognizes that one of the distinctive strengths of ritual is its ability to "involve individuals more openly and deeply" in their communities and welcome others into one's crises in life.[114] However, Hogue falls short of fully reconciling the dispensation he allows for privacy regarding "sensitive matters" and his wariness of individualism.

This is not to say that a pastor should not provide comfort for a divorcing couple or affirm that the steadfast presence of God is present in their pain. It is unequivocally a part of the church's calling to comfort those undergoing life's crises, including divorce. The caution here is against the impulse to ritualize a situation indiscriminately for humanistic ends without reflecting deeply on how this ritual fits within or affects the broader ritual infrastructure of the Church. When there is no ritually honest space for a liturgy in a particular situation, pastors have recourse to other means of pastoral care.

Some may also find that this insistence that all Christian rituals find their primary aim in the worship of God to be overly restrictive and dogmatic. On the other hand, one could argue that it is this very theocentric focus that makes rituals *Christian*. There are an abundance of rituals in which people take part, even on a daily basis, that are not aimed at the worship of God. However, it is in part the very mission of the Church to re-orient the world toward Her very purpose. Her rituals are one of the significant ways in which that mission is achieved. To formulate a "Christian" ritual directed primarily towards human felt needs at the expense of worship is only to introduce the patterns of the world into the church. One can have such rituals and they may be beneficial, but they would not be Christian. Without holding rigidly to the standard of ritual honesty, Christian rites lose their distinctive prophetic and formative power.

A Pastoral Ritual Hermeneutic Approach

As an alternative approach, this study will posit that the Eucharistic liturgy is the foundation of ritual care. This move is one that follows Schmemann, who sees in the reflex to create ad hoc rituals for each life occasion a false supposition "that the traditional worship can have no 'relevance' to these themes and has nothing to reveal about them, and that unless a 'theme' is somehow clearly spelled out in the liturgy, or made into its 'focus,' it is obviously outside the spiritual reach of liturgical experience."[115] This is not to say that

100 *Chapter 3*

traditional liturgies cannot be modified, nor new rituals created *ex nihilo*, but rather that the primary pastoral task of ritual care is of shepherding parishioners to know and shape their lives and situations through the interpretive key of the Eucharist.[116] Here, I will expound on what this entails and how it eschews the shortfalls of humanistic liturgies.

This push for a hermeneutic approach to ritual care is not to an exercise in interpreting and making sense of the Eucharistic liturgy. While engagement with and a growing knowledge of the Eucharist is necessary in this process, pastoral ritual hermeneutics is the converse task of the Eucharistic liturgy exegeting the lives of the faithful.[117] Willimon notes a similar phenomenon at work that is inherent to worship, as he contends, "As God is being revealed to us through our acts of worship, our deepest selves are being revealed as well."[118] To this statement one might add that it is not only our deepest selves, but the true nature of our circumstances, our communal identities, and the world itself that also are being revealed.

The pastor's role in the process is twofold, involving both the management of the liturgies, as well as direct guidance of the congregation. The former includes such responsibilities as maintaining the integrity of the church's ritual infrastructure. The pastor accomplishes this by ensuring that liturgies are ritually honest, directed first towards the worship of God. He maintains coherence among the rites of the church, bound by a Eucharistic consciousness and directed towards a common vision of God, humanity's mission, and the world. The minister also ensures that worship richly appeals to the senses and is not reduced solely to a rousing of the mind and emotions. In this first role, the pastor endeavors to be a thoughtful and attentive liturgist.

The pastor's other prominent role in ritual care involves direct guidance of the congregation. It is here that I wish to devote considerable attention. The hermeneutic aspect of the pastoral ritual process becomes most apparent in the counseling and catechizing of parishioners. Both within the liturgy and without, the minister aids the congregation in understanding its life in light of the Eucharist. This can be accomplished privately in counseling or by bringing forth the symbolic elements of the liturgy in homilies or in an "instructed Eucharist."[119] In each of these cases, parishioners are guided through the task of reading their pains, joys, questions, and confusions through the lens of the liturgy. This is an answer to Ramshaw's admonition that "we must live our way more deeply into the Christian symbols, the language of liturgy, so that we can bring those symbols to human experience without reducing or distorting experience."[120] In this task, the pastor's role is not simply to confer upon a congregational life its self-understanding in light of the Eucharist, but to build within the assembly a liturgical consciousness and fluency.

Of course, the hermeneutic process is not solely a discursive exercise. The goal is not always to arrive at a clear understanding of one's life or situation that can be articulated in concrete terms. More than anything the process involves submission. It is the faithful bringing of one's life, will, and even body under the formative power of the liturgy. As much as it is making sense of one's life circumstances in light of a theology of the Eucharist, it is also the giving over of one's anger, fear, and confusion to the taste of consecrated bread or to the sound of shuffling feet as fellow parishioners make their way to the altar rail. Chapter 2 made the assertion that traumas can be ambiguous and ineffable. Some traumatic memories are embedded chiefly in the body and not in any coherent manner in the mind. One of the benefits of liturgies is that they can meet worshipers at this same somatic and pre-reflective level.[121]

The pastor's task of guiding a congregation hermeneutically also includes the direction of parishioners in their *orientation* towards worship. This is an underappreciated aspect of ritual care. So much of ritual care literature is devoted to the formation and execution of liturgies that little attention has been given to the importance of how parishioners relate to them. For all that a liturgy can convey and accomplish in the life of a church can be undermined, its meaning and purpose even subverted, by the actions of its parishioners. I have alluded briefly to this above.

This position is validated in part by Schmemann, who writes:

> The liturgy of the Eucharist is best understood as a journey or procession. It is the journey of the Church into the dimension of the kingdom. . . . The journey begins when Christians leave their homes and beds. They leave, indeed, their life in this present and concrete world, and whether they have to drive fifteen miles or walk a few blocks, a sacramental act is already taking place, an act which is the very condition of everything else that is to happen. For they are now on their way to constitute the Church, or to be more exact, to be transformed into the Church of God.[122]

The Orthodox theologian suggests that the sacramental actions of the liturgy begin with the departure of the faithful from home as they journey to constitute the Church. Liturgical acts then are not confined between the "Entrance" and the "Dismissal." Consider one's decision to abstain from worship or leave a congregation due to the pain, embarrassment, or shame of divorce (to return to the example above). The divorcee's act of self-recusal can serve as a liturgical act that counters the aim and meaning of Eucharistic worship. For instance, by this act of withholding from the Eucharist, divorce may be construed ritually as the unbridgeable barrier between individuals, as well as individuals and God.[123]

102   *Chapter 3*

All this is to highlight the centrality of managing a congregation's relationship to worship in the act of ritual care. Assuming that the divorced couple attend the same church, a critical act of ritual care would be for the pastor to encourage the two to return to the Eucharistic liturgy, even as divorcees.[124] This would be their "divorce ritual," so to speak. Though no different than any other Sunday worship in form, this particular liturgy would carry a different, perhaps greater, meaning, not only for the divorcees but the congregation as a whole. Though divorced, the two eat of the same loaf and drink from the same cup.[125] Not only does bringing the divorced couple to the table maintain the integrity of worship, it enhances it. To an extent the presence of divorcees more emphatically conveys the dynamic truth of the Eucharist for the church than without it. Guiding a congregation's orientation to worship is an important facet of the meaning-making that occurs during ritual that is paramount for pastoral care.

To close, the following will briefly summarize how the centralization of the Eucharistic liturgy in ritual care helps to circumvent many of the shortfalls found in humanistic liturgies. The most obvious is that ritual honesty is more likely to be preserved, as the traditional liturgy is directed towards the worship of God in the Eucharist. Such an approach also avoids the possible ritual contradictions that can arise with the formulation of humanistic liturgies. Centralization of the Eucharist provides greater coherence to the ritual infrastructure of the Church.

For these reasons, the pastoral hermeneutic approach also resists the atomization of the church that becomes a potentiality in the humanistic mode. When aimed first at worship, rituals are necessarily open to the community of faith at-large. Even in occasional rites, there would be no private events; all are drawn to the central feature of the Eucharist. Through continuity and repetition, the assembly is conformed to a shared set of values, behaviors, identity, and vision of the world.

As a final point: this approach does not compromise the pastoral quality of ritual for the sake of maintaining ritual integrity. All of ritual care literature speak to the help ritual provides people in coping with difficult circumstances.[126] They do not all provide a clear rationale for why this is so. Willimon, however, offers the following: "By providing a patterned, purposeful, predictable way of behaving in the midst of crisis, by symbolically focusing our attention upon norms, beliefs, and sentiments regarding our ultimate concerns, religious ritual gives us a way through crises that might otherwise overwhelm us."[127] Ritual, as Willimon understands it, provides a sort of stability in the midst of vulnerable moments. Jean-Claude Larchet sees a similar phenomenon at work in the care that earlier monks provided for the infirm. He writes:

The Fathers had the possessed/insane reside in the monastery until they were cured, desiring to have them under their care at all times. By having them reside in the same place as the monks (as for example St Athanasius the Athonite who lodged Matthew in the very cells of the brothers in whose care he placed him), it is equally probable that they sought to integrate them into the *regular cycles of the monastic life so they could acquire a more organized and materially structured existence.*[128]

One can assume that the "regular cycles of monastic life" involved a highly liturgical and ritualized existence. The hermeneutic approach to ritual care more than the humanistic, provides grounding in the patterned and the predictable, while drawing attention to norms and ultimate concerns. If what Willimon posits is true, then the hermeneutic approach with its basis in the Eucharistic liturgy may prove to be more effective in addressing the pastoral needs of crisis situations. When unexpected tragedy strikes and one's life is no longer as it was before, the liturgy provides ongoing stability, familiarity, and a container for the messiness of existence, while directing one's eyes towards the highest good.

This chapter provided an exploration of two bodies of relevant literature. The first is a collection of veteran care literature that either addresses combat-related guilt or moral injury. The second is a compilation of works, here characterized as "ritual care" literature. As no work on veteran care extensively addresses the use of rituals and none of the ritual care texts speak to moral injury, it was necessary to assess both with a keen eye towards the possible intersection of these fields. Both bodies of literature served as conversation partners and offered theoretical building blocks for the model of ritual care proposed in the final portion of this chapter. Chapter 4 will provide a picture of these principles in application as well as a synthesis of the cumulative insights of previous chapters.

NOTES

1. Matsakis, *Back from the Front*, 175.
2. Ibid.
3. Ibid., 382.
4. Ibid., 97.
5. Ibid.
6. Friedman and Slone, *After the War Zone*, 98.
7. Ibid., 103.
8. Brett Litz, Nathan Stein, Eileen Delaney, Leslie Lebowitz, William P. Nash, Caroline Silva, and Shira Maguen, "Moral Injury and Moral Repair in War Veterans: A

104 Chapter 3

Preliminary Model and Intervention Strategy," *Clinical Psychology Review* 29, no. 8 (2009): 702.

9. Ibid.

10. Litz et al., "Moral Injury and Moral Repair in War Veterans," 703.

11. Ibid.

12. Ibid.

13. Ibid., 704.

14. Ibid.

15. Shira Maguen and Brett Litz, "Moral Injury in the Context of War," PTSD: National Center for PTSD, December 23, 2011, accessed March 18, 2018, http://www.ptsd.va.gov/professional/co-occurring/moral_injury_at_war.asp.

16. Shira Maguen, "Killing in War: Research and Treatment," PowerPoint presentation, San Francisco VA Medical Center, 2016.

17. Matt J. Gray et al., "Adaptive Disclosure: An Open Trial of a Novel Exposure-Based Intervention for Service Members with Combat-Related Psychological Stress Injuries," *Behavior Therapy* 43, no. 2 (2012): 409.

18. Gray, "Adaptive Disclosure," 410.

19. Ibid.

20. Jason Nieuwsma, Robyn Walser, Jacob Farnsworth, Kent Drescher, Keith Meador, and William Nash, "Possibilities within Acceptance and Commitment Therapy for Approaching Moral Injury," *Current Psychiatry Reviews* 11, no. 3 (2015): 196.

21. Nieuwsma et al., "Possibilities within Acceptance and Commitment Therapy for Approaching Moral Injury," 196.

22. Ibid., 197.

23. Ibid.

24. Ibid.

25. Ibid., 198.

26. Maguen, "Killing in War: Research and Treatment."

27. Gray, "Adaptive Disclosure," 412.

28. Paul D. Fritts, *Adaptive Disclosure: Critique of a Descriptive Intervention Modified for the Normative Problem of Moral Injury in Combat Veterans.* Seminar paper. Yale Divinity School (April 29, 2013), 1.

29. Kinghorn, "Combat Trauma and Moral Fragmentation," 65.

30. Ibid., 65–66.

31. Ibid., 66.

32. Kinghorn may find in the example of St. Theodosius a hint of the proper "teleological frame" in the face of suffering. The *Life of St. Theodosius* describes the saint's disposition towards the monks under his care: "He taught others to have courage and to hold on to the good in the face of their suffering. He in fact thought that in some of these cases it was better to be patient than to wish to be delivered from one's difficulties, for the first course of action achieved impassibility while the second proved that one lacked courage. Also he did not struggle to heal the ill person but advised him on how to hold on to the good with generosity and offer to God humble thoughts prompted by our miserable condition." [*Life of St Theodosius*, 42–44, cited

in Jean-Claude Larchet, *Mental Disorders & Spiritual Healing: Teachings from the Early Christian East* (Hillsdale, NY: Sophia Perennis, 2005), 76.]

33. Kinghorn, "Combat Trauma and Moral Fragmentation: A Theological Account of Moral Injury," 66.

34. Nieuwsma et al., "Possibilities within Acceptance and Commitment Therapy for Approaching Moral Injury," 197–98.

35. Ibid., 195.

36. Kinghorn, "Combat Trauma and Moral Fragmentation: A Theological Account of Moral Injury," 65.

37. Paul D. Fritts, *Adaptive Disclosure: Critique of a Descriptive Intervention Modified for the Normative Problem of Moral Injury in Combat Veterans*, 18.

38. Ibid., 19.

39. Ibid., 18.

40. Ibid.

41. Litz et al., "Moral Injury and Moral Repair in War Veterans," 702.

42. Shira Maguen et al., "Impact of Killing in War: A Randomized, Controlled Pilot Trial," *Journal of Clinical Psychology* 73, no. 9 (March 10, 2017): 1002–1003.

43. Ibid., 1002.

44. Shira Maguen, "Moral Injury and Killing in Combat Veterans: Research & Clinical Implications." Cyber seminar transcript, 11/19/2015.

45. Though Willimon's later article is titled "Ritual and Pastoral Care" (2002), he still does not engage ritual theorists in that work and continues to favor the words "worship" and "liturgy."

46. William H. Willimon, "Ritual and Pastoral Care," in *The Conviction of Things Not Seen: Worship and Ministry in the 21st Century*, edited by Todd E. Johnson (Grand Rapids: Brazos Press, 2002), 100.

47. William H. Willimon, *Worship as Pastoral Care* (Nashville, TN: Abingdon, 1979), 47–48.

48. Willimon, "Ritual and Pastoral Care," 100, 108.

49. Ibid., 115.

50. Ibid., 48.

51. Ibid.

52. Ibid.

53. Ibid., 100.

54. Elaine Ramshaw, *Ritual and Pastoral Care* (Philadelphia: Fortress Press, 1987), 13.

55. Elsewhere, Ramshaw writes, "Despite what so many of our carefully organized ministry programs . . . may seem to suggest, ritual and pastoral care are not separate activities which must be brought into a carefully negotiated relation. . . . Rather, they each involve the other necessarily, so that one without the other is no more than a caricature of itself. Liturgy without pastoral care is bad liturgy, and pastoral care dissociated from ritual and symbol is perhaps good psychotherapy, but certainly deficient pastoral care." [Elaine Ramshaw, "Ritual and Pastoral Care: The Vital Connection" in *Disciples at the Crossroads: Perspectives on Worship and Church Leadership*, ed. Eleanor Bernstein, C.S.J. (Collegeville, MN: The Liturgical Press, 1993), 92.]

56. Ramshaw, *Ritual and Pastoral Care*, 26–28.

57. Herbert Anderson and Edward Foley, *Mighty Stories, Dangerous Rituals: Weaving Together the Human and the Divine* (San Francisco: Jossey-Bass, 2001), 30.

58. Ramshaw, *Ritual and Pastoral Care*, 15.

59. Ibid., 25.

60. Anderson and Foley, *Mighty Stories, Dangerous Rituals*, 13.

61. Ibid., 14.

62. David Hogue, *Remembering the Future, Imagining the Past: Story, Ritual and the Human Brain* (Eugene, OR: Wipf & Stock, 2009), 121, 129.

63. Ibid., 186.

64. Ibid., 127.

65. Ibid., 130.

66. Ibid., 142–43.

67. Ibid., 139–40.

68. Susan Marie Smith, *Caring Liturgies: The Pastoral Power of Christian Ritual* (Minneapolis, MN: Fortress Press, 2012), 9.

69. Ibid., 9–10.

70. Hogue, *Remembering the Future, Imagining the Past*, 124.

71. Ramshaw, "Ritual and Pastoral Care: The Vital Connection," 92–93.

72. Ibid., 92.

73. Willimon, *Worship as Pastoral Care*, 48.

74. Anderson and Foley, *Mighty Stories, Dangerous Rituals*, ix–x.

75. Hogue, *Remembering the Future, Imagining the Past*, 121, 129, 130, 186.

76. Ibid., ix–x.

77. Smith, *Caring Liturgies*, 9–13.

78. Hogue, *Remembering the Future, Imagining the Past*, 185.

79. Willimon, *Worship as Pastoral Care*, 48.

80. Ibid., 116.

81. Willimon, "Ritual and Pastoral Care," 100.

82. Ramshaw, *Ritual and Pastoral Care*, 22–23. See also 15–16.

83. Willimon, "Ritual and Pastoral Care," 108.

84. Willimon, *Worship as Pastoral Care*, 97.

85. Irenaeus, *Against Heresies* 4.20.7.

86. The *Westminster Shorter Catechism* reflects this same notion with its opening question and answer: *What is the chief end of man? Man's chief end is to glorify God, and to enjoy him forever.*

87. Ramshaw, *Ritual and Pastoral Care*, 15–16. Also, Willimon, *Worship as Pastoral Care*, 48, 100.

88. That being said, according to my theological anthropology, which I draw from Schmemann, I understand the worship of God as a universal human need that cannot be replaced by any other act.

89. Ramshaw, *Ritual and Pastoral Care*, 13–14.

90. According to the Eucharistic Prayer found in the *Book of Common Prayer*, the assembly that partakes in Holy Communion offers itself as a sacrifice to God, a sacrifice of praise and thanksgiving. According to tradition, this is the appointed means by

which the church remembers the death and resurrection of the Son of God, as well as offers thanks for these salvific acts. This is why I presume, as I do in chapter 2, that the Eucharistic liturgy is the paradigmatic form of worship.

91. Alexander Schmemann, *For the Life of the World: Sacraments and Orthodoxy* (Yonkers, NY: St. Vladimir's Seminary Press, 1973), 118, 120, 125.

92. Wittgenstein, *Remarks on Frazer's Golden Bough* (1993), 128; cited in Johannes Quack, "Bell, Bourdieu, and Wittgenstein on Ritual Sense," in *The Problem of Ritual Efficacy*, edited by William Sax, William Sturman, Johannes Quack, and Jan Weinhold (Oxford: Oxford University Press, 2010), 179.

93. This is in part my answer to those who might wonder whether ritual approaches to care would be effective or well-received by people from non-liturgical church traditions. I (following Schmemann and Wittgenstein) contend that the issue would not be that these people are not liturgical. The issue would be that they are not familiar with the liturgies of a specific tradition. A part of ritual care would be to build a person's ritual fluency so as not to just receive the liturgies of the church, but to also inoculate her from the more insidious liturgies of the world.

94. St. Thomas Aquinas, *Summa Theologiae*, Prima Secundae Q. 2.

95. Seligman argues that it is not the mode of ritual to express the sincere or authentic feelings and views of its participants. Instead, rituals create an "as if" world or a "shared subjunctive universe" serving not as "the vehicle for self-expression or self-fulfillment." This squares with a Christian view of the sacraments. See Adam B. Seligman, *Ritual and Its Consequences: An Essay on the Limits of Sincerity* (Oxford: Oxford University Press, 2008), 8–10. Schmemann writes, "[T]he Church herself is thus the sacrament in which the broken, yet still 'symbolical,' life of 'this world' is brought, in Christ and by Christ, into the dimension of the Kingdom of God, becoming itself the sacrament of the 'world to come'" . . ." [Schmemann, *For the Life of the World*, 151.] This understanding of ritual serves as a challenge for some of the creative liturgies presented by Susan Smith and Hogue. Hogue for instance gives an example of a divorce ritual [*Remembering the Future*, 139–41], which despite its therapeutic benefit, seems to project an "as is" vision of reality far from the "sacrament of the 'world to come.'"

96. James K. A. Smith, *Desiring the Kingdom: Worship, Worldview, and Cultural Formation* (Grand Rapids, MI: Baker Academic, 2009), 32–33.

97. For instance, James K. A. Smith uses the mall as an example of a secular religious institution throughout his book *Desiring the Kingdom*. Smith describes the mall as a cathedral replete with its own liturgies, icons, and pilgrims.

98. Willimon, *Worship as Pastoral Care*, 115, 130.

99. While the second one (p. 139) actually precedes the first (pp. 140–41) in the chapter, it seems to refer to a climactic point in the ritual and so I have arranged it as such.

100. Hogue, *Remembering the Future, Imagining the Past*, 140–41.

101. Ibid., 139.

102. I wish to draw attention to the intentional use of the word "If" at the beginning of this statement. I concede that if a church does not understand the wedding as a signifying and sharing "in the mystery of that unity and fruitful love which exists

108   *Chapter 3*

between Christ and his Church," there may be less of a contradiction seen in the existence of a Christian divorce rite. I nevertheless advance this point as I presume this to be the most common understanding of a wedding/marriage in the Christian tradition.

103. Hogue, *Remembering the Future, Imagining the Past*, 141.

104. Ramshaw makes a similar argument from the perspective of communal norms and ethics. She writes: "It is ritual's role in affirming the central meaning-structure of the community which gives it normative, ethical force. Part of the symbolic world view presented in ritual is the tradition's understanding of good and evil, its models of the good person, its image of a just society. This normative dimension can never be separated out from the ritual functions of bonding the community or linking it with the transcendent. Even a ritual which has no explicit normative statement must carry implicit assumptions and images of what is right and valued. This means, for instance, that one cannot bless any activity without raising the normative question of how that activity—whether battle, inauguration, or second marriage—conforms to the tradition's understanding of justice and love." (*Ritual and Pastoral Care*, 26.)

105. Hogue, *Remembering the Future, Imagining the Past*, 140.

106. Ibid., 143.

107. Ramshaw, "Ritual and Pastoral Care: The Vital Connection," 93, see also Willimon, *Worship as Pastoral Care*, 48.

108. Hogue, *Remembering the Future, Imagining the Past*, 138.

109. Ibid., 139.

110. Ibid., 141.

111. Willimon, *Worship as Pastoral Care*, 130.

112. Hogue, *Remembering the Future, Imagining the Past*, 141.

113. Ibid.

114. Ibid., 142.

115. Schmemann, *For the Life of the World*, 125.

116. As noted above, I am not agnostic to the fact that there are various theological understandings of the Eucharist. I do not intend to present here a definitive or recommended understanding of the Eucharist or the Eucharistic liturgy. Such would be a separate, lengthy, and presumptuous task. The interpretive moves I make here and following do come from a particular theological location from which I stand. The primary focus of this presentation, however, is the method—this hermeneutic approach to ritual care—and not the resulting interpretations made. In chapter 4 I commend the Church community's use of experience, scripture, and tradition (inspired by the Wesleyan quadrilateral—the use of *reason* too should be implied), as a means of arriving at interpretations in service of ritual care and provide an example of how that could be done.

117. I find that the type of personal exegesis I propose here is akin to social psychologist Timothy Wilson's notion of introspection. Wilson writes:

"Introspection is more like literary criticism in which we are the text to be understood. Just as there is no single truth that lies within a literary text, but many truths, so are there many truths about a person that can be constructed.

The analogy I favor is introspection as a personal narrative, whereby people construct stories about their lives, much as a biographer would. We weave what we can observe (our conscious thoughts, feelings, and memories, our own behavior, the reactions of other people to us) into a story that, with luck, captures at least a part what we cannot observe (our nonconscious personality traits, goals, and feelings)." [Timothy D. Wilson, *Strangers to Ourselves: Discovering the Adaptive Unconscious* (Cambridge, MA: Belknap, 2004), 162.]

Therefore, my notion of "exegeting" should not be understood narrowly as interpretation alone. There is a constructive and formative aspect to this, which I will expound further in this chapter. What I am offering to Wilson's model of introspection is the use of the Eucharist as an interpretive key.

118. Willimon, "Ritual and Pastoral Care," 100.

119. Wherein a pastor may designate certain days each year to provide commentary on the liturgy as it is underway during worship.

120. Ramshaw, "Ritual and Pastoral Care," 93.

121. By contrast, the process of creating a one-off humanistic ritual presumes that one knows what one needs. Such a ritual is catered towards a specific aim, and, at best, one will acquire just that. Yet people are not always the best adjudicators of what they need and such a narrow vision for a ritual forecloses on the possibilities resident within cycles of regular corporate worship. Moreover, the orientation towards ritual creation is potentially contrary to the mode of submission posited here. It may arise from a desire to determine one's own meanings and achieve one's desired ends on one's own terms apart from a wider community of faith. While worship in the form of the Eucharistic liturgy may not directly speak to proximate concerns, it appeals to human beings at a deeper level, as a satisfaction of human nature and ultimate desires. Schmemann would state that behind these proximate desires are ultimately a desire for God [*For the Life of the World*, 14–15].

122. Schmemann, *For the Life of the World*, 26–27.

123. The absence of the divorcee, acknowledged consciously or unconsciously by the congregation, may serve as an impetus for a pattern of behavior within the community that further reinforces this assumption. Despite the instrumental role of the celebrant, the liturgy is fundamentally and unavoidably *leitourgia*, the work of the people.

124. That is not to say that one's shame and embarrassment are forgotten or disregarded in the process of ritual care. As I have stated before, the use of ritual care does not obviate or replace the need for traditional pastoral counseling. The ritual care process also entails processing and understanding one's circumstances, including shame, in light of the Eucharist to the benefit of the sufferer and the congregation at-large. Moreover, one's shame is brought to the liturgy, as with anything else. This is not shame brought in spite of the sufferer's intent to worship, but shame brought as an act of worship.

110   *Chapter 3*

125. Ancient penitential rites allow for a penitent's need to abstain from the Eucharist for a time and yet still participate in a meaningful way in worship. When the circumstances of a divorce make participation in the communion rite ritually dishonest, divorcees may have similar recourse to this ancient model of participation. More will be stated on this matter in the following chapter.

126. See for instance, Hogue, *Remembering the Future, Imagining the Past*, 143, and Willimon, *Worship as Pastoral Care*, 100.

127. Willimon, *Worship as Pastoral Care*, 100.

128. Larchet, *Mental Disorders and Spiritual Healing*, 82.

Chapter 4

Non-humanistic Ritual Care for Moral Injury

A Pastoral Theological Commentary

In this chapter, I conduct a pastoral theological commentary and analysis of St. Gregory the Wonderworker's graded penitential rite.[1] This is likely the ritual to which Brock,[2] Grundy,[3] and Kinghorn[4] refer when they speak of the penitential practices afforded to military veterans by the ancient church, though non-existent today. None of them necessarily advocates that this specific rite be re-instituted by Christian communities, though all of them seem to suggest that the absence of a rite for veterans is an oversight by the Church. Despite this seeming consensus, there has not been significant exploration into St. Gregory's rite for the study of moral injury, except to state with some wistfulness that such a rite once existed within the Church. In addition to the fact of its frequent mention by Christian investigators of moral injury, this rite is also explored here as it serves as a historical example of a liturgy used for military veterans that fits the principles of ritual honesty set forth in this study. Not only will this chapter present the graded penitential rite as an example of a ritually honest Christian practice, it will also demonstrate how such a ritual can be at the same time pastorally and therapeutically effective. This investigation will begin by providing a historical analysis of the ritual in order to understand its relevance to moral injury and pastoral care. This will be followed by a pastoral theological commentary on the form of the ancient penitential rite itself.

112 *Chapter 4*

THE ANCIENT GRADED PENITENTIAL DISCIPLINE
AND THE RITUAL CARE OF VETERANS

This section provides some historical background for the ancient practice referred to as the graded penitential discipline. This is not intended to be an exhaustive treatment of penitential texts or the early church's stance on military participation. After introducing St. Gregory's canonical epistle, the focus of this section will be limited to third- and fourth-century texts that refer to penance in the form of the bishop's graded penitential rite for military veterans who have shed blood. The purpose of this historical exploration is to suggest that this particular discipline was intended not solely for punishment or the remediation for sin, but also as a pastoral means for addressing moral injury. This particular ritual will be the subject of the subsequent pastoral theological analysis and commentary.

The graded form of penitential discipline emerged in the third century at a time when the penitential process began to mirror the probationary period placed upon catechumens preparing for baptism. What resulted is a "graded" penitential process in which the penitent advances in grades from a position outside the church inward until she is invited to partake of the Eucharist once again. Two of our third-century primary texts depicting this discipline are the *Didascalia* and St. Gregory the Wonderworker's *Canonical Epistle*. The latter document in particular provides a comprehensive and efficient summary of the penitential process:

> The "weeping" takes place outside the door of the worship space; there the sinner has to entreat the faithful who are entering to pray for him. The "audience" is inside the gate in the vestibule area, where one who has sinned has to stand until "the catechumens," and then leave. "For when one has heard the Scripture and the instruction," it says, "let him be put out, and not deemed worthy of the prayer." The "submission" is when someone, after standing within the church door, leaves with the catechumens. "Standing with" is when one stands along with the faithful, and does not leave with the catechumens. Finally comes "participation" in the Holy Communion.[5]

Penitential practices had existed prior to the emergence of this form of penance involving excommunication, fasting, and public confession. The graded form appears to be the first system of penance that involved an intentional and ordered abstention from communion. The practice spread over the course of the fourth century and extant texts reveal that many influential fathers of the church prescribed this discipline to address a variety of circumstances within the church. One of its uses was for Christians who had participated in combat as soldiers. The most explicit reference to this use is St. Basil's

Canons in the fourth century (ca. 374). In these texts, he writes, "Our fathers did not reckon killings in war as murders, but granted pardon, it seems to me, to those fighting in defense of virtue and piety. Perhaps, however, it is well to advise them that, since their hands are not clean, they should abstain from communion alone for a period of three years."[6] Given the prevalence of St. Gregory's rite at the time, one can presume that Basil's imposition of a three-year ban from communion involves the penitent making her way from the grade of "weeping" to "standing with" over the course of those years before "participation" in Holy Communion. This is a significant text not only in its reference to the graded form of penance in the context of military service, but in its ambiguous rationale for this ordinance. The passage seems to imply that even in the cases of pardonable "killing" or "fighting," penance is still recommended. This immediately brings to the forefront the question of the purpose of penance.

Penance as it is understood today in the *Catechism of the Catholic Church* is described as follows: "Those who approach the sacrament of Penance obtain pardon from God's mercy for the offense committed against him, and are, at the same time, reconciled with the Church which they have wounded by their sins and which by charity, by example, and by prayer labors for their conversion."[7] Participation in penance today implies that an offense has been committed by the penitent, thus creating the need to offer remediation. Basil's *Canon 13*, however, advises the imposition of a penance (a severe one, no less) even where the Church Fathers see no transgression committed. In order to make greater sense of this seeming paradox, two other texts are worth investigating.

The *Canons of Hippolytus*, a church order roughly contemporary with St. Basil's *Canons*, also makes reference to both military service and penitential abstention from the Eucharist. It states, "A Christian must not become a soldier, unless he is compelled by a chief bearing the sword [i.e., conscription]. He is not to burden himself with the sin of blood. But if he has shed blood, he is not to partake of the mysteries, unless he is purified by a punishment, tears, and wailing. He is not to come forward deceitfully but in the fear of God."[8] This canon dovetails nicely with Basil's, even if it seems to take a more hardline stance against military service. While Basil assumes Christian participation in some fighting, even to the point of killing, the church order asserts that Christians should not even become soldiers, except when compelled by authority. Like Basil, perhaps, the *Canons of Hippolytus* nevertheless sees Christian participation in soldiering as an unavoidable reality. The threshold at which veterans must refrain from "the mysteries" is when they "shed blood." There appears to be still greater parity here with Basil's final penitential prescription. Though the church order does not set a term limit for abstention, both sets of *Canons* see it as a necessity due to a sort of uncleanliness caused by participation in combat. The occasion for penance is that Basil's veterans have hands that are "not clean," while the church order speaks to soldiers needing time to be "purified."

One final patristic witness worth visiting is that of St. Isidore of Pelusium, dated approximately a century after Basil's. His statement on the matter of military service is a simple one, but no less befuddling, and for nearly the same reason. He writes that while "it is permissible to kill your enemy in battle, and although we erect triumphal arches for the victors and honor them, slaying in war is not free from blame."[9] The paradox is starkest here as he says killing in war is not only permissible, but even honorable, *and yet it is not free from blame.*

Among these three witnesses there is a general sense that for a Christian to kill in war is permissible or, perhaps, an inevitability. The *Canons of Hippolytus*, the outlier among the three, unequivocally discourages military service and the "sin of blood," but nevertheless depicts Christian conscription and even the shedding of blood as a seeming foregone conclusion. This sort of concession to the powers that be is a far cry from the subject of Tertullian's *De Corona* just a century earlier, in which a Christian is commended for his defiance of serving the emperor as a soldier, even in the face of punishment.[10] The *Canons* also seem to betray Tertullian's contemporary, Origen, who argues in his *Contra Celsum*, that Christians have been taught not even to defend themselves against their enemies.[11] An optimistic reader of Isidore, Basil, and the *Canons of Hippolytus*, may interpret the killing and shedding of blood referenced in these texts as pertaining to those acts *in defense of others*. In fact, John McGuckin interprets Basil's "defense of virtue and piety"[12] as referring to the latter, the act of protecting the weak.[13] Yet even with these dispensations given to Christian soldiers who shed blood in war, these fathers collectively describe the act as requiring some form of remediation. How does one reconcile these seemingly contradictory positions?

Basil and Isidore appear to adjudicate the act of killing in war on two levels. The first level attends to the legality of the act. At this level, the language of lawfulness and permissibility is used in relation to killing in war. Naturally, participating in war for the interests of one's government would not break any secular codes of law. The underlying concern at this level then appears to be whether the act transgresses *biblical* law, namely the sixth commandment. Basil observes a distinction being made between types of killing, the prohibitive form being *murder*. According to the bishop, some believed "killings in war" *not* to be classifiable as "murders."[14] In other words, the sixth commandment, interpreted as referring primarily to murder, is not broken in such circumstances.

Without getting into the technicalities of what constitutes "murder," one can at least assert that some in the early church believed that the context of war can present conditions in which it is lawful to kill. What makes the statements of Basil and Isidore provocative is that they believed, even still, that without technically engaging in any impermissible or unlawful acts (that is, even according to the *Mosaic* law), "slaying in war is not free from blame" and those engaged in such acts ought to abstain from communion. The apparent contradiction that arises from these declarations is that killing the enemy on the battlefield can be at once permissible (even praiseworthy), but not free from blame; fighting in defense of virtue and piety is pardonable, yet still requires penance. This second level of adjudication goes beyond whether an act transgresses any one of the Ten Commandments.

Verkamp finds that Augustine's conception of "concupiscence" provides a model for reconciling the early church's approach to sin and penance, particularly in the case of those who engage in lawful warfare. According to Verkamp, Augustine believed that an underlying "beastly desire" or "lust" wears against humanity's spiritual freedom, due to original sin, such that one's mind and flesh is never totally obedient to one's will.[15] Most know Augustine's concupiscence in regard to his reflections on sexual desire, but as the Church Father himself relates, this disorder applies to other areas of human life as well.[16] With regards to the matter of participating in lawful military conflict, Verkamp explains, "Though 'lawful and right,' and therefore certainly not sinful in any formal sense, the justifiable anger vented in the struggle against the vice of one's enemies nonetheless unleashes a certain 'bestial desire,' disturbs the warrior's 'peace of mind,' and leaves him in a certain state of 'depravity' from which he needs to be purified by the performance of one or another penance."[17] Therefore, the act is not unlawful, but participation in, say, killing one's enemies stirs within one "beastly desires" that sully the warrior. What I regard as two levels of adjudication, Verkamp frames, via Augustine, as a distinction between guilt and shame. As Verkamp understands it, "Whereas guilt is aroused by the transgression of boundaries set by the conscience and is accompanied by fear of destructive reprisal, shame occurs when an idealized goal is not reached and carries with it the threat of abandonment."[18] The assumption then is that penance here can be used to address the shame, if not the guilt, of a lawful killing.

Verkamp's recognition of a distinction between guilt and shame is helpful here, though I would not go so far as to invoke Augustine's understanding of concupiscence to reconcile the Fathers' views. Instead, I appeal to the aforementioned conception of sin as a failure of vocation. If sin were merely the transgression of the Ten Commandments, one would be befuddled by St. Basil's suggestion to recommend penance for *lawful* killings. From Verkamp's perspective, while the act may not bring the stain of guilt, it may

116   *Chapter 4*

elicit shame—the failure to realize the ideal in one's life. Verkamp, however, does not explicitly detail what the "idealized goal" of the Christian soldier should be. To say that this ideal is the *worship of God* (humanity's ultimate vocation) would actually bring Verkamp's understanding of shame close to my presentation of moral injury. In other words, to kill in war may not technically be classifiable as murder. It may even be a praiseworthy act if done in defense of virtue and sobriety, as in ensuring the safety of the weak. To take a life, in any situation, however, can hardly be considered a worshipful act. In fact it is a perversion of worship, a form of idolatry. According to Hauerwas, "The sacrifices of war are a counter-liturgy to the sacrifice at the altar made possible by Christ. Christians believe that Christ is the end of sacrifice—that is, any sacrifice that is not determined by the sacrifice of the cross—and therefore we are free of the necessity to secure our existence through sacrificing our and others' lives on the world's altars."[19] In these terms, the sacrifices of war then are worship of a different kind. Moreover, it still transgresses the very nature of humans and for what they were intended.[20] As a result, one can avoid breaking a law (civic or Mosaic)[21] and yet find oneself in a state of sin.[22]

Just as this study seeks to broaden the conception of sin, it also strives to expand the notion of penance. What the Church Fathers present in the graded penitential practice is not merely a medium for punishment and remediation of sin, but a model of ritual care. One of the insights drawn from contemporary research on killing is that human beings have a natural resistance to killing other human beings.[23] Moreover, the majority who do kill will be traumatized, or morally injured, by it.[24] Research seems to suggest that this is normative of people from all cultures and eras in human history.[25] If this is the case, one can assume the veterans called to the graded penitential rite for having shed blood are not disinterested participants. They are likely burdened by their actions, guilt-stricken, morally injured. It matters not that certain bishops at the time viewed killing in war as permissible. One Vietnam veteran I met at a VA clinic stated that his own experience of killing had led him to the profound, gut-wrenching realization that "God did not intend for human beings to kill one another." This was not his view going into war.

There is evidence in the above witnesses that pastoral care for the distraught soldier may have been their intent in administering penance. Recall that the *Canons of Hippolytus* do not set a specific term for penance but instruct that the condition upon which the soldier may return to the "mysteries" is purification by punishment, as well as *tears and wailing*. This sounds as though the bishop is giving the veteran time to grieve and mourn his actions in war. One can assume that this may be the case for Basil as well. It seems particularly incongruent to remark that the "defense of virtue and piety" is pardonable, and yet levy a three-year ban from communion. Again, the intent may not be simply to punish these soldiers, but it may reflect an understanding of the difficult and long process ingredient in wrestling with the trauma of killing.

Finally, one must consider where Isidore sees the source of "blame" to be, if killing the enemy is at once permissible and lauded by society. As a chaplain, I have encountered numerous veterans who have seen the "enemy" fall by their hand. Knowing that these were lawful killings, directed by a superior or done to protect self or a comrade, does not take away the pangs of guilt or shame for having ended another's life. Even when they believe that God has forgiven them, they cannot rid the interior voice that condemns them for having committed this evil. Perhaps the blame that Isidore observes is the one the soldier directs at himself.

This brief historical treatment of the usage of the graded penitential rite in the third and fourth centuries sought to reconcile the seeming incongruities found in the statements of the Fathers above, that is, between the permissibility of killing in war and the need for penance. The argument posited here is that coherence between the two can be found in two ways: (1) by demonstrating that an act can be at once lawful according to both civic and Mosaic laws, and yet still fall short of the Christian ideal (here, understood to be the fundamental human vocation to worship); and (2) by arguing that penance in these cases is not primarily a penalty for sin, but a means of addressing the pastoral needs of veterans. The following commentary will delve more deeply into those pastoral aspects of the graded penitential rite.

PASTORAL THEOLOGICAL COMMENTARY ON THE GRADED PENITENTIAL RITE

This remainder of the chapter will be dedicated to conducting a pastoral theological commentary on St. Gregory the Wonderworker's graded penitential rite. The following reflections are focused more narrowly on interfacing this ancient penitential discipline with a variety of research and the experiences of veterans surrounding moral injury today. This exercise is intended to explore in greater detail how ritual and current clinical theories validate, challenge, and inform one another, particularly in the realm of moral injury. Secondarily, some of the commentary will provide occasion for demonstrating what I have termed "pastoral ritual hermeneutics," by fleshing out interpretive possibilities where the ritual intersects with the moral injury experience in poignant ways. Overall, this section seeks to understand how a ritual grounded in the Eucharistic liturgy (a *non*-humanistic ritual) could function pastorally for the morally injured, given what we know of moral injury today.

This treatment of St. Gregory's rite should not be taken as an endorsement for the wholesale reintroduction of the graded penitential discipline into the

118 *Chapter 4*

church today. One reason such a recommendation should be approached with caution is because rituals are formed within a social, cultural, and historical milieu. One of the main differences between the third century and our present time is that they lived in a much more ritualized society where Gregory's rite may have fit more organically within the larger ritual infrastructure of the church. To bring this penitential system into any church today would be to put "new wine into old wineskins" (or in this case, vice versa), as the saying goes.[26]

That being said, there are certain practices and theological perspectives associated with the rite that would likely be beneficial if applied to our current circumstances. Thus, the remainder of this chapter is dedicated in part to using the graded rite as a springboard for seeing the possibilities of non-humanistic liturgies for pastoral care. In particular, it will point to some ways earlier practices can serve as resources for ritual care today, even if they cannot be assumed in whole.

The following commentary will be organized in segments, each aligned with a grade or stage in St. Gregory's penitential rite. At certain points material will be drawn from the *Didascalia*, another contemporary source for the graded penitential rite, to compensate for the paucity of detail in the *Canonical Epistle*'s economical language. These texts too will be the subject of analysis. With each grade, the commentary will revolve around a theme or feature drawn from the details of those associated texts. Though some of the segments build upon the insights of those that precede them, they are for the most part independent of each other. The first begins with *confession* and is followed then by each of St. Gregory's five grades.

Confession: The Danger of Disclosure

Confession is not formally one of the five steps of St. Gregory's graded penitential rite, but it is an implied stage in the process. Recall that, according to the *Canons of Hippolytus*, a Christian soldier is expected not to "burden himself with the sin of blood."[27] There is nevertheless an addendum stating that "*if he has shed blood*, he is not to partake of the mysteries . . ." (one translation states "*if it can be shown* that he has shed blood he should stay away from the mysteries . . .").[28] There is some process by which a bishop learns the nature of the penitent's acts. It is also by this disclosure that the length of the penance is determined, and the penitent is rebuked and instructed.[29] This act of disclosing one's sins is older than St. Gregory's rite and it has been conducted differently at different times and locales.[30] This brief section will explore the significance of confession for the morally injured and how current clinical studies replicate and validate this ancient practice as a means for restoration.

Non-humanistic Ritual Care for Moral Injury 119

For morally injured combat veterans, the practice of confession can be more than the simple rote recounting of one's perceived errors. It can be a frightening yet instrumental step towards one's recovery. For one, it implies connection. As discussed earlier, there is an inherent difficulty to sharing morally injurious experiences, as well as a tendency for the morally injured to isolate themselves. Coming to confession involves connection with a moral authority and/or a community. Connection and dialogue with a moral authority also happen to be two elements of Litz's proposed treatment plan for moral injury.[31]

For the morally injured, the disclosure of one's perceived sins entails the recollection of some of one's most traumatic experiences. This is what makes confession such a perilous proposition. And yet, sharing one's stories and revisiting one's traumas are commended regularly as necessary steps to recovery for moral injury in particular and trauma in general. Shay writes:

> There is a growing consensus among people who treat PTSD that any trauma, be it loss of family in a natural disaster, rape, exposure to the dead and mutilated in an industrial catastrophe, or combat itself, will have longer-lasting and more serious consequences if there has been no opportunity to talk about the traumatic event, or express to other people emotions about the event and those involved in it, or to experience the presence of socially connected others who will not let one go through it alone. This is what is meant by communalizing the trauma.[32]

Litz adds, "Disclosing, sharing, confessing is fundamental to repair. In doing so, the vets learn that what happened to them can be tolerated, [that] they're not rejected."[33]

As a result, treatment plans for moral injury ordinarily revolve around focused revisitations of morally injurious events. For Litz, one of the two routes for "moral repair and renewal" is "psychological- and emotional-processing of the memory of the moral transgression, its meaning and significance, and the implication for the service member."[34] Adaptive Disclosure for moral injury involves, an "imaginal exposure exercise . . . devoted to emotionally processing the war memory."[35] Shay, however, has a caution for the kind of listening that takes place in clinical environments. He writes, "All too often, however, our mode of listening deteriorates into intellectual sorting, with the professional grabbing the veterans' words from the air and sticking them in mental bins. To some degree that is institutionally and educationally necessary, but listening this way destroys trust."[36]

I have met with more than one veteran who chafed against this type of "listening." One veteran in particular shared that he was fed up with psychiatrists repeatedly asking him the same questions, while appearing to be more focused on their computers than the other human being in the room.

120   *Chapter 4*

Some questions he also found to be insensitive, such as, What was the most traumatic or difficult event you experienced? For all of the events were bad and yet deeply sacred and personal, he related. The ambiguity of such a statement was not lost on him, but such ambiguity demands careful attention and reflection. He did not feel such a question should be addressed so flippantly by an inattentive clinician just checking off items on a list.

In this way, the confessional model perhaps has an advantage. The church is no clinic with time-sensitive appointments. The confessor is no disinterested stranger, whose only relationship to the patient is a transactional one contingent upon the veteran's illness. The penitential rite begins with confession not so that the veteran can be unsaddled and once again live life autonomously now free from his burdens. The penitent's sins are brought forth as a necessary first step to be drawn more deeply into community with God and her neighbor. Confession implies ongoing relationship.

This model of confession is also not entirely deaf to the specific concerns and intentions of the clinical approaches presented above. As the penitential process unfolds, the veteran does not go through this trial alone,[37] he is not rejected,[38] and the ritual provides the penitent ample space for "processing" morally injurious events,[39] though within the hermeneutic framework of the Eucharistic liturgy. In some ways, one might argue that the penitential model more substantially addresses these concerns. The commentary on the subsequent grades will expound in detail how this may be so.

Grade of Weeping: Grieving and Discipline

The "weeping" takes place outside the door of the worship space; there the sinner has to entreat the faithful who are entering to pray for him.[40]

When you see somebody sinning be angry at him, and demand that they cast him out. And when he is cast out they should be angry at him, and argue with him, and keep him outside the church. And then they may come in and plead for him. For our Saviour likewise pleaded with his father for those who sinned. Thus is it written in the Gospel: "My father, they do not know what they are doing or what they are saying. But if it is possible, forgive them." And then, bishop, demand that he come in, and enquire of him whether he repents. And if he is worthy of return to the church appoint a period of fasting for him in accordance with his transgression, two weeks or three or five or seven, and speaking all that is righteous in admonition and instruction so send him away and let him go, Rebuke him, and say to him that he should be by himself in his humiliation, and that in the period of his fasting he should pray and beseech that he be found worthy of the forgiveness of sins, as it is written in Genesis: "Have you sinned? Be silent and your repentance will be with you and you shall have power over it." To Miriam, the sister of Moses, also it was said by the Lord, when she had spoken

Non-humanistic Ritual Care for Moral Injury   121

against Moses and afterwards repented and had been found worthy of forgiveness: "If her father had spat in her face she should have been ashamed and to be separated from the camp for seven days before coming in." It is required that you too should act thus, that you put out of the church those who promise to repent of their sins, as is right on account of their transgressions, and then receive them again as merciful fathers.[41]

The *Grade of Weeping* marks the commencement and first stage of Gregory's penitential rite. The *Didascalia* provides a contemporary, more detailed account of this stage, which is included above. In this more exhaustive text, the first grade coincides with the assignment of penance for the sinner. Here, this segment will address two elements of the penitential process that are brought forth in these passages: mourning and the demanding nature of the penitential assignment. In this pastoral theological commentary of these aspects of the rite, I will argue that both are essential in the renewal of veterans from moral injury.

Weeping and Mourning

That Gregory explicitly calls the first grade that of "weeping" may seem no more than an incidental detail. Some may construe this as an arbitrary name that best describes in sum the trappings of the penitential process as a whole, rather than reflecting at any point the actual disposition of the penitent. In other words, this "weeping" or "mourning" (as other translations call it) is expressed only ritually, not with sincerity.[42] If this is the case, some would find this approach to ritual problematic. Ramshaw, for one, has levied a charge against the Church Fathers for their "Stoic suspicion of all strong feeling, including rage, sexual passion, and even grief," as a result of which "we have little or no room in our ritual/symbol system for legitimate anger or for sexual feeling, and sadness or fear are often cast as a lack of faith."[43] This has grave implications for ritual care. Ramshaw is convinced that, "There can hardly be any greater obstacle to connecting ritual and pastoral care than the fact that our liturgies ignore or stigmatize so much of natural human feeling."[44]

Ramshaw's point is an important one and her judgment regarding the ritual and symbolic systems of today may ring true. Whether this is a legacy of the Church Fathers' penchant for Stoicism, however, can be challenged. Already, we have noted the admonishment in the *Canons of Hippolytus* that a soldier who has shed blood "is not to partake of the mysteries, unless he is purified by a punishment, *tears, and wailing.*"[45] There, weeping is an instrumental part of the penitential process, such that its very evidence is the measure by which the length of penance is determined. In the century prior, the *Didascalia* similarly uses the penitent's expression of grief as the prerequisite for resuming

122   *Chapter 4*

communion with the faithful. It states, "And then, as each repents and shows forth the fruit of repentance [i.e. weeps],[46] accept him into the prayer as you would a pagan. And just as you baptize a pagan and at that time receive him, so lay the hand on this man while everyone is praying for him, and then bring him in and allow him to communicate with the church."[47]

There is good reason to believe that these are not just features unique to the graded penitential rite, but existed in the tradition that preceded it. In the period in which Marcus Aurelius was writing his *Meditations*, St. Irenaeus relayed an account of a woman who "spent her whole time in the exercise of public confession [*exomologesis*], *weeping over and lamenting* over the defilement which she had received" when she was seduced by a Gnostic.[48] Later in the second century, Tertullian would expound further what this "*exomologesis*" entails. He writes:

> *Exomologesis*, then, is a discipline which leads a man to prostrate and humble himself. It prescribes a way of life which, even in the matter of food and clothing, appeals to pity. It bids him to lie in sackcloth and ashes, to cover his body with filthy rags, to plunge his soul into sorrow, to exchange sin for suffering. Moreover, it demands that you know only such food and drink as is plain; this means it is taken for the sake of your soul, not your belly. It requires that you habitually nourish prayer by fasting, that you *sigh and weep and groan day and night* to the Lord your God, that you prostrate yourself at the feet of the priests and kneel before the beloved of God making all the brethren commissioned ambassadors of your prayer for pardon.[49]

It appears then the outward expression of lament has been part of the penitential process and perhaps the Christian ethos from early on. Given the continuity between his rite and the previous ones, one might even surmise that the penitent in St. Gregory's rite was expected to "weep and groan" while she "entreats the faithful."

These texts may not convince those like Ramshaw that the histrionics presented therein are not just that, mere theater. While there is no way to prove apodictically one way or another, the following arguments will assert that there is a place for both sincere and non-sincere expressions of lament in ritual care. This is particularly true in the care of morally injured veterans. Here, I will approach this notion of mourning from the perspective of *Acceptance and Commitment Therapy* (ACT) and relate in turn how this model fits with Christian pastoral theological assumptions.

Mourning is closely related to confession. Whereas confession requires the disclosure of the details of one's failings, mourning (in the "sincere" form) requires the disclosure of one's emotions tied to them. Drawing from the

Non-humanistic Ritual Care for Moral Injury 123

principles of ACT, Nieuwsma believes that being present with such emotions is necessary to moving beyond MI. He states:

> This kind of openness to experience may assist the patient in seeing that thoughts and emotions themselves are not dangerous. Being present to emotion is often informative, and in the case of moral injury, emotions such as guilt can actually be important to understanding how one might choose to live in the future. Guilt is not the enemy. It should be noted however, that we are also not suggesting that patients "wallow" in guilt; this is not a request to experience pain for pain's sake. Rather, we are asking patients to be aware of their emotional states, open up to them, and choose values as their guide to living.[50]

To the veteran's benefit, the form of the graded rite is such that it provides dedicated time and space to foster this sort of presence with one's emotions.

This ritual provision for mourning is particularly important for morally injured veterans. As veterans tend to want to avoid recalling the details of morally injurious events, they just as much wish to avoid the gut-wrenching emotions associated with them. Yet the ACT approach deems the avoidance of negative thoughts and emotions as causing only additional suffering.[51] This presupposition is founded on ACT's belief that "human suffering is inevitable and normal."[52] Therefore, attempts to eliminate negative emotions at every turn can be perceived as both fruitless and harmful.

It should be no surprise then, that "'curing' mental health problems, or suffering in general, is not the primary aim of ACT."[53] Instead, the objective is to foster values-based living. Yet in pursuit of this aim, studies have shown that this process does indeed reduce the symptoms of mental illness as a "secondary benefit."[54] This unique therapeutic perspective offers a clinically validated therapeutic model that connects well with Christian theological assumptions.

Nieuwsma is in agreement with theologians like Schmemann, who take for granted suffering within this life. The theologian writes in strikingly similar terms, "The religious outlook considers disease rather than health to be the 'normal' state of man. In this world of mortal and changing matter suffering, sickness and sorrow are the normal conditions of life."[55] Therefore, even in the work of pastoral care, there ought by no means to be this reflex to reduce all suffering or weeping.[56] Instead ACT invites us to be present with those painful emotions while striving for a higher aim.

ACT offers a potential model for a pastoral theology that looks upon the reduction of emotional suffering as only a secondary purpose or by-product to another otherwise higher aim. Willimon's understanding of "worship as pastoral care" seems to provide the most natural theological corollary to the ACT model. He writes, "My thesis is . . . not that we should use the liturgy as

124 *Chapter 4*

a new method of pastoral care but that the liturgy itself and a congregation's experience of divine worship already functions, even if in a secondary way, as pastoral care. The pastoral care that occurs as we are meeting and being met by God in worship is a significant by-product that we have too often overlooked."[57] The difference between Willimon's aims and Nieuwsma's is that the Christian liturgy aspires towards worship, while Acceptance Commitment Therapy is directed towards values-based living. Though not entirely unrelated, they are still fundamentally different. In the following discussion of non-sincere ritual expressions of mourning, I will demonstrate how ritual care can also achieve Nieuwsma's values-based living as another "secondary benefit."

Training the Non-weeping

If weeping, or mourning, is an essential step in the penitential and recovery process for MI, what of those who simply cannot feel grief or guilt over their transgressive actions? There are two populations of veterans that may find themselves in this category. Grossman cites research that the few who are not resistant to killing or driven insane by war conditions that would normally debilitate 98% of the population are already aggressive psychopaths.[58] On the other hand, there are also those who have been psychologically debilitated by war and have learned to become unfeeling as a defense mechanism.[59] Such people who can function effectively within society would not be a concern for the clinical world. The imposition of penance in the ancient world, however, was not contingent upon whether the veteran exhibited grief over his actions. The condition upon which a veteran was given to the graded penitential rite was whether he shed blood or not. What relevance then does St. Gregory's rite have for the emotionally numb or the sociopath? Here I will explore the notion of ritual as a potential site of affective formation.

Speaking of medieval penances, Verkamp states that it is conceivable that the church imposed penances to *stir up feelings* of shame when such was absent in a warrior.[60] There is no reason to believe that this may not have been conceivable for the earlier church as well. Such a practice would dovetail with Mark Searle's view that liturgy is essentially a "rehearsal of Christian attitudes."[61] (Initially, Searle had described it as a rehearsal of *right* attitudes.)[62] This Catholic liturgist explains, "Liturgy will not leave us on an emotional high because that is not its purpose. But regular, persevering participation and growing familiarity with liturgy's images and gestures will eventually shape our attitudes, our thoughts, and even our feelings."[63] Therefore, the liturgy is not simply a place to give air to one's true feelings and attitudes. It is also the environment where the proper feelings and attitudes are cultivated. It is therefore conceivable that the sociopathic or emotionally avoidant

Christian could participate in the ritual gestures of mourning with hopes that one day she would inhabit this disposition in earnest.[64]

Social psychologist Timothy Wilson validates this possibility, citing William James as a precursor to such thinking. According to Wilson, "James argued that the perception of environmental events triggers bodily responses, which then trigger conscious emotions; 'we feel sorry because we cry, angry because we strike, afraid because we tremble.' In his famous example, we do not meet a bear and run because we are afraid; we meet a bear, run, and then experience a post-hoc fear that played no causal role in our fleeing—much like the 'whoosh' of fear I experienced after regaining control of the rental car."[65] In other words, even in a human being's normative responses to outward stimuli, gestures precede the emotions associated with them. To this point, Wilson later adds, "the more frequently people perform a behavior, the more habitual and automatic it becomes, requiring little effort or conscious attention. One of the most enduring lessons of social psychology is that behavior change often precedes changes in attitudes and feelings."[66] Wilson did not seem to have rituals in mind when he shared this insight. Yet rituals may prove to be the ideal locus for the formation of feelings and attitudes with their formalized, repetitive actions.[67]

Consider for instance the gestures of mourning and lament that have been ingredient in the ancient penitential practices of the church. Both St. Gregory's *Canon* and the *Didascalia* above describe the penitent "entreating" and "beseeching" the faithful for prayer. In the previous generation, Tertullian describes the process of *exomologesis* as involving lying in sackcloth and ashes, fasting, groaning, weeping, and bowing before presbyters.[68] There is no indication that these were necessarily expressions of genuine emotion. These gestures of mourning can be construed as ritual acts, whose purpose is not simply to emote one's effusive feelings, but to practice and habituate the right response to one's sins. If Wilson is correct, the one for whom such feelings do not come naturally can learn to inhabit them through ritual rehearsal.

This promotion of actions in spite of dissonant feelings is not foreign to therapeutic models for treating moral injury. The ACT process is one that similarly promotes values-based living in spite of one's emotional state. ACT has been widely used in the VA in recent years and found to be an effective response to the effects of trauma on veterans. In the program, veterans are asked to identify values that are most important to them and encouraged to take what ACT calls "committed action" to live out those values.[69]

Consider for instance, the common story of a veteran that values community above all else, who nevertheless finds that her relationships over the years have been compromised due to her unwillingness to leave her home. The veteran does not necessarily enjoy being at home, but due to trauma this is where she feels most comfortable and safe. While her anxieties are to an extent quelled by this hermetic lifestyle, she has become increasingly depressed due to her loneliness. The decision to take committed action would be made by weighing which of these perceived values is more important—the value of community or the feeling of safety. The veteran would then be encouraged to make decisions consonant with her most cherished values even if she did not "feel like it," such as accepting a lunch date with a friend that requires her to leave her house. The result may be that her anxieties about leaving her home are reduced and she becomes the kind of person that makes relationships a priority, as consonant with her values.

Psychological theories validate what theologians posit regarding the formative nature of ritual participation. Moreover, ACT helps to provide an explanation for why ritual penance can be effective for moving veterans past moral injury by living according to their Christian values, even in the presence of contrary feelings. With this in mind, I turn from the matter of mourning to the demanding nature of the penitential assignment.

Sternness

One of the most potentially off-putting aspects of the ancient penitential rite to modern sensibilities is the seeming harshness of it. The *Didascalia* implores twice to "be angry at [the penitent]"[70] and then to "rebuke him," even inviting the church to "argue with him."[71] I will explore here two possible pastoral purposes to this sternness towards the penitent. Having discussed how the graded penitential ritual can be formative of the penitent's affections, I will discuss here how the same can be true for the witnessing congregation. Next, I will comment on how a firm stance towards a veteran's transgressive actions is necessary in her recovery from MI.

The first point to be made in light of the prior discussion is that this harshness by the community also should be construed as a ritual act and not merely the venting of unbridled disgust by a congregation. Recall how, at the time, killing in war for some was considered a praiseworthy act.[72] Therefore, it is conceivable that for at least some in the congregation such sternness against a veteran would not be their natural inclination. The *Didascalia* nevertheless prescribes "anger" and "rebuke" as necessary for the penitential process. This may be an indication that the liturgy should be viewed as a "rehearsal of Christian attitudes" not only for the penitent, but the community as a whole. Should a witness to the veteran's weeping experience feelings of sympathy, she is still to act "as if"[73] she is appalled by his shedding of blood as per the dictates of the *Didascalia*. Through ritual repetition this act is to instill within the parishioner the proper attitude towards killing, perhaps praiseworthy in some respects, but nevertheless a reflection of humanity's failure to fulfill its vocation in the world.

The compartmentalization and timing of these prescribed affective gestures lends further credence to this view that they are in fact ritual acts. Note that the *Didascalia* portrays a sort of back and forth in which the penitent is cast out and taken to task outside the church. As soon as the parishioners enter the church, however, they are to plead for him.[74] That the community is tasked collectively with directing "anger" and "arguing" toward the penitent one moment, and then offering a compassionate prayer for the penitent the very next, signals that these may not have to be (and are not intended to be) sincere gestures. This ritual drama will continue to unfold as the penitent journeys through the remaining grades. Again, one can see this as a process of shaping attitudes, thoughts, and feelings.

Paradoxically, the morally injured today welcome a measure of sternness with regards to their actions. It is often the case that no one is more condemnatory of the veteran than the veteran himself. What the veteran needs is someone to take his transgressions as seriously as he takes them himself, not someone to offer simple absolution. My own experience in the VA validates this point that veterans who have killed or committed atrocities in war often do not want their deeds to be taken lightly. It can be isolating to carry the moral burden of having committed such a serious act known to very few in the world. To dismiss a veteran's morally injurious experiences in war with such phrases as "You were just following orders" or "You had to do what you had to do to survive" or "You weren't yourself at the time" can amplify the veteran's feelings of isolation. Such comments only reaffirm the veteran's belief that no one understands their struggle and that they are in fact alone. The veteran wants the gravity and pain of what they have done heard and understood first. To acknowledge the seriousness of, say, killing, is to begin to understand the moral pain carried by the one who killed. This principle may be best illustrated in a relevant encounter I had with an Air Force veteran who was distraught over some of her past actions. Despite the many reassurances of others that she had not done anything wrong, for years she could not shake this persistent feeling of guilt. It was not until she was invited to a period of fasting over her sins that she felt the closest to God than she had been in years and the most peace she had experienced since the incident. It was not until she engaged in a physical and spiritual discipline that took seriously her actions and addressed directly her sins that she was relieved of some of her moral injury.

Length of Penance

The length of penances in the ancient world is another seemingly harsh measure that I will argue bears both a theological and pastoral logic. Until the High Middle Ages, it was standard form that one was reconciled after confession *and the completion of assigned penance.*[75] Though there is documentation of a reconciliation immediately following confession (without the completion of penance) as early as the late ninth century,[76] this practice did not become a fixture until the twelfth century and is the general model that exists today.[77] The lengths of penances were not always consistent in the early church and they appear to have reached their peak with St. Basil, reflected in his three-year penance for those who have killed in war.[78] Such a measure would be unheard of today. Yet something seems to be lost in both the inversion of the penitential order and the curtailing of penitential sentences. This may be especially true when working with the morally injured.

Immediate reconciliation runs the same risk noted above of minimizing the offenses of the penitent. Susan Smith affirms the importance of proclaiming forgiveness when ritually addressing a transgression, but "if it comes too soon," she cautions, "it could be experienced as 'cheap grace' and fail to restore the person to full personhood in Christ."[79] When dealing with morally injured veterans, Brock sees within this practice even more complex problems:

> Premature forgiveness may be cathartic and offer emotional relief, but receiving such forgiveness requires amnesia about the full extent of harm that war inflicts. Facile forgiveness interferes with veterans facing the truth of what they did. It may offer anesthesia for the pain of moral injury, but premature forgiveness can create an addiction to relief, and it can reinforce a need to tell horror stories, enact guilt, and solicit forgiveness. This cycle relieves moral responsibility temporarily instead of building the lifelong strength to live with it.[80]

Delayed reconciliation ensures that the veteran knows that her grievances are taken seriously, and it allows her a dedicated season to process and heal from her injuries in a structured and intentional manner. Again, this is a period of growth and formation not only for the penitent but also for the participating congregation as a whole. The indulgent use of time is a feature of ancient rites largely absent in rituals today.

The virtue of Basil's penitential prescription for war veterans lies not only in its length, but in its limit. Basil's three-year penance may seem cruel and unusual, but to a Vietnam veteran that has spent the last fifty years mired in guilt, it is a grace. The parameters imposed by ritual set limits on the morally injured person's inclination to reside in an interminable state of preoccupation with one's guilt and trauma. That is not to say that a veteran is guaranteed to cease feeling guilty following the penitential term, but she has something tangible to look back upon with a sense of accomplishment and finality. Following her own period of penance, the Air Force veteran discussed above states that she thinks back to her fast when she senses her guilt creeping back into her consciousness and it gives her some comfort. Prior to this fast she did not have the same experience to lean upon.

Isolation

What is perhaps the most salient feature of the grade of weeping is the exclusion it imposes on the sinner. In this grade, the penitent is conspicuously positioned outside the door of the church. Again, what appears to be a harsh measure carries pastoral and theological import particularly when approached pastoral-hermeneutically as proposed here.

It is important first to establish that the penitent's exclusion is not a shunning or excommunication. In fact, it is quite the opposite. Consider for instance the morally injured who are already prone towards excessive levels of isolation. I have spoken with a number of veterans who, despite their devout faith, are reluctant to attend church due to their own feelings of uncleanliness or unworthiness. Even as the penitent assumes the position of exclusion in the *Grade of Weeping*, the penitent is being invited to play an active role in a ritual drama that incorporates the participation of the entire community of faith. This means that the veteran is obliged to come to the assembly regularly to participate in the rite. For the morally injured in particular, such ritual participation actually serves as a protection against a veteran's self-imposed and often destructive form of isolation.

This invitation to the ritual does not deny the penitent's sobering assessment of her actions or imply an offer of what Susan Smith refers to as "cheap grace." Even while participating in the work of the liturgy, the exclusionary position would serve to validate a morally injured veteran's feeling of unworthiness. She need not enter the church, but she is still part of the liturgy, a member of the community. Moreover, as the remaining grades reveal, the penitent is placed on a clear trajectory towards the Eucharist, a path that will not let her abide in this state indefinitely. Outside the liturgy and left to their own devices, the morally injured are at risk of condemning themselves to an indefinite state of solitary confinement.

What is referred to here as a ritual drama has a pedagogical component for the assembly as a whole.[81] The grade of weeping offers a visual and experiential reminder of what happens to those who sin. This particular aspect of the rite, the physical removal from the interior of the church, offers an example of where hermeneutics plays a role in ritual care. One can interpret this ritual separation, for instance, as demonstrating that sin drives a wedge between themselves and the Body of Christ, known in the liturgy through the Eucharist and the community of believers. Yet there is not only a caution here, but also a source of hope. Though the penitent is temporarily removed from the Mysteries, what his continued participation in the community and their

130   *Chapter 4*

pleas on his behalf convey is that sin does not ultimately remove him from the grace of God. Through the process of pastoral ritual hermeneutics, the minister can assist the congregation in coming to learn and experience these meanings in a poignant way.

This balance (or ambiguity) between the seriousness of sin and the grace of God is one that needs to be held together delicately for the morally injured. The veteran desires that the gravity of his acts is respected and acknowledged, and yet that those acts do not deem him ultimately hopeless and lost. This seemingly paradoxical balance is not conveyed easily through discourse, even more so to the morally distressed. Yet the ritual provides the congregation the opportunity to know this truth visually, which the penitent will come to know viscerally. This highlights the important task in ritual care of helping to build the ritual consciousness of the congregation and shepherding it to understand its life in the context of the liturgy.

Grade of Audience: Faith and Solidarity

> The "audience" is inside the gate in the vestibule area, where one who has sinned has to stand until "the catechumens," and then leave. "For when one has heard the Scripture and the instruction," it says, "let him be put out, and not worthy of prayer."[82]

> By no means, however, are you, bishop, to prevent them from entering the church to hear the word. For not even Our Lord and Savior shunned or cast out tax-collectors and sinners, he even ate with them. . . . Therefore have involvement with those who are convicted of sins and who are in sickness; associate with them, and take care of them, and speak to them and comfort them and keep hold of them and enable them to return.[83]

Like each grade in St. Gregory's penitential rite, this step marks something of a milestone in the ritual drama. The penitent moves from a space of relative isolation outside the church to join a community of catechumens inside the building. The pastoral theological commentary on the rite will continue here to explore two particular themes highlighted by the rite that are relevant to the care of the morally injured. The first is the reconstruction of faith and the second is solidarity.

Reconstruction of Faith

Scholars have noted that the graded penitential rite is based on the ritual of the catechumenate. In this ancient practice of initiation, the catechumens made their way towards baptism over a period of time in a succession of grades.[84] St. Gregory's *Canonical Epistle* reflects the convergence of these parallel processes as the penitent actually joins the catechumens in the grade of "Audience" or *Hearer of the Word*.[85] This association between a catechumen and a penitent is theologically compelling, though no rationale for the conflation of these statuses is explicitly laid out. What the experience of the morally injured offers is one explanation for how the penitential process might be associated with religious initiation. This correlation also highlights the potential pastoral benefit of a ritual like St. Gregory's for the morally injured.

One of the commonly recognized symptoms of moral injury is a change in or loss of spirituality.[86] This is reflected in the *Moral Injury Symptom Scale*, which includes such items as "I wondered what I did for God to punish me," "I wondered whether God had abandoned me," "I questioned God's love for me," and "I questioned the power of God,"[87] all of which are thoughts not uncommon for the morally injured to have. As these statements exhibit, morally injurious experiences have a way of shattering one's fundamental spiritual assumptions.[88] The penitent's association with the catechumenate then is appropriate. For many veterans, moral injury marks a starting over and a rethinking of foundational beliefs about one's faith. What St. Gregory reminds us of is that in times of moral crisis, people need the allowance and space to rethink the foundational tenets of their faith.

Some pastoral care providers may be tempted to minimize the morally injured person's sudden questioning of long-held beliefs as a temporary crisis of faith that will pass with time. There will be a tendency then to address the traumatic circumstances alone, assuming that once those matters are settled, the veteran will return to her faith. St. Gregory's rite offers a reminder that a reconsideration of the fundamentals of one's faith must necessarily come alongside the remediation of grievous sins. Moreover, it posits that the healing from sin requires a re-entrance into the faith, a reminder of one's baptism. To cast the attachment of the penitent to the catechumenate as a punishment of humiliation or demotion would then be overly reductive. The ritual offers validation of the morally injured person's self-perception as a spiritual novice in a time of subversion and provides the time, space, and community for that person to undergo a reformulation of his faith.

While the penitent's joining of the catechumenate points to the need for faith reconstruction after sin, the step also reminds us of the role solidarity plays in sin and restoration from it. In the remainder of this section, we will explore further the importance of community and solidarity in the experience of and rehabilitation from moral injury.

132   Chapter 4

Solidarity

Appendix A recounts the spirit of a Christian era marked by an intense sense of solidarity. Given the third century provenance of the graded penitential rite, one can assume that this form of penance is shot through with the same ethos. Evidence of this emerges from the *Didascalia* when it enjoins the faithful now to "have involvement" with the penitents, "associate with them," and "keep hold of them."[89] One might even capture a hint of this in Gregory's text as his penitents are situated with the catechumens. Community support and solidarity can play a vital part in the healing of moral injury. Solidarity, however, can be a double-edged sword, as will be detailed below. The following sections on solidarity will endeavor to illuminate the whys and hows of solidarity in both the precipitating and remedying of MI. I will begin by presenting two ways that an innate sense of solidarity may be implicated in inducing MI itself. This point will then anticipate the following—that is, in view of the inherent solidarity of humankind, all are implicated in the sins of war. Such a position makes the penitential rite an appropriate and logical means of addressing the phenomenon of moral injury. This section will close with some perspectives on why communal support is necessary for the healing of moral injury.

Solidarity between Perpetrator and Victim as a Source of Injury

Successful participation in war necessitates the radical "other-ing" of one's enemies. As Tick writes, "When we go to war, we declare that we are not and cannot be at one with the other."[90] In order to bring oneself psychologically to kill a member of one's own species, the combatant must believe that the enemy is different than herself, perhaps not even human. In the rituals of war, enemy combatants are transubstantiated into "towel heads," "camel jockeys," "sand niggers," and "hajjis."[91] In the act of ending an other's life, however, there is a dramatic reversal. This is the great irony of the divisiveness of war. Tick explains:

> We think of killing as the opposite of intimacy. Yet as these stories indicate, and as veterans have confessed to me for decades, the act of taking a life is profoundly intimate, one that engenders a lifelong bonding to the other. Some survivors of war feel closer to those they killed during warfare or to the wounded men or corpses they tended than to anyone living with whom they have been intimate before or since. Some feel that they are bonded forever through the act of taking a life to those whose life they have taken or through the sacrifices comrades made for each other on the battlefield.[92]

No matter the extent to which one dehumanizes the enemy, the solidarity of all peoples seems to be written in the consciousness of veterans and made manifest particularly following a killing. This is illustrated in Richard Holmes's account of a Marine company that killed nineteen and wounded four North Vietnamese. He writes, "Some . . . reached the bottom level of reflection and came to see the young Vietnamese they had killed as allies in a bigger war of individual existence, as young men with whom they were united throughout their lives against the big impersonal 'thems' of the world. . . . In killing the grunts of North Vietnam, the grunts of America had killed a part of themselves."[93]

What makes killing in war particularly traumatic is the immediate identification warriors make at times between the people they kill with loved ones in their lives. This is a peculiar phenomenon that I have witnessed in more than one veteran. I spoke with one Puerto Rican veteran who lamented having to kill an Afghan combatant who was the age of his daughter. An African-American veteran shared with me the difficulty of being commanded to kill a Vietnamese civilian who reminded him suddenly of his own grandfather. More than one veteran has shared with me that they have had nightmares reliving such scenarios in which the faces of their victims are replaced by those of their own family members. One veteran has had a recurring nightmare in which he would remove the cloth covering the face of a deceased man lying on the side of a Vietnamese road only to find his own face staring up at him. One would wager that identifications like these between one's intimate associations (including oneself) and virtual strangers of another land would not normally be made in other circumstances. Perhaps there is something in human nature that wishes to remind us in moments of violence that we are not just fellow members of a species, but we are connected in a far more intimate way.

As I have argued above, moral injury cannot simply be caused by the violation of one's core moral beliefs. Many a veteran who has been morally injured has gone into war with the view that it is morally acceptable to kill enemy combatants. On the other hand, one would be hard pressed to find a veteran who feels it is morally acceptable to kill one's own family members. Yet, that is exactly what people seem to become when we take their lives. Moral injury may be described, at least in part, as arising from what Aristotle calls *anagnorisis*, or recognition.[94] This is the point of reversal in a Greek play, the moment when Oedipus suddenly realizes he killed his father and married his mother. Through the revelatory, even sacramental,[95] quality of killing, the true nature of all humankind is made known and fiercely injures the warrior. The truth that all human beings are in fact family is what renders warriors tragic heroes.

134 Chapter 4

Solidarity between Bystander and Perpetrator as a Source of Injury

The historical theological analysis of St. Gregory's graded rite above offered an explanation for why penance might be prescribed even for those who—according to some bishops like St. Isidore and St. Basil's "fathers"—did not act unjustly in war. These penitential prescriptions are directed at those who shed blood but did so in service to a just war or acted in defense of "virtue and piety." The argument above is that even just actions resulting in the shedding of blood do not preclude the possibility of the warrior suffering from moral injury.

Current theorizers of moral injury offer a related situation in which warriors can be morally injured even when they have *not* directly perpetrated harm against another. Here, armed personnel are removed one step further from any form of culpability as these have not even shed blood by their own hands. Instead, these troops were injured by virtue of *bearing witness* to such acts. Litz, Drescher, and Kinghorn argue that moral injury can arise from "failing to prevent, bearing witness to, or learning about acts that transgress deeply held moral beliefs and expectations,"[96] which also includes bearing witness to the aftermath of violence and human carnage.[97] It is for this reason that I state in my own definition that moral injury can result from *encountering* and not just participating in sin. That caregivers observe this recurring phenomenon within veterans reveals that there is a tendency amongst warriors not only to identify intimately with their victims, but also with other known or unknown perpetrators to the extent that they would be personally injured morally by it.

Again, there is a peculiar tendency amongst humans in moments of great violence to show solidarity with others in such a way that contributes to the disruption of one's body, soul, and spirit. Though solidarity may be the source of the "sting" in moral injury, below I discuss how it may also be its salve.

Solidarity between Community and Perpetrator as a Source of Healing

Pastoral theology has come to recognize increasingly the importance of community in providing pastoral care. In a penitential ritual context, the importance of community in the rehabilitation of the penitent may be even more pronounced. From the ancient perspective, the role of the community is to help carry the burden of guilt (both felt and forensic) held by the perpetrator. In one aspect, the graded penitential process can be viewed as the means by which the guilt held by individuals is gradually assumed by the community at large.[98] This is an essential step in the rehabilitation of moral injury. War guilt

A Mystical Solidarity

is too much for one to carry. That the morally injured are prone to bearing this burden on their own anticipates the devastating nature of this phenomenon in the lives of veterans. Through this ritual process both the community and the penitent come to see that all share the guilt of the sins of war. Here I will discuss how this is true both mystically and practically.

A Mystical Solidarity

Two particular features of ancient penitential rites are likely to bewilder moderns. The first is their public nature. The second is the collective outpouring of emotion by the community as attested in a number of pre-modern Christian texts. A common scene emerges over a number of these accounts:[99] As the penitent publicly expresses her remorse, the bishop and congregation join her in groaning and weeping aloud. At first glance it may seem that the community is moved to pity over the penitent's state, which in itself is a remarkable act of solidarity. This may in fact be the case. However, a more extensive review of penitential texts, ancient through the Middle Ages, results in a slightly more nuanced picture. There is a consistent call for the Christian to *identify* with sufferers. Note for instance Sozomen's fifth-century account of a Roman penitential practice in his *Ecclesiastical History*: "It is observed with great rigor by the Western churches, particularly at Rome, where there is a place appropriated to the reception of penitents, in which spot they stand and mourn until the completion of the services, for it is not lawful for them to take part in the mysteries; then they cast themselves, with groans and lamentations, prostrate on the ground. The bishop conducts the ceremony, sheds tears and prostrates himself in like manner; and all the people burst into tears and groan aloud."[100] Paulinus writes a contemporary account of a similar practice by the Bishop of Milan in his *Life of St. Ambrose*: "He would rejoice with those who rejoiced, and weep with those who wept; in fact, whenever anyone confessed his sins to him in order to receive penance, his tears were such as to draw tears even from sinners. For he thought it proper to prostrate himself with the prostrate."[101] In Sozomen's and Paulinus's accounts, the bishops do not simply weep for the penitent but actually *prostrate alongside him*.[102] Identification with another's sins may mean, on the one hand, that another's sins remind one of his own. On the other hand, it can mean that the other's sins *are one's own*. I wish to pursue the latter interpretation in the Christian tradition.

This sort of identification with another's sins has been inspired in part by such biblical texts as Romans 12 and 1 Corinthians 12, often cited by the very Church Fathers who advocate this type of solidarity. The basis for this belief is that all members of the church are parts of one body in which Christ is the head. Therefore, if one suffers, all suffer, and if one rejoices, all rejoice.[103] This

136   *Chapter 4*

sentiment finds its height in the fourth- and fifth-century monastic tradition, as expressed in the *Sayings of the Desert Fathers*: "The old men used to say that we should each of us look upon our neighbor's experiences as if they were our own. We should suffer with our neighbor in everything and weep with him, and should behave as if we were inside his body; and if any trouble befalls him, we should feel as much distress as we would for ourselves."[104] It would appear that for some, "our neighbor's experiences" include their sin. This is certainly the case for Dorothy Day and the Catholic Worker movement of the twentieth century.

Day asserted that all people "are members or potential members of the Mystical Body of Christ."[105] Day would go on to apply this doctrine to the wars and conflicts of her generation. She found in the Mystical Body of Christ her justification for shouldering the guilt of others, even those whose actions she did not support. William Cavanaugh summarizes her position as follows: "If we are all members of the same body, it is not so easy to separate the guilty from the innocent. The commutability of pain in the body also implies the commutability of guilt, the sharing of blame for the conflict to which Dorothy Day saw the mystical body as the solution. It is precisely for this reason that Day so often prescribed penance as the antidote for war, penance not only for *them*, but also for *us*."[106]

Penance then is necessarily a corporate process, not only because communal care is effective care (which it is). The penitential *leitourgia* must be the work of the people because all are implicated in the transgressions of the individual. The penitent undergoing the graded ritual process is analogous to the identified patient in family systems theory, whose symptoms are actually indicative of a problem in the family itself.[107] Again, her exclusion must not be viewed as the quarantining of a contaminant from an otherwise pristine body. The body of Christ is "the place where sin is absorbed and healed by the very process of love by which members assume the burdens of each other's sins, both the consequences of those sins and the guilt for them."[108] The penitential liturgy provides a ritual means for facilitating this process.

If the first sting of moral injury is the sudden bond with one's victim or a perpetrator, the second would be having to carry *alone* the weight of bloodshed. For the bystander who is morally injured by bearing witness to atrocities, the problem is not that she carries the guilt of another, but that she carries it alone. The solidarity found in the ancient ritual reminds the penitent that mystically she is not alone in bearing sin. She need not shoulder alone the moral burden of one's or another's actions, including that bond with the dead. In turn, what it reminds the remaining church is that they need not look upon a sinner with a sense of moral superiority or a pious form of pity. The sins of another are one's own, and all must be penitent. The doctrine of the

Non-humanistic Ritual Care for Moral Injury   137

Mystical Body of Christ ultimately binds a community closer together in the face of the divisive power of sin.

A Practical Solidarity

While the doctrine of the Mystical Body of Christ provides sufficient theological justification for assuming the guilt of others' actions, there are practical reasons for doing so as well in the instance of war. Here I wish to summarize briefly the various positions on why civilian communities can be viewed as complicit in the actions of war, further justifying the sharing of guilt.

First, one can take a broader perspective in terms of causality. One can point to the beliefs, ideologies, and dispositions rampant the world over that create the breeding ground for conflicts. It is from this standpoint that the *Catholic Worker* ran a headline in 1939 that read, "We are to Blame for the New War in Europe." The article went on to explain, "The blame rests on the peoples of the entire world, for their materialism, their greed, their idolatrous nationalism, for their refusal to believe in a just peace, for their ruthless subjection of a noble country . . . Hitler is incidental; the war must have come sooner or later under the circumstances."[109] Again, war is merely a symptom of a disease that plagues the entire globe, a disease from which all suffer.

Just three years after that publication, Day would write that "we must all admit guilt" by virtue of "our participation in the social order which has resulted in this monstrous crime of war."[110] This "participation in the social order" can be construed more narrowly in terms of one's civic, political, and economic engagement in society. This falls under what Nancy Sherman refers to as the "weak sense of moral responsibility."[111] When considering the atrocities of war, this includes paying taxes that fund those conflicts, voting for hawkish candidates, or even providing young people the intellectual and physical capabilities to engage in combat.[112] To some, reaping the benefits of war also makes civilians and noncombatants morally responsible for them. Cavanaugh for instance argues that even if we condemn wars fought for access to cheap oil, we are complicit in these wars if that oil fuels the cars we drive.[113] Such is the nature of the human web that all are in some way connected to the actions of war, even to those conflicts most appalling to civilian sensibilities. If one takes a step back or goes deep enough into the chain of causality, one will find that there are cogent reasons for why all are worthy of doing penance for war.

Thus far, this section has proffered both theological and practical reasons for the congregation to share in the sinner's guilt during the penitential process. The congregation's participation is necessary by virtue of its complicity in the actions of war. However, there is also a significant pastoral and

138   *Chapter 4*

therapeutic benefit seen in corporately assuming the guilt of the morally injured. This will be discussed in the following segment.

Community as Healing

As noted above, various experiences can lead to moral injury. However, one of the most paradigmatic acts leading to moral injury is killing. Moreover, the conditions for such a counterintuitive act only can be produced by an entire world that pathologically orients itself to things other than God. Therefore, it is the world's sin that is the driving force behind killing in war, the result of which can be a painfully intimate bond with one's victim—that is, solidarity with the very life one has ended. Such a burden is too heavy for any one person to carry. And yet, it is the immediate impulse for the morally injured to do just that, while the rest of society seems happy to accommodate. Below, I will summarize the insights of those attentive to veterans' needs who have recognized the importance of a community in addressing the problems of combat trauma. Thereafter, I will provide some reasons why ritual in particular is an ideal means by which communal care is conveyed to the morally injured.

On more than one occasion, clinicians and other stakeholders in the care of veterans have observed the benefits of communal support for healing the wounds of combat trauma. While discussing PTSD, Shay asserts, "In the case of a physical wound what counts is physical nutrition; in the case of a psychological injury what counts is *social* nutrition."[114] (It is important to remember that Shay elsewhere describes moral injury as a "psychological injury."[115]) Matsakis also testifies to the importance of "social support and love and acceptance received from others" for veterans transitioning to civilian life.[116] The psychologist points to families as an important source of this, stating, "Veterans who come home to families that embrace them with open arms and do not shame them for showing signs of combat trauma are much more likely to adjust to civilian life without long-term symptoms than veterans whose families berate or reject them for their reactions to having been in a war. It has been found, for example, that PTSD-afflicted combat vets who perceive support from their families have more hope than those who feel unsupported."[117] Again, while Matsakis offers PTSD as an example, her concern is for veterans "showing signs of combat trauma," which would include phenomena like MI.

Perhaps most relevant to this discussion is Peter Marin's account of an interaction he had with a Vietnam veteran. The journalist shares that he was accosted one day by this veteran after giving a talk about guilt and the Vietnam War. The veteran was irate as he thought Marin was attributing the guilt of war exclusively to veterans like him. Marin sought to clarify his position and paraphrased his response to the indignant man as such: "[Y]es, the vets were guilty, but many of us had been guilty also, and that we were guilty not only for the war, but for countless public and private acts whose consequences had been pain or suffering for others. It was all of us, I tried to say, who ought to struggle to come to terms with human fallibility and culpability. The vets were not alone in that, or ought not to be alone in that. It was a struggle all men should share."[118] To this response Marin saw that the veteran visibly "relaxed."[119] From experiences such as these, Marin learned, "What he needed, as do all the vets, was not only a way of thinking and speaking about his life, but *the willingness of others to consider their lives in the same way*."[120] What Marin sees is that veterans need not only people to sympathize with their plight, but also a community to share in their condition. Spiritual burdens, no less than physical burdens, are lightened when the weight is borne jointly with others.[121]

These appeals to community are met with sobering challenges, not the least for veteran populations. Not all have family or family on whom they can rely for support. Furthermore, as Matsakis's comments suggest, not all communities are sympathetic or understanding of a veteran's needs upon returning from war. Moreover, one may be hard pressed to find a community willing or able to express solidarity with a veteran's war-guilt as Marin has. Herein lies the strength of ritual for the support of morally injured veterans.

Rituals are typically regular, reliable, and communal events. Even in the absence of friends or family, the Eucharistic liturgy can be found on a weekly, even daily basis in most locales. Moreover, as Susan Smith attests, "Christian worship rites are neither planned nor celebrated alone."[122] A ritual participant is necessarily connected to a community. As H.P.V. Renner further states, in ritual, private experiences are gathered into the communal experience of the group.[123] Renner is not alone in recognizing the unifying effect of rituals. Hogue writes, "Rituals are instruments of belonging, proclaiming our solidarity with others more than our difference and uniqueness."[124] For Hogue, this is not merely a fanciful sentiment. His research into neuroscience further validates this claim. He writes, "During ritual or meditation, input into that area of the brain decreases, resulting in a breakdown of the sense of separation between self and others. Our experience of connectedness with others, including God—of belonging—shows up in our brains as well. We might, in fact, think of worship as an experience of extended empathy."[125] Therefore, what is declared symbolically in the Eucharist is also experienced on a neurological level between participants in the liturgy. Rituals then do not require the eloquence of a journalist like Marin to convey one's solidarity with a veteran.

Further comparison between ritual solidarity and Marin's own experience exposes some of the limitations of speech. Public talks, whether they be sermons, speeches, or seminars like his, are largely unilateral affairs and deeply vulnerable to selective attention and misinterpretation. In Marin's case, it

140   Chapter 4

was not until he spoke privately with the veteran that mutual understanding was achieved. Even then, as helpful as it may have been to the veteran,
solidarity was expressed conceptually, as an idea. There is no indication in
his article that this expression of solidarity with the veteran occurred beyond
that one time.

In contrast, solidarity is reinforced regularly in the liturgy. It is known not
merely on an intellectual level, but bodily and spiritually. Moreover, ritual
participation is not the expression of the *idea* of solidarity, it *is* solidarity. It
is important to note that ritual solidarity is not only for the penitent or the
morally injured veteran. In the graded penitential rite, even the non-penitents
present at each Eucharistic liturgy have their "private experiences" assumed
into the "communal experience of the group."[126] It is not only that the sufferers have their burdens shouldered by the church, but the sufferer also bears
the joys and pains of others. This too sets ritual solidarity apart from that
experienced in non-sacramental approaches to solidarity.

The need to reconstruct one's faith and share the burden of guilt in solidarity with a community can be particularly pronounced in the lives of the morally injured. Gregory's graded system of penance offers an example of how
ritual can satisfy these needs. What ritual solidarity reminds us, however, is
that the formation that occurs within penance is not for the penitent alone,
but for the whole church. One of the distinctives of ritual care is that it never
just rehabilitates an individual, but it is always transforming the imagination
of a community.

Grade of Submission: A Pastoral Ritual Interpretation

> The "submission" is when someone, after standing within the church door,
> leaves with the catechumens.[127]

With the *Grade of Submission*, the penitent continues his progression towards
the Table as he finds himself now within the nave of the church. Gregory's
laconic description reflects no substantial change from the prior grade, save
for the placement of the penitent with respect to the building. Notably, in each
of the first three grades, Gregory situates the penitent in relation to a "door."
First, the penitent is "outside the door of the worship space," then he is "inside
the gate [or door] in the vestibule area,"[128] and finally, as a *Submission*, he is
"within the church door."[129] Though Gregory gives no direct indication as to
the significance of this motif in his *Canonical Epistle*, the image of "the door"
has carried significant biblical and liturgical meanings within the tradition.
Doors also carry significant meaning to veterans today. Using this motif, I
will offer an example of how life experiences, scripture, and tradition can be

Non-humanistic Ritual Care for Moral Injury 141

drawn together for the purpose of ritual care. In this exercise I again intend to model the task of pastoral ritual hermeneutics proposed in this study.

Doors in the Veteran Experience

Since I began my work as a VA chaplain, every veteran I have known with combat trauma has had a preoccupation with doors. This is a product of the veteran's military training, as well as a hypervigilance developed while enduring a variety of perilous situations.[130] This phenomenon is exemplified well by comments made on an online PTSD forum:

> *Claire:* Yep, I prefer to sit with my back to the wall looking into the room. I sleep in the corner of the room. Its [*sic*] just another symptom. I look for the escape route all the time. When I feel myself doing this I'm working on trying to accept that I am safe where I am. I'm really bad at the [therapist's office]. I need to be in the corner, near the door when I'm there!

> *YoungAndAngry:* I always sit closest to the exit, doesn't matter where it is . . . And I don't like it when people invade my space. Up until very recently . . . whenever my therapist held open the door for me to enter . . . I would literally "jump" through the door way [*sic*] . . . it almost felt like an obstacle each time . . . even though I trust him, I still must sit close to the door. Oh yeah, and every where I go, I can describe the door to you . . . 'cause it's what I spend most of my time staring at.[131]

For veterans like these, doors are both escape routes in moments of danger, as well as potential entry points for outside threats. While such preoccupations are more commonly associated with PTSD (fear-based trauma) and not moral injury proper, I have seen this same hypervigilance within veterans who have been referred to me for MI. This results from a number of reasons. First, those who have killed in combat more often than not have been attacked as well. This is a reason why PTSD often runs hand-in-hand with MI. Second, a veteran who may have killed while never having her life threatened may be hypervigilant for fear of retribution, whether from her victim's associates or from God/fate. This is akin to Freud's "savage" returning victoriously from war and yet living in fear of the "avenging spirits of the slain."[132] Finally, the morally injured may be hypervigilant simply because they have a keen sense of the fragility of life. Whether the veteran witnesses loss of life at her own hands or another's, such intimate exposure to death can signal to the morally injured that her life or that of her loved ones can be extinguished just as easily at any moment.

My experience with these veterans has revealed that an ambivalent relationship to doors can create in turn an ambivalent relationship to churches. More than one veteran has shared that she would like to return to church, but

142 *Chapter 4*

she does not feel safe in such crowded and enclosed areas. If the veteran does attend, she might, like those veterans in the PTSD forum, sit in the back near the exit and leave early. This poses a potential challenge for veteran participation in the rites of the church.

Following this theme, I will discuss how ritual, scripture, and tradition can converge to help shape and orient the Christian imagination through a pastoral ritual hermeneutic.

Doors in Ritual, Scripture, and Tradition

As I have noted before, one of the strengths of using ritual in pastoral care is the intentional involvement of the body for the restoration and formation of people. Because rituals posit not only a certain vision of humanity or the divine, but also that of the world, Christian worship can shift one's orientation toward the material world, or creation, as well. As Schmemann puts it, worship reveals to us the true meaning of the world:

> We need water and oil, bread and wine in order to be in communion with God and to know Him. Yet conversely . . . it is this communion with God by means of "matter" that reveals the true meaning of "matter," i.e., of the world itself. We can only worship in time, yet it is worship that ultimately not only reveals the meaning of time, but truly "renews" time itself. There is no worship without the participation of the body, without words and silence, light and darkness, movement and stillness—yet it is in and through worship that all these essential expressions of man in his relation to the world are given their ultimate "term" of reference, revealed in their highest and deepest meaning.
>
> Thus the term "sacramental" means that for the world to be means of worship and means of grace is not accidental, but the revelation of its meaning, the restoration of its essence, the fulfillment of its destiny . . . Being the epiphany of God, worship is thus the epiphany of the world; being communion with God, it is the only true communion with the world; being knowledge of God, it is the ultimate fulfillment of all human knowledge.[133]

In the world of trauma, doors are possible avenues for safety, as well as invitations for potential danger. The nature of trauma is such that it invests even the mundane, like a door, with dynamic meaning in ways that are life-changing. One of the reasons that such attributions can be so stubbornly persistent is that a non-sacramental perception of the world offers no alternative meaning to "the door." A door is simply a door. In a vacuum of significance, anything else that can forcefully assert its own meanings upon something will do so.

Schmemann, however, suggests that worship has a way of revealing the highest and deepest meaning of a thing, even "renewing" it. One can then posit that with Gregory's attention towards doors in his *Canonical Epistle*, they are brought into the realm of the "sacramental." This penitential ritual offers the possibility for something as mundane as a door to have new meaning. A hermeneutic approach to ritual care may entail guiding a veteran to negotiate such meanings as she participates in liturgies. Scripture and tradition are two resources from which to draw symbols and meanings to counter those of the world.

Scripture would be a natural first key for unlocking the deeper meanings of the world in the Christian imagination. A veteran struggling with ambivalence regarding doors during the liturgy may be guided to the New Testament, where doors are common images used by Jesus, particularly to signify entrance into the Kingdom of Heaven. The most well-known, may be Jesus's illustration of the door being opened to those who "ask," "search," and "knock."[134] The door plays a central role in Jesus's parables as well, with a door being shut to the foolish bridesmaids,[135] as well as to those outside the owner's house.[136] In one case Jesus teaches his followers to be like watchful slaves who would open the door for their master when he knocks.[137] Finally, in another well-known image, Luke's Jesus exhorts a crowd to "enter through the narrow door."[138] Again, guidance of the veteran in this manner would not be simply an intellectual exercise or a "Bible study" of sorts but rather a discussion in conversation with the veteran's own stories as well as her felt experiences in the liturgy.

The wider Christian tradition may also bring something to bear on the veteran's experiences. Liturgically, doors have a more prominent place in the Eastern Orthodox Church than in any other. In the Divine Liturgy, the deacon calls out, just prior to the recitation of the creed, "The doors! The doors! In wisdom, let us attend!"[139] According to Lawrence Farley, this is a call to ensure that the catechumens and non-communicants have left and that the doors to the church building have been closed.[140] This is an exclusionary practice, "to keep out those who had no spiritual right to attend the gathering of the holy Church around its Lord."[141] As another Orthodox priest explains, the exclusion ensures that only those who have recited the Creed at baptism may recite it at the liturgy.[142] At a symbolic level, it is also stated that the doors represent in a way the Church's eschatological separation from the world.[143] When viewed in this fashion, the deacon's call in the Divine Liturgy resonates with the Kingdom images presented in the New Testament.

These doors had practical purposes within Orthodox liturgical history as well. Despite the assumed connection between the call and the creed in the Divine Liturgy today, Farley claims that the deacon's call existed long before the inclusion of the creed in the liturgy. According to Farley, the call's original purpose was actually to signal the doorkeeper to guard the main entrance of

144   *Chapter 4*

the church. The intent was to keep out certain unwanted intruders—namely Roman soldiers. In the pre-Nicene church, to offer the Eucharist was a capital offense and so the lives of the worshippers were placed at risk for participation in the liturgy.[144] The call therefore had the practical purpose of preventing the interruption of worship and ensuring physical safety for congregants. Whether this story is true or merely apocryphal, this image along with the other liturgical and biblical associations discussed above might have particular resonance for traumatized veterans today.

The aim of incorporating scripture and tradition into the practice of the liturgy is to enrich the participant's imagination regarding the material world, even for such mundane objects as doors. By stepping into the ritual drama of the liturgy, the veteran is stepping into a new framework of meaning from which to shape and interpret her own beliefs, attitudes, feelings, and life experiences. For the traumatized veterans whose relationship to doors is fraught, this change in orientation towards these objects may be a helpful practice. Through the liturgy, the veteran may come to see the doors of the church as icons of the entrance to the Kingdom of Heaven. The veteran also may find comfort and solidarity in the ancient Christians who stood in church with anxiety over whether intruders would come bursting through the doors. And whether the door represents entrance into the Kingdom or an inroad for intruders, the veteran may come to find that fear is in fact the proper posture to have when entering church. Not only is the veteran's orientation towards doors changed, so too is her orientation to her own fears. As this interpretive exercise shows, the point is not necessarily to replace or eradicate the veteran's anxieties surrounding a particular object. The veteran's fears may themselves be the point of contact that situates her more deeply within the tradition and practices of the church.

Grade of Standing with: Ritual Narrativity in Care

> "Standing with" is when one stands along with the faithful, and does not leave with the catechumens.[145]

Heretofore I have used the phrase "ritual drama" to describe the ritual process the penitent undergoes in Gregory's rite. There is something undoubtedly theatrical about rituals and liturgies. It is no surprise that scholars of late have noted the similarities between rituals and narratives, but the correspondence between the two may not be more pronounced than in the graded penitential rite. By the time the penitent arrives at the *Grade of Standing with*, one will have the sense that the penitent has reached a climactic point and completed something of a narrative arc. This section will explore first the narrative qualities of ritual in general and then those of Gregory's rite in particular.

The Narrativity of Rituals

Over the years, scholars have increasingly noted the connection between rituals and narratives. This interest in the correlation between the two has produced a scholarly tome dedicated to the topic titled *Ritual and Narrative*. The edited volume draws perspectives from various fields of inquiry. In one article, an English philologist, Vera Nünning, enumerates twelve levels of "interfaces" and ten "functions" shared by narratives and rituals.[146] Three points from that list are particularly relevant to our discussion. Nünning observes that narratives and rituals share a narrative sequencing;[147] create and change worlds;[148] and serve in the maintaining, constructing, and modifying of existing cultural memory.[149] I will expound later on how these come to bear in ritual care.

This correlation between ritual and narrative has not been lost on religion scholars. Their insights seem to dovetail and build upon Nünning's own observations. For one, Nünning notes not only the narrative structure of rituals, but also that stories are often told within rituals.[150] Theologian James K. A. Smith would argue further that implicit in the liturgy itself is a story.[151] Furthermore, all of what Nünning meticulously relays in her twenty-two points seem ingredient in Anderson and Foley's claim that "Narrative and ritual are the larger vehicles by which we define meaning in life, communicate that meaning to others, and give order to individual and communal activity."[152] Across the theoretical landscape there appears to be a general acceptance regarding the relationship between these two basic phenomena in human life.

Gregory's rite perhaps more than most bears what Nünning calls a "narrative sequencing."[153] Like Joseph Campbell's hero, Gregory has the penitent embark on a journey,[154] cross a (in this case, literal) threshold,[155] enter "The Belly of the Whale,"[156] before achieving "The Ultimate Boon."[157] Story consultant and writer Christopher Vogler famously adapts Campbell's mythic pattern to fit a three-act structure as a model for dramatists.[158] In Vogler's amendment of the hero's journey, he recasts the "The Belly of the Whale" as the "Approach to the Inmost Cave,"[159] an apt description of where the penitent finds herself in the *Grade of Standing with*. To Campbell, this stage of the hero's journey is likened to a "passing of a worshiper into a temple where he is to be quickened by the recollection of who and what he is";[160] he undergoes a metamorphosis.[161] In Vogler's model, "The Approach to the Inmost Cave" occurs at the start of the second-act crisis point.[162] Vogler summarizes this moment as follows: "The hero comes at last to the edge of a dangerous place, sometimes deep underground, where the object of the quest is hidden. Often

146   *Chapter 4*

it's the headquarters of the hero's greatest enemy, the most dangerous spot in the Special World, the Inmost Cave. When the hero enters that fearful place he will cross the second major threshold."[163] Given what we have discussed thus far, this would be an accurate portrayal of the morally injured person's graded journey into the "belly" of the sanctuary in pursuit of her Eucharistic "boon." Below, I will expound further the narrative structure of Gregory's rite, particularly as it frames the life story of the penitent.

The Story of the Graded Penitential Rite

In the space of worship, one's own stories are confronted by the narrativity of the ritual. Anderson and Foley write, "Understanding our story in relation to God's story is necessary for persons of faith."[164] Stepping into the liturgy is, in a way, a stepping into God's story. Anderson and Foley's appeal to "understanding our story" highlights the hermeneutic task that ought to come to the fore in ritual care. In the end, stories need to be interpreted. As stated above, the minister may guide the parishioner in bringing to bear the story of God resident within the liturgy on the stories of worshipers. Here, I will demonstrate how understanding Gregory's rite as a story shapes the way one understands the rite, and in turn informs and validates the stories of those who participate in it. In this case I will use as an example the story of morally injured veterans.

When the graded rite is viewed in light of the narrative framework of Campbell and Vogler, movement towards the "belly" of the church would have to be seen as a movement towards potential danger, not of relief, as one might expect. As counterintuitive as this might seem, if one were to use the perspectives of veterans like "Claire" and "YoungAndAngry" such a description would be accurate.[165] In a world where every person and place bears a possible threat, the church building would look like a trap. This is not an interpretation only fitting for morally injured veterans undergoing penance. Approaching the Mysteries (Campbell's "Ultimate Boon" or Vogler's "Reward") can be seen as a danger for all penitents and the catechumens with them. A sense of danger may arise from the possibility of rejection by God or the church for one's past actions. For the initiates or those returning to the faith, it is the danger of making a fundamentally life-altering commitment.

Furthermore, grade four marks a turning point at which the penitent ceases to leave with the catechumens. In the previous two grades, the penitent would stand with the catechumens by a door and depart with them before the rest of the congregation participates in Holy Communion. In light of the "danger" awaiting the penitent, this practice of repeated self-recusal may depict ritually the hesitancy that resides (or should reside) within the penitent.

Rather than stay with the novices at the *Grade of Standing with*, the penitent now joins the "faithful" and no mention of the penitent's relationship to the door is made from this point forward. The penitent steps out alone away from the catechumens to join this new cadre of worshipers. One can imagine that at this juncture, the penitent also has moved away from the door to a more central position in the nave. It is as if to say that this is the stage where the penitent is no longer a spiritual novice; she need not fixate upon doors. There should no longer be a need to plan escape routes or fear outside invaders this side of the eschatological barrier. Instead, the veteran's only focus is the Eucharist. Table 4.1 illustrates this narrative arc and the sudden shift that occurs between grades three and four.

Within Vogler's framework one can see the shaping of a narrative that at this point is approaching its climax. In the section that follows, I will expound on the relevance of the narrative features of ritual for pastoral care.

Counter-Narratives in Ritual and Therapy

To this point, this study has made recurring claims regarding the formative nature of ritual participation. For instance, I have cited the social psychological insight that "behavior often precedes changes in attitudes and feelings."[166] I have also appealed to liturgist Mark Searle's description of liturgy as a "rehearsal of Christian attitudes."[167] To this I might add James K. A. Smith's argument that liturgies are the places where desires are formed.[168] All this has been to say that rituals, like Gregory's penitential rite, are not simply forums for self-expression or symbolically conveying truths. Rituals are also arenas in which people's beliefs, attitudes, desires, and feelings are fashioned. This feature of ritual has been explored in some measure in the commentary on the *Grade of Weeping*. Here I will discuss another means by which rituals shape participants pastorally, that is, in the way that they offer counter-narratives to those stories animating one's life.

Table 4.1

	Grade I: Outside Church	Grade II: Inside the Gate or Narthex	Grade III: Inside the Nave	Grade IV	Grade V
Positioned with Door	√	√	√		
With Catechumens & Goes Forth with Catechumens		√	√		
With Faithful				√	√

148   *Chapter 4*

According to Alasdair MacIntyre, "Man is in his actions and practice, as well as in his fiction, essentially a story-telling animal."[169] As Anderson and Foley state, stories are the means by which we communicate and construct meaning.[170] "Telling stories or fashioning a narrative," they go on to write, "are not, at their root, just speech patterns but life patterns—not simply a way of talking to explain the world or communicate ourselves, but a way of being in the world that, in turn, becomes the basis of our explanations and interpretations."[171] There is something then about one's story that is fundamental to one's being. Wherever one's story goes, so goes one's very life, for better or for worse. According to Narrative Therapy, problems arise when a person actively participates in the performance of stories that are unhelpful, unsatisfying, dead-ended, or when "these stories do not sufficiently encapsulate the person's lived experience or are very significantly contradicted by important aspects of the person's lived experience."[172] *Counter*-narratives then are those that can realign one's story, one's life even, in a preferred direction.

Counter-narratives are a central feature of narrative therapy. Narrative therapy emerged from systematic family therapy and is intentionally postmodern in orientation.[173] One of the main tasks of narrative therapy is the re-storying and re-authoring of one's life stories.[174] With the aid of a therapist, the client labors to challenge any unexamined socially and culturally influenced beliefs that may be harmful.[175] Counter-narratives are those that disrupt problem-saturated narratives dominant in one's life. While this approach to therapy may not be familiar to many, this task of re-authoring narratives in some ways is foundational to the work of psychotherapy as a whole. As Wilson states, "In short, psychotherapy seems to be a beneficial process whereby clients adopt a *new narrative* about their problem that is more helpful than the story they told before."[176]

Notably, this logic behind the counter-narrative is not entirely absent within ritual studies. By noting the narrativity of rituals, Nünning sees a similar function inherent within rituals. She writes, "The seventh function, which we have termed the 'cultural-memory function,' relates to narratives and rituals as important media of cultural remembrance as well as of the construction and modification of existing cultural memory. This includes the creation of 'counter-narratives,' which aim at criticizing, delegitimizing or even superseding existing memories."[177] There is a marked similarity between the function of narrative therapy's counter-narrative and Nünning's. While Narrative Therapy seeks to deconstruct harmful beliefs, Nünning's rituals function to criticize, delegitimize, and supersede existing memories.[178] Encountering a formative story then seems to be part and parcel of both Narrative Therapy and ritual, but how this encounter takes place can vary considerably.

Unlike with ritual, Narrative Therapy's approach is primarily a dialectical one. This is reflected in the therapeutic process, which includes telling the story, naming the problem, using externalizing language, considering social and political issues, employing "relative influence questioning," deconstructing of "unique outcomes," taking a position on the problem, and re-telling the story.[179] In contrast, ritual's pastoral efficacy might be found in ritual's ability to provide rich, immersive counter-narratives for its participants. Ritual's narratives are conveyed not just orally, but through music, movement, images, smells, taste, and touch. These sensory features are not alternative means for communicating what can otherwise be relayed dialectically. Instead, they often speak what cannot be spoken in words. As discussed in chapter 2, there is a certain knowing that can only be known through the body. Moreover, rituals create space for those ambiguities in the human experience that escape articulation. It is in this manner—through holistic means—that "rituals shape our stories."[180]

The most pronounced difference between narrative therapy's use of the counter-narrative and ritual's approach to the counter-narrative advocated here is their aim. In narrative therapy, the therapist mines the problem-saturated stories of a client to highlight "unique outcomes," moments that counter the dominant narrative.[181] The hope is to direct the client towards living out "preferred narratives."[182] The implication is that the preferred narrative is one of the client's own choosing.[183] In ritual care the counter-narratives are inherent in the liturgy itself. They may be multivalent, but they are not narratives of the participant's own choosing. They may not even be "preferred."

The contrasting roles of the therapist and bishop in Narrative Therapy and St. Gregory's penitential rite, respectively, may best illustrate this difference. In the postmodern therapeutic environment, the therapist does not assume the position of "expert."[184] Her role is decentralized.[185] The therapist may ask questions, but it is the client who determines the direction of the intervention.[186] In Christie Neuger's application of narrative theory to pastoral counseling, she writes, "[T]he counselor doesn't know where the counseling is supposed to go and operates from this sense of not knowing."[187] Instead, the client ultimately determines which narratives are "unhelpful" and "unsatisfying," and which are "preferred."[188] Despite being situated unavoidably in a position of power,[189] the therapist seeks to avoid imposing her beliefs on the client.[190]

As expressed in the *Didascalia* passages cited above, the bishop unequivocally wields and demonstrates authority over the penitential process. These texts suggest that in the graded rite, the penitent ultimately advances at the whim of the bishop. One can imagine that this could occur at the expense of the penitent's own "preferred narrative." If a penitent may never see herself beyond grade three, either due to fear or a sense of unworthiness, it may be the minister's pastoral discretion to advance her to grade four, "as if" she was ready to stand with the faithful. This is part and parcel of what ritual does.

150 *Chapter 4*

Seligman sees "ritual as a subjunctive—the creation of an order *as if* it were truly the case."[191] This is not coercion, but formation.

While narrative theorists may decry this practice as replicating "the effect of the dominant culture's privileged knowledges and practices on those in subjugated positions," one may interpret this direction as a pastoral one. A deeply morally injured veteran may never choose willingly to return to communion or accept a state of forgiveness despite the message of the gospel. A penitent who may feel unworthy of standing with the "faithful" may be trained through the ritual process to live into her status as one who is worthy. Rather than simply being told that she is forgiven, she is invited into a sensory-rich story of forgiveness.[192] Again, this alludes to the formative nature of ritual processes.

Counter-Narratives and Moral Injury

Thus far, I have discussed the formative potential of both narratives and rituals in the lives of people by means of counter-narratives. Here, I turn to the particular relevance of counter-narratives for moral injury from both a clinical and theological perspective.

In his work with moral injury, Litz does not speak directly of "counter-narratives," but he comes close when he asserts the need for "countervailing experiences"[193] in the lives of morally injured veterans. Litz maintains that "there are two routes to moral repair and renewal: (a) psychological- and emotional-processing of the memory of the moral transgression, its meaning and significance, and the implication for the service member, and (b) exposure to corrective life experience."[194] It is in pursuit of the latter that counter-narratives seem to find their importance for the morally injured. In Litz's assessment, morally injured veterans have negative beliefs about themselves and the world. These include beliefs that they are tainted, unforgivable, and deserve to suffer. Litz states that these dire judgments "tend to be very rigid and resistant to disconfirmation," but suggests that they can be "examined and challenged."[195] This is achieved by "exposure to corrective life experience."[196] For Litz, this may entail "doing good deeds and . . . seeing others do good deeds, as well as by giving and receiving care and love."[197] Because of the acute nature of these judgments about themselves and the world, the morally injured need "an equally intense real-time encounter with a countervailing experience."[198]

Given this assessment, one may have the sense that a discursive approach to challenging the morally injured person's negative valuations may fall short. The descent into moral injury can come in the wake of physical injury, a sense of betrayal, and the sights, sounds, smells of war. When Litz calls for an "equally intense real-time encounter,"[199] one wonders if he is not asking for an experience that is just as physically, spiritually, and emotionally engaging, to counter the veteran's trauma. While there may be few experiences in the world that can match those of war, the liturgy has some distinct advantages over conventional talk therapy in this respect.

The liturgy answers Litz's perceived need for countervailing experiences on three levels: the sensual, the personal, and the global. First, as I have described above, the liturgy captures not only the intellect and the imagination but appeals to the various senses. At the liturgy, the indelible sounds, smells, and sights of war are met with hymnody, incense, and iconography proclaiming the peace of God. Second, on a personal level, the worshiper would have recourse to "care and love" from the worshiping community, as well as liturgical declarations of absolution, both being "real-time" encounters that challenge any self-directed condemnation. Third, the veteran's disillusionment with the world can also find a countervailing experience in the liturgy. From the perspective of Nünning, rituals are said to be the place that worlds are constructed and changed.[200] Theologically, the prototypical Christian ritual, the Eucharistic liturgy, is understood to be the place where worshipers encounter the Kingdom of God.[201] As William Cavanaugh writes, "In the liturgy we are able to see the world, to imagine it as it really is, which is to say, as it will be and already is in the eyes of God."[202] This is a world in which war has no part.[203] A veteran seeking reprieve from a world of violence may find it, even if only a foretaste, in the Kingdom present at the Eucharistic liturgy.

In total then, the liturgy offers for the veteran a tangible narrative of peace, forgiveness, and love to counter those harmful narratives instilled by participation in war. It may not seem at first glance that the "story" of the Eucharistic liturgy would be immediately relevant to the concerns of moral injury. By beginning with Litz's clinical assessment of the morally injured, I have demonstrated how the liturgy-as-counter-narrative could meet the perceived psychological needs of the morally injured. Here, I will close this discussion with a brief note on how, theologically, the liturgy for some serves as a natural counter-narrative to war.

For certain theological ethicists, Christian worship is inherently antithetical to war. As Stanley Hauerwas puts it, "the Christian alternative to war is worship."[204] The issue is not that war is diametrically opposed in form and function to worship. In fact, it is their similarities that make war such a natural comparison and competitor to worship. According to Cavanaugh, war is a parody of the Eucharist in two ways. For one, war, like the Eucharist, has a unifying effect on a people. War unites a nation against another, while making one's country an object of devotion. The Eucharist also unites; however, it does so transnationally, bringing disparate peoples into the single Body of Christ.[205] It is from this standpoint of the Eucharist that we can affirm, as

152 Chapter 4

Dorothy Day does, "all men [and women] are members or potential members of Christ's Mystical Body."[206] Second, war, like the Eucharist, carries with it a strong notion of sacrifice. War calls for both the sacrifice of self and the enemy for one's country.[207] The liturgy, however, entails self-surrender and participation in the sacrifice of Christ.[208] Though similar in function, both posit fundamentally conflicting visions of the world. This is what makes the liturgy a natural counter-narrative to war, not only for the individual morally injured, but for societies as a whole.

Considering the narrativity of rituals opens up the possibility of understanding ritual care through a Narrative Therapeutic framework. In particular, liturgies can be seen as potential "counter-narratives" that subvert the problem-saturated stories of worshipers. Viewed in this light, the Eucharistic liturgy presents a fitting answer to the morally injured person's needs for experiences that counter those of war, as seen from a psychological perspective. At the same time, a theological understanding of the Eucharist and war also present them as naturally countervailing forces to one another. As Anderson and Foley state, "Rituals shape our stories."[209] Here we see that they shape our stories not only at a personal level, but for communities at large.

Grade of Participation: Trauma Recovery and Ritual

Finally comes "participation" in the Holy Communion.[210]

> . . . And then, as each repents and shows forth the fruit of repentance, accept him into the prayer as you would a pagan. And just as you baptize a pagan and at that time receive him, so lay the hand on this man while everyone is praying for him, and then bring him in and allow him to communicate with the church, for the imposition of the hand shall take the place of baptism for him, as whether by the imposition of a hand or by baptism they receive participation in the Holy Spirit.[211]

Gregory's penitential rite ends with the *Grade of Participation*. This grade marks two milestones for the penitent, reflected in the two texts above. First, as denoted in the name itself, the penitent is now able to participate in Communion.[212] Second, as the *Didascalia* details, the penitent is received back into the community. That a notion of "reconnection" plays a prominent role in the final stage of the penitential rite is one of several points of resonance with standard plans for trauma recovery. In this final stage of analysis, I will explore medical models for trauma recovery and their points of contact, as well as significant differences, when viewed alongside Gregory's penitential rite. I will begin by outlining current approaches to trauma recovery. This summary will demonstrate how Judith Herman's three-stage model for

Non-humanistic Ritual Care for Moral Injury 153

trauma recovery undergirds Litz's treatment plan for MI. I will then discuss the ways the trauma recovery process, as understood in the clinical world, and the graded penitential rite share points of contact, bear some considerable difference, and have the potential to inform one another in meaningful ways. The primary aim of this section is to highlight again some of the clinically validated pastoral benefits of ritual care for MI.

The Clinical Model for Trauma Recovery

Judith Herman's *Trauma and Recovery* has long been the standard for the treatment of trauma in the clinical world. Her three-stage recovery process has played a role in the care of veterans and, as I will discuss below, has been adapted for use with the morally injured. Shay and Matsakis are two veteran care providers who have looked to Herman in their work. In lieu of offering my own initial summary of Herman's text, I have produced a table that outlines Herman's stages in Shay and Matsakis's own words. Table 4.2 reflects some of their interpretations and emphases in light of their respective concerns for veteran care.

Herman's book is concerned primarily with "simple PTSD" or fear-based trauma. In other words, her book presupposes a client that has been a victim, not a victimizer. Her references to her primary subject as "victimized people"[213] and "survivors" in need of empowering make this clear.[214] Such characterizations do not seem as appropriate for, say, perpetrators of violence against others. Yet this has not prevented clinicians like Shay from using her model in his work with the morally injured.

Herman's Three Stages as the Basis for MI Treatment

Litz too seems not to have shied away from Herman's model in his proposed treatment plan for MI. Though Litz's program is spread over eight

Table 4.2. Judith Herman's Three-Stage Trauma Recovery Process

	Jonathan Shay[a]	Aphrodite Matsakis[b]
Stage One	Establishment of safety, sobriety, and self-care	Creating safety: making one's world as safe as possible
Stage Two	Trauma-centered work of constructing a personal narrative and of grieving	Uncovering the trauma and feeling the feelings
Stage Three	Reconnecting with people, communities, ideals, and ambitions	Reconnecting with one's self and others

[a]Shay, *Odysseus in America*, 168.

[b]Matsakis, *Back from the Front*, 380.

154 *Chapter 4*

steps, it appears to be an adaptation of Herman's work. Litz's eight steps are as follows:

- Step one: Connection
- Step two: Preparation and education
- Step three: Modified exposure component
- Step four: Examination and integration
- Step five: Dialogue with a benevolent moral authority
- Step six: Reparation and forgiveness
- Step seven: Fostering reconnection
- Step eight: Planning for the long haul[215]

In what follows, I demonstrate the correlation between Litz's MI treatment plan and Judith Herman's trauma recovery model for two reasons. First, by recognizing Litz's reliance on Herman's work, the psychologist's approach to (and its limitations in) MI treatment is better understood. Second, establishing that Herman's model is at the core of MI treatment justifies its use as a conversation partner for MI work in ritual care.

Despite the seeming discrepancies, there are indications that Herman's three-stage plan is the foundation of Litz's treatment plan for MI. Litz's step one corresponds with Herman's first stage of recovery, which in her own words involves "a healing relationship."[216] As Herman writes, "Recovery can only take place in the context of relationships; it cannot occur in isolation."[217] The therapeutic relationship is one of those "healing relationships" (and by no means the only or necessarily the best relationship for recovery, Herman adds).[218] Similarly, for Litz, "Connection" entails "a strong working alliance," namely, "a strong and genuinely caring and respectful therapeutic relationship."[219] This, he says, is "critical" due to the delicate nature of moral injury. This is still just one component, though an important one, in establishing "safety" for the traumatized veteran in the first stage of recovery.

The remaining steps of Litz's programs find more ready correlations with Herman's model. In Herman's second stage of recovery, the survivor tells the story of her trauma.[220] This stage may also involve the "flooding technique," a treatment by which the patient is exposed to a controlled reliving of the traumatic experience.[221] This correlates directly with Litz's "Modified exposure" and "Examination and integration" steps. For both clinicians, this stage has several aims. First, repeated exposure to the traumatic experiences is intended to alleviate the intensity of their trauma on the patient.[222] Second, the processing of these experiences opens the patient to the possibility of relating to them in a new way.[223] (This is akin to Narrative Therapy's trading of problem-saturated stories for preferred narratives.) Finally, this process allows patients to integrate these traumatic moments into their lives in a way that they no longer take center stage. The traumatic moment becomes relativized as just one moment amongst many in a person's life, an event now situated in the past, where it belongs.[224]

Herman and Litz both use the term "reconnection" to describe what happens in the final stages of recovery in their respective plans. For Herman, reconnection is multifaceted. It entails gaining possession of and reconnecting with one's self.[225] This is not a return to some sort of normative period in one's life prior to the traumatic incident. Herman sees this stage as a mourning the loss of the old and pursuing the new.[226] The patient also comes to terms with the meaning of the trauma and may begin opening herself to intimacy with others again.[227] For Litz, "reconnection" revolves primarily around this latter notion of the term. For him, central to this stage is pursuing "positive and healing relationships outside of therapy."[228] As a secondary component, Litz states that therapists may also incorporate a discussion of spirituality at this point in a way that supports the underlying aims of the treatment.

Again, Herman's work seems to serve as the standard model for approaching trauma in the clinical world. This appears to be true even when addressing the trauma of moral injury. Litz's elaborations on the standard trauma recovery model (particularly the "Dialogue with a benevolent moral authority," and "Reparation and forgiveness" steps) appear to be driven in part by the need to adapt the process to address the specific concerns of perpetrators, as opposed to victims of violence. Nevertheless, Herman's three stages remain at its core. In the following section, I will place this foundational model for trauma recovery in conversation with Gregory's graded penitential rite.

Trauma Recovery and the Graded Penitential Rite

Before beginning this comparative analysis, I must note that by juxtaposing the trauma recovery model with Gregory's rite I am not implying that they belong in the same analytic category. This is not intended to be a comparison of two treatment plans or two healing rituals for moral injury. I understand that the two are fundamentally different *things* or phenomena within the world. Where I do find commonality that justifies a conversation between the two is that both provide a medium by which healing is offered to the morally injured (even if "healing" may be defined differently in both arenas). The goal here is not only to highlight differences either, but to see how the clinical model's understanding of trauma and the human response to it can illuminate and inform those of the penitential world and vice versa.[229] This analysis will begin with greater points of resonance between the two and close with a discussion of major points of departure. For the most part I will be tracking the two in their sequential orders.

156   Chapter 4

Herman's recovery model begins with ensuring safety for the patient, which includes establishing a therapeutic relationship. The commentary on the *Grade of Weeping* above has already argued the point that a penitent's participation in the rite, even in its early stages of ritual exclusion, can be a form of "safety," particularly for the morally injured. Participation in the rite connects the penitent to a community, resisting the tendency for the morally injured to seclude and engage in self-destructive behaviors. The penitent's "therapeutic relationship" is not only with the presiding bishop, but with the worshiping community as a whole. Exclusion also validates the veteran's need for separation and for her sins to be taken seriously, while placing limits on the extent to which the veteran may pursue both. Moreover, the penitent is given a clear path for a way forward, beyond the mire of self-loathing and punishment, a requirement established in Litz's step two, "Preparation and education." The clinical model in some way provides language for what occurs early in the penitential rite; that is, it offers "safety" by providing accountability and a way forward.

In the second stage of trauma recovery the patient is invited to tell the story of her trauma. The process requires the "reconstruction" of the traumatic narrative. Reconstruction is needed as traumatic memories are often detached, fragmented and incoherent.[230] For Herman and Litz, transformation of the story also means reconsidering harmful beliefs associated with traumatic (e.g. morally injurious) experiences.[231] The goal is not to purge the traumatic memory from one's consciousness but to integrate it into one's life story.[232] At this stage, the patient must assimilate a fully-fleshed and truthful account of the event, one from which she can move forward.[233]

Herman and Litz highlight the formidable challenges this second stage entails. The first challenge for the morally injured veteran in the reconstruction process is moving the traumatic narrative from a place of incoherence to coherence. The veteran must then strike a tenuous balance, constructing a narrative that on the one hand countenances the veteran's real participation in a transgressive act and on the other hand "accommodates" the veteran. By this, Litz means that

> [t]herapists should help service members and new veterans to process the event in a way so that accommodation, *but not over-accommodation*, can occur. Rather than coping with a morally injurious event by denying it or excessively accommodating it, what is needed is a new synthesis—a new way to view the world and the self in it that takes into account the reality of the event and its significance without giving up too much of what was known to be good and just about the world and the self prior to the event (and what can be revealed in the future).[234]

One of the strategies Litz offers for maintaining this balance is helping the veteran to accept the notion of an "imperfect self" and that one is not defined in whole by a particular moment or act.[235] This is undoubtedly a challenge when that one act is something as grievous as ending another's life.

To say that the process of healing necessitates the reconstruction and integration of a traumatic memory offers a constructive standpoint from which to analyze St. Gregory's rite. In the juxtaposition of the two, one is led to wonder whether St. Gregory's rite involves a similar task that facilitates the penitent's restoration. I will demonstrate here that there is indeed an essential process of narrative reconstruction and integration within the ancient rite, though of a different manner. Moreover, I will posit that in this undertaking, the penitential rite offers an alternative to the unwieldy balance that Litz seeks to maintain between accommodation and over-accommodation.

One of the first steps in the penitential process is a form of storytelling, that is, the confession of one's sins. This is the story of an individual, acting presumably on his own, claiming responsibility for his sins. It is from this standpoint that the penitent steps into the drama of St. Gregory's rite. The terms "reconstruction" and "integration" describe well what happens to the penitent's narrative as he undertakes this ritual journey. In the liturgy, narrative reconstruction is not a move from incoherence to coherence, however. It is a move from the personal to the communal. In the course of St. Gregory's penitential rite, the sins confessed at confession are gradually assumed by the congregation, the Body of Christ, as a whole. Here, reconstruction and integration are one and the same. Integration is not assimilating an acceptable version of traumatic events into one's life story. In the liturgy, integration is assimilating one's life story into the shared narrative of the church.

This perspective offers an alternative to trying to strike a balance between accommodation and non-accommodation. The danger of accommodation is making light of the veteran's transgressive acts, which would appear at once dismissive in the eyes of the veteran and ethically irresponsible. The danger of non-accommodation, facing down and holding one accountable for the real horrors committed, is that this may be a burden too much for the veteran to bear. One cannot help but think that arriving at a "new synthesis" will require compromising to some extent truth for the sake of the veteran, or the veteran for the sake of truth. The penitential model allows preservation of both the veteran and the truth. On the one hand the sin is confessed openly, the veteran is called to publicly mourn for an extended period of time while refraining from Communion, and the community is exhorted to be stern with the penitent. As discussed in the *Grade of Weeping*, the church's attitudes and beliefs towards sin are being molded through these ritual acts. On the other hand, while the gravity of sin is being acknowledged, the responsibility for that sin is being assumed gradually by the congregation as a whole and the penitent

158   *Chapter 4*

is eventually brought back to Communion. In St. Gregory's rite the horrors of sin are fully recognized, but then the burden of sin is no longer the veteran's alone to carry. What a theological perspective presents to the clinical model is a deeper notion of solidarity in sin, which I addressed above with the *Grade of Audience*.

The third stage of recovery, "Reconnection," offers another point of resonance with the penitential rite. In both cases, this final stage involves the reestablishment of relationships. As in the penitential rite, Herman and Litz acknowledge that after trauma, one must ease into relationships in a sort of progression. Litz writes, "Patients should generate a list of the people in their world who are (or were) important to them and who have (or had) a positive influence in their lives. The individuals (or groups) should be arranged in a hierarchy based on the expectations of difficulty in relating *in light of the moral injury*. The patient should be encouraged to move up the hierarchy incrementally and systematically and learn something useful and growth-promoting in each instance."[236] Herman recognizes that reconnection may entail, especially for survivors of abuse, family disclosures and confrontations as well. These too must be approached "incrementally and systematically." Herman offers as a way of analogy a comparison between this process and self-defense training for survivors. Herman details one particular self-defense program for women, in which these survivors are put through increasingly aggressive attacks that they are taught to repel. She comments, "Just like self-defense training, direct involvement in family conflicts often requires a series of *graded* exercises, in which the survivor masters one level of fear before choosing to proceed to higher levels of exposure."[237] Herman's words draw an immediate correlation with Gregory's penitential rite.

The point is not simply that the two processes involve incremental steps towards engagement with a community. There is a connection to be made in the rationale behind these approaches. As suggested earlier, there is a tendency to view the graded ritual as beginning the penitent's transformation from a place of disenfranchisement. The assumption is that the penitent is excluded from community as a form of punishment, and it is only over the course of the penance that she earns her rights to be part of the community again. I have countered this view before, but the trauma recovery model offers perhaps another means by which to understand the graded nature of Gregory's rite. As the clinical model seeks to ease the patient into potentially conflictual relationships, the rite gradually accustoms the penitent to receiving grace and all that grace entails. The self-defense program for survivors again provides a fitting analogy: "By choosing to 'taste fear' in these self-defense exercises, survivors put themselves in a position to reconstruct the normal physiological responses to danger, to rebuild the 'action system' that was shattered and fragmented by trauma. As a result, they face their world more confidently."[238]

Participation in the penitential ritual is a choosing to "taste" grace, forgiveness, and acceptance. In the graded rite, the morally injured would find that their normal physiological, psychological, and spiritual responses to liturgical "communion" (in both senses) are reconstructed. These do not come easily for the morally injured. At one point Herman says that reconnection is like "entering a new country,"[239] which from a liturgical standpoint carries appropriate overtones. The grades in the ancient rite account for the penitent's needs to re-inhabit *incrementally* certain tastes, norms, and customs, namely those of the Kingdom. As in the trauma recovery model, this also pertains to reconnecting with certain relationships. One will notice that as the grades in the penitential rite progress, so does the level of intimacy. The penitent is first secluded, then placed alongside novices, and in the final grade, hands are lain upon her in prayer, and she partakes in the Eucharist. St. Gregory's rite highlights the importance of time and patience as a pastoral tool.

In the interfacing of the trauma recovery model and St. Gregory's graded penitential rite, this section has highlighted a number of resonances that nevertheless betray their distinctiveness from one another. In closing this segment, I will outline some of the more significant differences between these two approaches to healing. The first is their divergent understandings of this term, "healing." Litz's aim seems to be the remediation of psycho-bio-social "impairment," though he falls short of describing what that looks like.[240] Herman comes closer in describing the nature of what she calls "recovery." She writes, "The core experiences of psychological trauma are disempowerment and disconnection from others. Recovery, therefore, is based upon the empowerment of the survivor and the creation of new connections. . . . In her renewed connections with other people, the survivor re-creates the psychological faculties that were damaged or deformed by the traumatic experiences. These faculties include the basic capacities for trust, autonomy, initiative, competence, identity, and intimacy."[241] According to Herman then, healing occurs when two conditions are met: the patient is connected with others, and she is able exercise certain basic psychological capacities.

From a theological standpoint, I understand healing to be the restoration of one's humanity, whose fundamental vocation is the worship of God. Worship also requires engagement of the body, soul, and spirit, as well as participation within a community. Restoration of these components in one's life is thus important, but not the ultimate aim. Therefore, if a physically and psychologically fit man had strong social networks but did not orient his life towards the worship of God, he is still in need of healing according to this theological scheme. Any doctor, however, would deem such a man healthy. (Inversely, a

160   *Chapter 4*

man can be physically and psychologically disabled, but still be considered healed to an extent, if his life reflects the worship of God.) These differences in aims necessarily shape the means by which these aims are achieved.

This then brings attention to the differences in the very structure and form of the remediation processes juxtaposed here. While the trauma recovery programs have "steps" and "stages," they do not bear the narrative quality of the graded penitential ritual. While there is a logical progression to Litz's steps that unifies the whole, his treatment plan is essentially a collection of treatment strategies to reduce the debilitating symptoms of moral injury. Litz himself acknowledges a lack of a clear sequential order noting that "there will be substantial overlap in their application," and that certain steps are intended to occur throughout the treatment.[242]

St. Gregory's rite on the other hand bears a more narrative structure. As in psychotherapy, healing in ritual care involves adopting a "new narrative."[243] One finds one's vocation as a worshiper of Israel's God by inhabiting a particular narrative about oneself and the people of Israel. Because the very form of the graded rite is the healing narrative that the penitent inhabits, it is more rigid. For instance, there is no indication that anyone ever repeats a prior grade, only that some might linger at one stage longer before moving forward. One might say that to regress to a prior grade or to cease participation in the rite is in a way to tell an incoherent or untruthful story.[244] While the liturgy is for the penitent and the people, it is not ultimately a story about them. It is ultimately a story about God's work in history. In this way, the penitent participates in a story already in progress and does not dictate its outcome. In contrast to the clinical model, worship is not "patient-centered care."[245] This is clear in their contrasting approaches.

Finally, there is a fundamental difference between the two in the manner that community is integrated into care. The purpose of drawing attention to the differences here has not been necessarily to favor one or the other. In this case, however, there will be one critique to levy against the trauma recovery treatment plans espoused by Herman and Litz. There is a marked dissonance between the unambiguous language touting the importance of relationships for trauma recovery and the near absence of proffered strategies for forming them. It seems enough for Herman and Litz to say that patients should connect or reconnect with people, without explaining how to do this. They also seem to presume that patients have people with whom to connect in their lives.[246] This seems to me to be a glaring omission, as I have known a number of veterans who are lonely, claim to have no friends, and have a formidable difficulty communicating with and relating to others.

In this way one can argue justifiably that the liturgical model is advantageous. From the moment the penitent participates in the liturgy, she is involved in a community. Though involvement in worship does not guarantee close relationships, the liturgy joins people in solidarity to share a common vocation. The one way in which the trauma recovery process does provide relationship is through the therapeutic relationship. This, however, is a temporary and transactional one, since the relationship is contingent upon the patient's illness and the therapist being compensated for her services. The church, in contrast, provides a universal and abiding communal presence.

Again, the aim of juxtaposing the two approaches to healing is not to imply that the ritual is a superior model for healing than the trauma recovery model. Ritual and medicine do not necessarily share a competitive space. At the same time, comparison between the two is not intended to create some sort of synthesis to provide a definitive treatment plan for moral injury. It would seem ideal that a morally injured veteran would receive both medical treatment *and* pastoral/ritual care. It should also be made clear that the main purpose for St. Gregory's rite was never to provide psychological comfort, let alone treatment for psychological trauma. As has been established above, the primary aim for the Christian liturgy, for ritual care, is worship. By bringing the two models into conversation, this study has explored how they might validate, challenge, and inform one another in their understanding of the morally injured and their healing.

CONCLUDING REMARKS ON THE PASTORAL THEOLOGICAL COMMENTARY

When rituals are viewed in the context of pastoral care, there is a temptation at times to view them narrowly in one of two ways. On the one hand, they may be looked upon as largely esoteric vestiges of a bygone era and wholly irrelevant to the Church's work of *cura animarum*. On the other hand, they may be reduced to therapeutic tools finding their worth primarily in the task of providing psychological comfort for their participants. In this chapter I have provided a pastoral theological commentary on and analysis of St. Gregory the Wonderworker's graded penitential rite in light of the pastoral issue of moral injury. The point of this exploration was not necessarily to commend this very ritual for the treatment of morally injured veterans today but to illustrate that a ritual, like St. Gregory's, directed first and foremost towards worship in the Eucharist, is no less pastorally helpful for it. Indeed, theocentric liturgies are also more theological, and what Willimon states regarding funerals he would likely claim of all liturgies, that as they "become more explicitly and intentionally theological they will become more pastorally helpful."[247] Below I will offer a concise summary of the pastoral and therapeutic benefits of St. Gregory's rite as detailed in the above sections of this

162   *Chapter 4*

chapter. I will then close with a brief statement regarding how St. Gregory's rite can be used as a model for ritual approaches to pastoral care today.

Pastoral and Therapeutic Benefits

As described in the introduction to this book, clinicians, ministers and theologians alike have recognized the need for a ritual response to moral injury. As such, entertaining the idea of responding ritually to moral injury is not novel in and of itself. Two of the main tasks of this study are to investigate more deeply (1) *why* rituals might be helpful in addressing moral injury, and (2) *what kind* of liturgies might serve as the most appropriate Christian pastoral responses to moral injury—two questions heretofore unanswered in any significant manner by veteran care providers and researchers. This study has culminated in a collection of essays found in this chapter to present a *kind* of ritual advocated in this study—one that is ritually honest—held in conversation with current medical and social scientific research to illustrate *why* such a rite might be helpful in addressing moral injury. In exploring the 'why' of the potential pastoral effectiveness of rituals like St. Gregory's rite, this chapter has yielded the following observations:

- (*Confession*) The ritual offers interpersonal connection/relationship (as opposed to isolation) and an opportunity to confess one's sins to a moral authority.
- (*Grade of Weeping*) The ritual offers ample space to mourn the past while actively embarking on a positive path forward. It also provides a context of affective formation for the penitent, as well as for the witnessing congregation, in order that the community might maintain the proper orientation towards sin.
- (*Grade of Audience*) The ritual directs the penitent through a process of faith reconstruction within the context of a community. It also provides the vehicle for the communal sharing of one's sin.
- (*Grade of Submission*) The ritual helps change the veteran's orientation to the world and her own fears, that they might be the means by which the veteran is more firmly rooted within the church and not avoidant of it.
- (*Grade of Standing with*) The ritual provides sensory-rich counter-narratives (or countervailing experiences) to shape the body, soul, and mind of the veteran to assume a status of forgiven-ness, when rational disquisitions or simply declaring one as "forgiven" seems to fall short.
- (*Grade of Participation*) The ritual fosters reconnection with the community as a whole while taking seriously the nature of one's sins. The graded nature of the rite also helps ease the veteran back into community.

Though the graded penitential rite is theocentric in orientation, it nevertheless yields the above pastoral and clinically validated benefits known for reducing the symptoms of this trauma and ultimately aiding one's restoration from moral injury. Despite the potential of St. Gregory's rite for addressing moral injury, I have noted above the challenges of applying a third century, near-eastern rite to present-day American churches. The graded penitential rite is nevertheless a helpful model of the "Principles of Ritual Care" outlined above. Even if the ritual cannot (or will not) be assumed as a whole in this modern Western milieu, there are certainly features of the rite itself that could be introduced into the ritual infrastructures of churches today. Below, I will speak to one feature in particular.

St. Gregory's Graded Penitential Rite in Pastoral Application

While a firm advocate of ritually honest liturgies, this study does not intend to foreclose on all possibilities for ritual construction. For this reason, chapter 3 introduced *principles* for ritual care and did not commend a specific rite for moral injury. Moreover, in this chapter St. Gregory's rite served as an *example* of the possibilities for theocentric ritual care, already resident within the church tradition. This chapter fleshed out some of the ways such a penitential process could address the needs of the morally injured, as experienced by veterans today. While I summarized all of the potential pastoral and therapeutic benefits of St. Gregory's rite above, here I will avoid conducting a summary of all of the *formal* aspects of the rite that would be worth replicating in the Church today. Such would be a more subjective task left for the pastor to discern based upon the individual congregation or faith community. Nevertheless, I will highlight one feature of the graded penitential ritual that should be considered in ritual approaches to pastoral care. This recommendation is made in light of the discussions in chapter 3 regarding theocentric/humanistic liturgies and ritual formulation.

One of the critiques levied against humanistic liturgies in chapter 3 is that they are directed primarily towards providing some therapeutic or practical benefit to its central participants. The result is a violation of ritual honesty and a general incoherence within the ritual infrastructure of a church community. In opposition to this approach, chapter 3 proposed that ritual honesty was achieved by making the Eucharist the ultimate focus in all Christian liturgies. This is a challenge for occasional rites, such as funerals and weddings, where participants ordinarily do not partake of Communion, and contemporary liturgies have trended in a more humanistic direction. The challenge is no less for penitential rites. St. Gregory's rite, however, offers one model for creating occasional rites that ultimately find their aim in the Eucharist.

164 *Chapter 4*

The Eucharistic liturgy is the paradigmatic form of worship. All other Christian rites are in some ways (or ought to be) a derivative of this central rite. Even in the absence of Holy Communion itself, all occasional rituals should have underlying them a Eucharistic consciousness. This is what binds all the Church towards a common vision of God, the world, and humanity. The third-century graded rite is an occasional rite formulated apart from the Eucharistic liturgy, but that nevertheless is anchored in it. *This is achieved by it serving as an adjunct to the weekly liturgy itself.* The penitential discipline actually occurs concurrently with the weekly Eucharistic liturgy at the site of the Church. As detailed above, the penitent begins outside the church and, as the drama unfolds over the period of the penance, the penitent moves spatially closer to the Communion table. The ingenuity of the penitential rite is that it utilizes the exterior of the church, the narthex, and the nave as additional liturgical spaces to accommodate the penitent (and catechumenate) by placing her on a pilgrimage towards the Eucharist. One might say that St. Gregory's rite is not necessarily a separate rite, but an addendum to the Eucharistic liturgy.

Therefore, what St. Gregory's rite offers to pastors engaged in the work of ritual construction today is another model[248] for formulating rites out of and connected to the Eucharistic liturgy itself.[249] In a way, little of one's creative faculties is taxed by this form of ritual construction. St. Gregory simply wrote a subplot to the main story that is the Eucharistic liturgy. By following the narrative logic of the central liturgy, the penitential rite can be said to have written itself. There is not even a separate ending written for this ancillary rite as it ultimately shares the climax found in the Eucharistic liturgy. This is perhaps the most direct way of carrying out the pastoral ritual hermeneutic task of shepherding parishioners to know and shape their lives and situations through the interpretive key of the Eucharist.

Even without advocating in whole the use of the graded penitential rite today, I have highlighted features of the ritual and ancient approaches to penance that would serve as wise models for today's Church. By interfacing moral injury and Gregory's rite, my goal was to illustrate new approaches to ritual care that could enrich the Church's task in caring for some of the most pressing concerns within our communities.

NOTES

1. Hereafter, this rite may be referred to as "St. Gregory's rite," "St. Gregory's penitential rite," "the graded rite," or "the graded penitential discipline," though all refer to the same general third century practice as detailed in St. Gregory's *Canonical Epistle* and the *Didascalia*.

2. Brock and Lettini, *Soul Repair*, xvii–xviii.

3. Christopher Grundy, "Basic Retraining: The Role of Congregational Ritual in the Care of Returning Veterans," *Liturgy* 27, no. 4 (2012): 32.

4. Warren Kinghorn, "Combat Trauma and Moral Fragmentation: A Theological Account of Moral Injury," *Journal of the Society of Christian Ethics* 32, no. 2 (Fall/Winter 2012): 68.

5. Saint Gregory Thaumaturgus, "Canonical Epistle," in *St. Gregory Thaumaturgus: Life and Works (Fathers of the Church; v. 98)*, translated by Michael Slusser (Washington, DC: Catholic University of America Press, 1998), 151.

6. Saint Basil, "To Amphilochius, concerning the Canons," in *Letters: Volume 2 (186–368)*, translated by Sister Agnes Clare Way with notes by Roy J. Deferrari (Washington, DC: Catholic University of America Press, 2008), 23.

7. *Catechism of the Catholic Church* 2.2.2.1422.

8. *Canons of Hippolytus* 14 in Paul Bradshaw, Maxwell Johnson, and L. Edward Phillips, *The Apostolic Tradition: A Commentary* (Minneapolis, MN: Fortress Press, 2002), 91.

9. Bernard Joseph Verkamp, *The Moral Treatment of Returning Warriors in Early Medieval and Modern Times* (Scranton, PA: Univ. of Scranton Press, 1993), 305.

10. Tertullian, *De Corona* 1.

11. Origen, *Contra Celsum* 3.8.

12. McGuckin's translation states "defense of *sobriety* and piety." See John McGuckin, "Nonviolence and Peace Traditions in Early & Eastern Christianity," *In Communion*, December 29, 2004, accessed March 18, 2018, http://incommunion.org/2004 /12/29/nonviolence-and-peace-traditions/.

13. Centuries later, Thomas Aquinas would make a similar claim that "a religious order may fittingly be established for soldiering, not indeed for any worldly purpose, but for the *defense of divine worship and public safety*, or also of the poor and oppressed . . ." [*Summa Theologiae* Pt. II–II, Q. 188, Art. 3, italics mine].

14. St. Basil, *Canon 13*.

15. Verkamp, *The Moral Treatment of Returning Warriors*, 34.

16. Ibid., 36.

17. Ibid.

18. Ibid., 37.

19. Stanley Hauerwas, *War and the American Difference: Theological Reflections on Violence and National Identity* (Grand Rapids, MI: Baker Academic, 2011), 56. If Hauerwas is correct, it is only appropriate then that the remedy for participation in war is participation in right worship.

20. One story that illustrates this dynamic well is that of one Desert Storm veteran I met at a clinic. The veteran stated that due to circumstances not directly related to his own actions, he had a young boy suffering in his arms. The veteran was outraged that, due to someone's negligence, a child would be placed in such a condition. As a "mercy killing" he shot the child. The veteran distinctly remembers the feeling of the child's life leaving him while in his arms. This event has troubled the veteran since. When asked if he saw this act as the lesser of two evils, he said, *no*, such an idea is "bullshit." There were no lesser of two evils in this instance, he said. The veteran knew that if he did not end the child's life, the child would likely suffer longer only to die

166 *Chapter 4*

anyway. Yet even in seeking to alleviate this child's suffering, he felt in his bones that taking this child's life was an unequivocal evil. The veteran, not directly responsible for the child's injury and knowing no better action than to take the child's life (a decision he does *not* regret), continues to struggle with moral injury today over the incident. Notably, this illustrates how the act of killing in itself is experienced as contrary to human nature, even if done mercifully and for a conceivably "good" reason. Though not a Christian in the traditional sense, the veteran's intuition here resonates with the argument regarding sin presented here. Many would not consider what the veteran did murder, or illegal. Some might even say that what he did was honorable. Yet what the veteran experienced in ending another's life is a sense that such an act was inherently sinful, contrary to human nature, and counter to the worship of God. Some may argue that the veteran's act was not sinful and that he should not feel guilty as he had no other option and he made the best decision given the situation. The moral burden the veteran seems to carry, however, is not necessarily his own (in his mind he acted morally given the circumstances), but that of the circumstances that created the situation. The veteran may not have had another choice, but at some point the people who created the situation in the chain of causality leading to that point probably could have taken a different path. This is akin to Peter Marin's "second category of moral pain" which he describes as "the world's pain." ["Living in Moral Pain," in *The Vietnam Reader*, edited by Walter H. Capps (New York: Routledge, 1991), 49.] The section on the *Grade of Audience* will speak to this phenomenon, wherein one has a tendency in moral injury to assume the burden of others.

21. If the sixth commandment is in fact only a prohibition of cold-blooded murder and does not encapsulate legal armed conflict.

22. Shay resonates with this desire to administer a rite (in his case, a "purification" rite) for veterans who have shed blood, however "blamelessly." [Jonathan Shay, *Odysseus in America: Combat Trauma and the Trials of Homecoming* (New York: Scribner, 2010), 25.] This also further illustrates the point made in chapter 1 using the words of Wright, who states that sin in is not "simply the breaking of moral codes," but "the missing of the mark of genuine humanness through the failure of worship." [N. T. Wright, *The Day the Revolution Began: Reconsidering the Meaning of Jesus's Crucifixion* (San Francisco: HarperOne, 2016), 86.]

23. See for instance Appendix B and David Grossman, *On Killing: The Psychological Cost of Learning to Kill in War and Society* (Boston: Little, Brown, 1996).

24. Grossman, *On Killing*, 50.

25. See Appendix B.

26. If anything, I might advocate that we become a more *intentionally* ritualized society so that such rituals could be received more readily and enrich the life of the church.

27. *Canons of Hippolytus* 14, italics mine.

28. Ibid.

29. *Didascalia Apostolorum* 2.16.

30. For instance St. Jerome speaks of the *public* confession of Fabiola's errors in his letter *To Oceanus*. [*Epist.* 77, *To Oceanus* (PL, 22, 692), cited in Paul E. Palmer, *Sacraments and Forgiveness: History and Doctorinal Development of Penance,*

Extreme Unction and Indulgences (Westminster, MD: Newman Press, 1961), 121.] In Paulinus's biography of St. Ambrose, however, the saint says of the Bishop of Milan's work as a confessor, "the sins which were confessed to him he would speak of to none but God only, to whom he made intercession, and thus he left behind a good example to priests who should come after him, that they should be intercessors before God, rather than accusers before men." [*Vita S. Ambrosii*, 39, cited in John Thomas Arthur Gunstone, *The Liturgy of Penance* (New York: Morehouse-Barlow, 1966), 38.] Paulinus's description sounds more akin to the private confessions held today in both the Catholic and Eastern Orthodox churches.

31. Brett Litz, Nathan Stein, Eileen Delaney, Leslie Lebowitz, William P. Nash, Caroline Silva, and Shira Maguen, "Moral Injury and Moral Repair in War Veterans: A Preliminary Model and Intervention Strategy," *Clinical Psychology Review* 29, no. 8 (2009): 702.

32. Shay, *Achilles in Vietnam*, 55.

33. Jane E. Brody, "War Wounds That Time Alone Can't Heal," *The New York Times*, June 6, 2016, accessed March 18, 2018, https://well.blogs.nytimes.com/2016/06/06/war-wounds-that-time-alone-cant-heal/.

34. Litz, "Moral Injury and Moral Repair in War Veterans," 701.

35. Matt J. Gray et al., "Adaptive Disclosure: An Open Trial of a Novel Exposure-Based Intervention for Service Members With Combat-Related Psychological Stress Injuries," *Behavior Therapy* 43, no. 2 (2012): 409.

36. Shay, *Achilles in Vietnam*, 4.

37. Shay, *Achilles in Vietnam*, 55.

38. Brody, "War Wounds That Time Alone Can't Heal."

39. Litz, "Moral Injury and Moral Repair in War Veterans," 701.

40. St. Gregory Thaumaturgus, *Canonical Epistle*, Canon 11.

41. *Didascalia Apostolorum* 2.16 in Alistair Stewart-Sykes, trans., *The Didascalia Apostolorum: An English Version* (Turnhout, Belgium: Brepols Publishers, 2009).

42. Here I have in mind the observations of Seligman when using the term "sincerity." [Adam B. Seligman, *Ritual and Its Consequences: An Essay on the Limits of Sincerity* (Oxford: Oxford University Press, 2008), 8–9.]

43. Elaine Ramshaw, "Ritual and Pastoral Care: The Vital Connection" in *Disciples at the Crossroads: Perspectives on Worship and Church Leadership*, ed. Eleanor Bernstein, C.S.J. (Collegeville, MN: The Liturgical Press, 1993), 102.

44. Ramshaw, "Ritual and Pastoral Care," 102.

45. *Canons of Hippolytus* 14, italics mine.

46. As translated by R. Hugh Connolly.

47. *Didascalia Apostolorum* 2.41.

48. Irenaeus, *Against Heresies* 1.13.5, italics mine.

49. Tertullian, *De Poenitentia*, 9, italics mine.

50. Jason Nieuwsma, Robyn Walser, Jacob Farnsworth, Kent Drescher, Keith Meador, and William Nash, "Possibilities within Acceptance and Commitment Therapy for Approaching Moral Injury," *Current Psychiatry Reviews* 11, no. 3 (2015): 196–97.

51. Ibid., 198.

168 *Chapter 4*

52. Ibid., 197.

53. Ibid.

54. Ibid., 198.

55. Alexander Schmemann, *For the Life of the World: Sacraments and Orthodoxy* (Yonkers, NY: St. Vladimir's Seminary Press, 1973), 101.

56. As Kinghorn suggests above, one needs to be able "to distinguish between suffering that aids in the realization of the good life and suffering that thwarts the achievement of these ends." [Kinghorn, "Combat Trauma and Moral Fragmentation," 65.]

57. William H. Willimon, *Worship as Pastoral Care* (Nashville, TN: Abingdon, 1979), 48.

58. Grossman, *On Killing*, 61, 180–81.

59. As Peter Marin writes, "Time and again one hears vets say about the war and its issues: 'It don't mean nothin'.' They struggle to empty the past of meaning—not because they are hardened to what happened or because it does not mean nothing, but because it is the only way they can preserve sanity in its shadow." [Marin, "Living in Moral Pain," 50.]

60. Verkamp, *The Moral Treatment of Returning Warriors*, 42.

61. Mark Searle, "The Sacraments of Faith," *Assembly* 5, no. 5 (1979): 54–55, cited in Stephen S. Wilbricht, *Rehearsing God's Just Kingdom: The Eucharistic Vision of Mark Searle* (Collegeville, MN: Liturgical Press, 2013), 28.

62. Mark Searle, "Liturgical Gestures" (Editorial), *Assembly* 6, no. 3 (1979) 73, 80, cited in Wilbricht, *Rehearsing God's Just Kingdom*, 30.

63. Mark Searle, *Called to Participate: Theological, Ritual, and Social Perspectives*, ed. Barbara S. Searle and Anne Y. Koester (Collegeville, MN: Liturgical Press, 2006), 62, cited in Wilbricht, *Rehearsing God's Kingdom*, 12.

64. If this is true, liturgies like St. Gregory's graded penitential rite can be the place in which a spirit and posture of *repentance* can be nurtured where previously absent. *Catechism of the Catholic Church* 1431 describes "Interior repentance" as "a radical reorientation of our whole life, a return, a conversion to God with all our heart, an end of sin, a turning away from evil, with repugnance toward the evil actions we have committed. At the same time it entails the desire and resolution to change one's life, with hope in God's mercy and trust in the help of his grace. This conversion of heart is accompanied by a salutary pain and sadness which the Fathers called *animi cruciatus* (affliction of spirit) and *compunctio cordis* (repentance of heart)."

65. Timothy Wilson, *Strangers to Ourselves* (Cambridge, MA: Belknap, 2004), 124.

66. Wilson, *Strangers to Ourselves*, 212. Wilson also cites the *Nichomachean Ethics*, in which Aristotle speaks of the primacy of action in the acquisition of virtues. His insights are no less relevant here. He writes, "We acquire [virtues] by first having put them into action . . . we become just by the practice of just actions, self-controlled by exercising self-control, and courageous by performing acts of courage." [Wilson, *Strangers to Ourselves*, 211–12.]

67. That being said, the eventual manifestation of Christian attitudes should not again be confused as the end or purpose of the liturgy. The penitential rite is not in any way less when the outward expressions of mourning remain insincere. In fact,

Seligman would argue that it is this "as if" or "could be" quality of ritual "that makes our shared social world possible." [Seligman, *Ritual and Its Consequences*, 7.] Rituals hold significance within a community for the way they allow participants to act "as if" certain ideal conditions exist. For an unremorseful veteran to state that he is repentant and then undergo the actions of mourning without feeling is not an undermining of ritual. It is part and parcel of ritual, even worship. Seligman actually sees an overemphasis on sincerity as being at odds with ritual. [Seligman, *Ritual and Its Consequences*, 8.]

68. Tertullian, *On Repentance* 9.3–4.

69. Nieuwsma et al., "Possibilities within Acceptance and Commitment Therapy for Approaching Moral Injury," 196.

70. R. Hugh Connolly translates the phrase "be stern with him."

71. *Didascalia Apostolorum* 2.16.

72. Recall again Isidore's statement in Verkamp, *The Moral Treatment of Returning Warriors*, 305. See also Athanasius's statement regarding killing the enemy in war in his *Letter to Amun*.

73. Again, I use this phrase in the sense that Seligman does, referring to the subjunctive quality of rituals. [Seligman, *Ritual and Its Consequences*, 7.]

74. This is a balance advocated by St. Cyprian in his letter to Antonian. Cyprian writes, "Neither should we be too unmerciful and stubborn in repelling them from penance: nor, again, too lax and easy in rashly allowing them to communicate." [Cited in Palmer, *Sacraments and Forgiveness*, 51.] One can imagine that these carefully prescribed gestures can also place a limit on those who wish to be unmerciful to the penitent.

75. The only exception is the deathbed reconciliation. [Paul E. Palmer, *Sacraments and Forgiveness: History and Doctrinal Development of Penance, Extreme Unction and Indulgences* (Westminster, MD: Newman Press, 1961), 171.]

76. Palmer, *Sacraments and Forgiveness*, 172, and Gunstone, *Liturgy of Penance*, 50.

77. Palmer, *Sacraments and Forgiveness*, 184.

78. Ibid., 71–72.

79. Susan Marie Smith, *Caring Liturgies: The Pastoral Power of Christian Ritual* (Minneapolis, MN: Fortress Press, 2012), 92.

80. Brock and Lettini, *Soul Repair*, 103.

81. Willimon writes, "Liturgy *is* education. The question before us . . . is not *whether* our people will learn when they worship. The question is, *What* will they learn when we lead them in worship?" [*Worship as Pastoral Care*, 123–24.] He qualifies his statement, however, by citing Westerhoff and Kennedy, who caution, "Some religious educators have made the serious mistake of speaking of teaching *by* or *with* the liturgy, thereby reducing the liturgy to a didactic act. To *use* the liturgy is to do it violence. Of course, we learn through the liturgy. . . . Our rituals shape and form us in fundamental ways. But our liturgies properly should be understood as ends and not as means." [In John H. Westerhoff and Gwen Kennedy Neville, *Learning Through Liturgy* (New York: Seabury Press, 1978), 91–92.]

82. St. Gregory Thaumaturgus, *Canonical Epistle*, Canon 11.

170   *Chapter 4*

83. *Didascalia Apostolorum* 2.40.

84. Palmer, *Sacraments and Forgiveness*, 59–60.

85. Ibid., 60.

86. Drescher et al., "An Exploration of the Viability and Usefulness of the Construct of Moral Injury in War Veterans," 9. See also Harold Koenig et al., "The Moral Injury Symptom Scale-Military Version." *Journal of Religion & Health* 52, no. 3 (September 2013): 10.

87. Koenig et al., "The Moral Injury Symptom Scale-Military Version," 10.

88. This is already a recognized symptom of PTSD as well. Evidence suggests that veterans in treatment for PTSD exhibit significantly more religious and spiritual struggles than their demographically matched counterparts, due to their experiences in war. See Nieuwsma, "Possibilities within Acceptance and Commitment Therapy for Approaching Moral Injury," 203.

89. *Didascalia Apostolorum* 2.40.

90. Edward Tick, "Healing the Wounds of War," *Parabola Magazine* (October 31, 2014), 115.

91. Phillip Martin, "Why So Many Iraqis Hate Us? Try 'Towel Head' On for Size," *The Huffington Post*, May 25, 2011, accessed April 09, 2018, https://www.huffingtonpost.com/phillip-martin/why-so-many-iraqis-hate-u_b_96330.html.

92. Tick, "Healing the Wounds of War," 118–19.

93. Richard Holmes, *Acts of War: The Behavior of Men in Battle* (New York: Free Press, 1989), 393.

94. Aristotle, *Poetics* XI.

95. For Schmemann, a sacrament reveals the true nature of something. [*For the Life of the World*, 102, 121.] By killing, a veteran learns the true nature of the bond between herself and the other. I also use this term because veterans often view these experiences not favorably, but as being indescribably sacred.

96. Shira Maguen and Brett Litz, "Moral Injury in Veterans of War," *PTSD Research Quarterly* 23, no. 1 (2012): 1.

97. Kinghorn, "Combat Trauma and Moral Fragmentation," 61, paraphrasing Litz et al., "Moral Injury and Moral Repair in War Veterans," 700.

98. Jean-Claude Larchet often sees this as the *modus operandi* of the communities of the Early Christian East. When dealing with the sinner, the sick, and the insane, the community is exhorted to intercede for these less fortunate as if their infirmities were the community's own. St. Theodosius was even said to have claimed responsibility for their faults, chosen to partake of their lot, and encouraged the community to do the same. Rather than blaming or excluding them, the community strived for greater union and integration with those who had fallen under misfortune. On this, see Jean-Claude Larchet, *Mental Disorders & Spiritual Healing: Teachings from the Early Christian East* (Hillsdale, NY: Sophia Perennis, 2005), 79–81. See also William T. Cavanaugh, *Field Hospital* (Grand Rapids, MI: William B. Eerdmans Publishing Company, 2016), 263.

99. See Appendix A.

100. Sozomen, *Ecclesiastical History* 7.16, translated by Chester D. Hartranft, quoted in Gunstone, *The Liturgy of Penance*, 31.

101. Paulinus, *Life of St. Ambrose* (PL, 14, 43), quoted in Palmer, *Sacraments and Forgiveness*, 91.

102. This is an example of how a ritual act can serve as a hermeneutic guide for the church. By virtue of mirroring the posture of the penitent, the bishop may be directing the church to see the shared guilt of the penitent with the church body. The Eucharist is still the hermeneutic key as the bishop's posture is also a Christological posture. In a sense it is a ritual representation of 2 Cor. 5:21. This also demonstrates that the pastor's hermeneutic role in ritual care can be fulfilled even absent of direct discourse.

103. Romans 12:15 and 1 Corinthians 12:26.

104. *The Sayings of the Desert Fathers* in Paul Evergetinos, *Collection*, vol. iii, ed. Victor Matthaiou (Monastery of the Transfiguration, Athens, 1964), 497.

105. "Aims and Purposes," *Catholic Worker,* Jan. 1939, p. 7, cited in Cavanaugh, *Field Hospital*, 262.

106. Cavanaugh, *Field Hospital*, 250.

107. Edwin H. Friedman, *Generation to Generation: Family Process in Church and Synagogue* (New York: Guilford Press, 2011), 13.

108. Cavanaugh, *Field Hospital*, 263.

109. "We Are to Blame for the New War in Europe," *Catholic Worker*, September 1939, pp. 1, 4, quoted in Cavanaugh, *Field Hospital*, 149.

110. Day, "Why Do the Members of Christ Tear One Another?" *Catholic Worker,* Feb. 1942, p. 7, quoted in Cavanaugh, *Field Hospital*, 259.

111. Nancy Sherman, *Afterwar: Healing the Moral Injuries of Our Soldiers* (New York, NY: Oxford University Press, 2015), 26.

112. Ibid.

113. William T. Cavanaugh, "An End to Every War," ABC*: Religion & Ethics*, January 19, 2016, accessed March 21, 2018, http://www.abc.net.au/religion/articles /2016/01/19/4390491.htm.

114. Jonathan Shay, *Odysseus in America*, 150.

115. Jonathan Shay, "Casualties," *Daedalus* 140, no. 3 (2011): 182.

116. Aphrodite Matsakis, *Back from the Front: Combat Trauma, Love, and the Family* (Baltimore, MD: Sidran Institute Press, 2007), 53.

117. Ibid.

118. Marin, "Living in Moral Pain," 48.

119. Ibid.

120. Ibid. Italics mine.

121. St. Augustine validates this principle: "Far be it, therefore, from us to refuse to hear even of the bitter and sorrowful things which befall those who are very dear to us! For in some way which I cannot explain, the pain suffered by one member is mitigated when all the other members suffer with it. And this mitigation is effected not by actual participation in the calamity, but by the solacing power of love; for although only some suffer the actual burden of the affliction, and the others share their suffering through knowing what these have to bear, nevertheless the tribulation is borne in common by them all, seeing that they have in common the same experience, hope, and love, and the same Divine Spirit." Augustine, *Letter 99.*

122. Smith, *Caring Liturgies*, 43–44.

123. H.P.V. Renner, "The Use of Ritual in Pastoral Care," *Journal of Pastoral Care & Counseling* 33, no. 3 (1979): 173.

124. David Hogue, *Remembering the Future, Imagining the Past: Story, Ritual and the Human Brain* (Eugene, OR: Wipf & Stock, 2009), 168.

125. Hogue, *Remembering the Future Imagining the Past*, 150–51.

126. Renner, "The Use of Ritual in Pastoral Care," 173.

127. St. Gregory Thaumaturgus, *Canonical Epistle*, Canon 11.

128. Other translation states "inside the door, inside the narthex."

129. St. Gregory Thaumaturgus, *Canonical Epistle*, Canon 11.

130. It may be no coincidence that both the processing of spatial relations and the imprinting of trauma occur on the same side (the right) of the brain. See Bessel Van Der Kolk, *The Body Keeps the Score: Brain, Mind and Body in the Healing of Trauma* (New York: Penguin Books, 2015), 298.

131. "Layout of Rooms—Back To The Walls, Doors In View," *My PTSD Forum*, February 6, 2007, accessed March 21, 2018, https://www.myptsd.com/threads/layout -of-rooms-back-to-the-walls-doors-in-view.1563/.

132. Sigmund Freud, "Thoughts for the Times on War and Death," in *The Standard Edition of the Complete Psychological Works of Sigmund Freud / On the History of the Psychoanalytic Movement; Papers on Metapsychology* (London: Hogarth Press, 1957), 295.

133. Schmemann, *For the Life of the World*, 121.

134. Matthew 7:7–8 and Luke 11:9–10.

135. Matthew 25:10.

136. Luke 13:25.

137. Luke 12:36.

138. Luke 13:24.

139. Lawrence Farley, "Conclusion: 'The Doors! The Doors! In Wisdom Let Us Attend,'" *Orthodox Christian Network*, July 14, 2014, accessed March 21, 2018, http: //myocn.net/conclusion-exclusion-the-doors-the-doors-in-wisdom-let-us-attend/.

140. Thomas Hopko, "The Orthodox Faith—Volume II—Worship—The Divine Liturgy—Love and Faith," *Orthodox Church in America*, accessed March 21, 2018, https://oca.org/orthodoxy/the-orthodox-faith/worship/the-divine-liturgy/love-and -faith. The text is taken from *The Orthodox Faith, Vol. II* (Yonkers: St. Vladimir's Seminary Press, 2016).

141. Lawrence Farley, "Conclusion: 'The Doors! The Doors! In Wisdom Let Us Attend.'"

142. Thomas Hopko, "The Orthodox Faith—Volume II—Worship—The Divine Liturgy—Love and Faith."

143. Lawrence Farley, "Conclusion: 'The Doors! The Doors! In Wisdom Let Us Attend.'"

144. Ibid.

145. St. Gregory Thaumaturgus, *Canonical Epistle*, Canon 11.

146. Nünning, "On the Narrativity of Rituals," in *Ritual and Narrative: Theoretical Explorations and Historical Case Studies*, ed. Vera Nunning (Bielefeld: Transcript-Verlag, 2014), 54–58 and 65–68.

147. Nünning, "On the Narrativity of Rituals," 55.

148. Ibid., 57, 68.

149. Ibid., 68.

150. Ibid., 55–56.

151. James K. A. Smith, *Desiring the Kingdom: Worship, Worldview, and Cultural Formation* (Grand Rapids, MI: Baker Academic, 2009), 88.

152. Herbert Anderson and Edward Foley, *Mighty Stories, Dangerous Rituals: Weaving Together the Human and the Divine* (San Francisco: Jossey-Bass, 2001), xiii.

153. Nünning, "On the Narrativity of Rituals," 55.

154. Joseph Campbell, *The Hero with a Thousand Faces* (Novato: New World Library, 2008), 45.

155. Ibid., 71.

156. Ibid., 83.

157. Ibid., 159.

158. My reference to the Hero's Journey here should not be taken as an endorsement of Campbell's belief in the "monomyth." What I seek to highlight by the comparison between Gregory's rite and the hero's journey is the narrative quality inherent within the sequencing of the graded penitential ritual. The comparison provides a way to see the steps in the penitential rite not as unconnected moments but as a coherent drama. Vogler's reframing of Campbell's journey makes this further evident.

159. Christopher Vogler, *The Writer's Journey: Mythic Structure for Storytellers and Screenwriters* (Studio City: Michael Wiese Productions, 2007), 13.

160. Campbell, *The Hero with a Thousand Faces*, 84.

161. Ibid., 85.

162. Vogler, *The Writer's Journey*, 8.

163. Ibid., 13.

164. Anderson and Foley, *Mighty Stories, Dangerous Rituals*, 12.

165. As much as the veteran-penitent is guided hermeneutically through the ritual process, in a hermeneutic approach to ritual care the veteran's experience could also serve as an interpretive key and guiding metaphor for the rest of the congregation. Witnesses to the penitential drama would be led to consider in what way should approaching the Table, or crossing the "eschatological separation" between the Church and the world be considered dangerous? In what way is this the appropriate posture when entering the church? In what way is the church a place of vulnerability and exposure? Such questions validate the experiences of penitents, as well as catechumens who may be experiencing fear for different reasons. At the same time, these discussions involve all congregants in a reflective process that builds liturgical consciousness and fluency. It is an answer to Ramshaw's call to "live our way more deeply into the Christian symbols, the language of liturgy, so that we bring those symbols to human experience." [Ramshaw, "Ritual and Pastoral Care," 93.]

166. Wilson, *Strangers to Ourselves*, 212.

167. Mark Searle, "The Sacraments of Faith," *Assembly* 5, no. 5 (1979): 54–55, cited in Wilbricht, *Rehearsing God's Kingdom*, 28.

168. Smith, *Desiring the Kingdom*, 32–33.

174 *Chapter 4*

169. Alasdair C. MacIntyre, *After Virtue: A Study in Moral Theory* (Notre Dame: University of Notre Dame Press, 1981), 216.

170. Anderson and Foley, *Mighty Stories, Dangerous Rituals*, 4–5.

171. Ibid., 11.

172. Jill Freedman and Gene Combs, *Narrative Therapy: The Social Construction of Preferred Realities* (New York: W. W. Norton & Company, 1996), 39.

173. Martin Payne, *Narrative Therapy* (Thousand Oaks: Sage Publications, 2006), 6 and 20.

174. Payne, *Narrative Therapy*, 19.

175. Ibid., 32.

176. Wilson, *Strangers to Ourselves*, 181.

177. Nünning, "On the Narrativity of Rituals," 67.

178. Ibid.

179. Payne, *Narrative Therapy*, 10–17.

180. Anderson and Foley, *Mighty Stories, Dangerous Rituals*, 27.

181. Freedman and Combs, *Narrative Therapy*, 89. See also Christie Cozad Neuger, *Counseling Women: A Narrative, Pastoral Approach* (Minneapolis: Fortress Press, 2004), 90, and Michael White and David Epston, *Narrative Means to Therapeutic Ends* (New York: Norton, 1990), 15.

182. Neuger, *Counseling Women*, 55, 87, 142–43. Freedman and Combs, *Narrative Therapy*, 39.

183. Freedman and Combs, *Narrative Therapy*, 118.

184. Payne, *Narrative Therapy*, 83.

185. Ibid., 133, 137.

186. Freedman and Combs, *Narrative Therapy*, 118.

187. Neuger, *Counseling Women*, 55.

188. Freedman and Combs, *Narrative Therapy*, 39.

189. Payne, *Narrative Therapy*, 138.

190. Freedman and Combs, *Narrative Therapy*, 57–58.

191. *Ritual and Its Consequences*, 20, italics mine.

192. I would argue that a penitent's willing participation in a ritual narrative not their own places them no more under the subjugation of dominant cultural practices than a person who is told they are worthy of forgiveness either by a priest or a therapist.

193. Litz, "Moral Injury and Moral Repair in War Veterans," 701.

194. Ibid.

195. Ibid. This language is already reminiscent of the Narrative Therapeutic task of challenging harmful beliefs, and the ritual function of criticizing, delegitimizing, and superseding of existing memories.

196. Ibid.

197. Ibid.

198. Ibid.

199. Ibid.

200. For instance, see Nünning, "On the Narrativity of Rituals," 57, 68.

201. Schmemann, *For the Life of the World*, 26, and McGuckin, "Nonviolence and Peace Traditions in Early & Eastern Christianity."

202. Cavanaugh, "An End to Every War."

203. Ibid.

204. Hauerwas, *War and the American Difference*, 68.

205. Cavanaugh, "An End to Every War."

206. "Aims and Purposes," *Catholic Worker*, Jan. 1939, p. 7, cited in Cavanaugh, *Field Hospital*, 262.

207. Cavanaugh, "An End to Every War."

208. Mark Searle, "Active Participation" (Editorial), *Assembly* 6, no. 2 (1979): 65, 72.

209. Anderson and Foley, *Mighty Stories, Dangerous Rituals*, 27.

210. St. Gregory Thaumaturgus, *Canonical Epistle*, Canon 11.

211. *Didascalia Apostolorum* 2.41.

212. Note how Gregory's penitential ritual is grafted onto the Eucharistic liturgy such that it organically leads the penitent back to the table for regular worship. This presents an alternative to creating separate occasional rites while maintaining the centrality of worship and the Eucharist. The streamlining of penance and the Eucharistic liturgy also allows for a more coherent narrative structure as discussed in the previous grade.

213. Judith Lewis Herman, *Trauma and Recovery: The Aftermath of Violence, from Domestic Abuse to Political Terror* (New York: Basic Books, 2015), 135ff.

214. Ibid.

215. Litz et al., "Moral Injury and Moral Repair in War Veterans," 702–4.

216. Herman, *Trauma and Recovery*, 133.

217. Ibid.

218. Ibid., 134.

219. Litz et al., "Moral Injury and Moral Repair in War Veterans," 702.

220. Herman, *Trauma and Recovery*, 175.

221. Ibid., 181–82.

222. Ibid., 183.

223. Litz et al., "Moral Injury and Moral Repair in War Veterans," 703.

224. Herman, *Trauma and Recovery* (2015), 195, and Litz et al., "Moral Injury and Moral Repair in War Veterans," 704.

225. Herman, *Trauma and Recovery*, 203.

226. Ibid., 196.

227. Ibid., 206.

228. Litz et al., "Moral Injury and Moral Repair in War Veterans," 704.

229. I am invoking here Swinton's pastoral theological method, a commitment to which I had established in the introduction to this book. The prioritization of theological aims necessitates that I understand healing as *the restoration of one's humanity whose primary vocation is to worship God*, even as I converse with and draw insights from the sciences. I follow Swinton in viewing that the sciences "offer complementary knowledge which will enhance and sharpen our theological understandings" [John Swinton and Harriet Mowat, *Practical Theology and Qualitative Research* (London: SCM Press, 2011), 85.].

230. Herman, *Trauma and Recovery*, 175. I have detailed this point in chapter 2.

231. Litz et al., "Moral Injury and Moral Repair in War Veterans," 703. See also, Herman, *Trauma and Recovery*, 178.

232. Herman, *Trauma and Recovery*, 175 and 181.

233. Litz et al., "Moral Injury and Moral Repair in War Veterans," 698, and Herman, *Trauma and Recovery*, 177 and 181.

234. Litz et al., "Moral Injury and Moral Repair in War Veterans," 703.

235. Ibid.

236. Litz et al., "Moral Injury and Moral Repair in War Veterans," 704.

237. Herman, *Trauma and Recovery*, 201, italics mine.

238. Ibid., 198.

239. Ibid., 196.

240. Litz et al., "Moral Injury and Moral Repair in War Veterans," 696, 705.

241. Herman, *Trauma and Recovery*, 133.

242. Ibid., 702.

243. Wilson, *Strangers to Ourselves*, 181.

244. To say that such would be an "untruthful story" is to place the notion of "ritual contradiction" in a narrative context. See the above discussion of divorce rituals under the section, "Pastoral Ritual Hermeneutics."

245. This phrase is a common refrain one will hear when working in a hospital.

246. Herman, *Trauma and Recovery*, 205.

247. Willimon, *Worship as Pastoral Care*, 116.

248. St. Gregory's is not the only occasional rite formulated as an extension of the Eucharistic liturgy. His *Canonical Epistle* makes reference to the process of Christian initiation that finds the Catechumenate on a similar journey towards the Table following baptism. Today, Eastern Orthodox weddings are often integrated into the weekly Divine Liturgy and not made a separate and private affair.

249. The task of formulating occasional rites in such a manner requires, as a prerequisite, understanding the occasion at hand, whatever it may be, in relationship to the Eucharist. Through this approach, ritual care can come to follow naturally the principles outlined above.

Chapter 5

Sin and Pastoral Theology

In this study I have brought together the two relatively untrodden fields of inquiry—moral injury and ritual care—into the realm of pastoral theology. As I noted in the introduction, it was psychiatrists and psychologists who first recognized the phenomenon of "moral injury" in veterans and began to study it for clinical purposes. In the first chapter I endeavored to take this largely clinical understanding of the term and redefine it for pastoral theological purposes. In chapter 2 I highlighted the unique challenges moral injury poses for conventional pastoral care and counseling. There, I offered several reasons why ritual provided a fitting response to this particular malady. With chapter 3 I explored two bodies of literature, one detailing combat-related guilt and moral injury and the other ritual care. My analysis of this literature offered a springboard for synthesizing three foundational principles for ritual care. In chapter 4 I offered a pastoral theological commentary on an ancient penitential rite that provided a platform for illustrating these principles in view of the particular needs of the morally injured.

In this final chapter I will summarize what I see as some of the inherent proposals my research offers for the future study of pastoral theology. The first is dedicated to the role of sin in pastoral theology, and the second argues for the incorporation of ritual as a normative feature in pastoral care.

SIN AND PASTORAL THEOLOGY

Obliquely related to the discussion of moral injury and ritual care is the important topic of sin and its place in pastoral theology. In this section I will briefly reflect on the implications of this study as it relates to the role of sin in the study of pastoral theology.

Sin as a Normative Subject for Pastoral Theology

Moral injury has been described popularly as resulting from a transgression of one's deeply held *moral beliefs*.[1] This study has redefined moral injury as a disruption in the body, soul, and spirit, resulting from encountering or participating in *sin*. It is from this standpoint that I justified a pastoral theological exploration of MI, and the use of ritual as a fitting pastoral response to it. By doing two tasks—first, casting moral injury as a pastoral theological issue and second, defining MI as a disruption caused by sin—I have in turn posited that sin is a pastoral theological issue. Though it was not my primary intent to argue for this position in my study, this assertion seems to be a right one. While sin is not a common area of reflection in pastoral theology today, I will argue here that to do so is not entirely unprecedented or unwarranted.

For one, I have already drawn comparisons to James Poling's pastoral theological work in chapter 2. Though Poling favors the term "evil" and expounds it from a largely psychological perspective,[2] he has trended in a similar direction as this study has on the matter. Poling's work with child sex abusers is particularly relevant as I do not merely propose that pastoral theology turns a greater focus on the concept of sin alone, but towards *those who sin*. Advocacy for further pastoral theological research that includes sin within its purview would simply be a continuation of a path followed by Poling.

Understandably, pastoral theology's attention towards perpetrators may seem something of a subversion of priorities. Melinda McGarrah Sharp once described pastoral theology as "a theological commitment to prioritize human suffering as a source for theological reflection."[3] Hence, care towards *perpetrators* of violence as opposed to *victims* of violence would appear anomalous. If there is anything this study of moral injury has revealed, however, it would be the profound level of suffering that sin can cause, even for the perpetrator. This is validated by Poling who sees that perpetrators of sexual abuse are in themselves injured people.[4] If McGarrah Sharp is correct, current definitions of pastoral theology already anticipate the inclusion of some perpetrators as subjects for pastoral care.

Finally, one may only need look to the ancient past to find the clearest precedent for the inclusion of sin in the domain of pastoral care. People have often tied pastoral theology's roots to the *cura animarum* or the ancient "care of souls" tradition, which Warren Reich describes as "the care of troubled persons whose difficulties—whether spiritual, mental, or physical—are approached in the context of the pursuit of the religious goals of life or, in nonreligious contexts, the search for ultimate meanings."[5] The phrase, he writes, reflects a "comprehensive idea of healing" which included such "helping acts" as "reconciliation (including penitential reconciliation for those who

Sin and Pastoral Theology 179

have sinned), sustaining (including compassionate consolation), and guiding (spiritual and moral guidance)."[6] Within this tradition, moral injury would find itself squarely within its scope of care and Gregory's penitential rite would be well within range of its many "helping acts."

Sin and Non-suffering

Given McGarrah Sharp's and Reich's descriptions of pastoral theology and the *cura animarum* respectively, there is one additional consideration to be made in light of this study of MI. Chapter 1 suggested that someone could be morally injured without feeling distress over her actions. The section went on to state that such a circumstance could be an indication of a more serious disturbance in the individual, someone in no less need of pastoral attention. Chapter 4 then explained how Gregory's penitential rite provided the means by which both guilt feelings and the absence of guilt feelings over one's transgressive actions could be addressed. Therefore, in my conception of moral injury, "injury" does not necessarily imply existential distress over one's condition. This causes potential conflict with McGarrah Sharp's "commitment to prioritize human *suffering*" and Reich's "care of *troubled* persons." If sin is a pastoral theological issue, is it so because it causes suffering or because it is sin? Taking the latter assertion to be true, I will address the implications that emerge as a result.

First, this study of moral injury beckons pastoral theology to clarify its aim. If what McGarrah Sharp deems a *prioritization* of human suffering implies a focus on human suffering *alone*, there is an inherent conflict with a pastoral theological commitment to address sin. Under this reading of McGarrah Sharp's description of pastoral theology, Poling would not be concerned theologically with the child sex abuser who has no remorse over his actions (which very well may be his position). On the other hand, if McGarrah Sharp's language of "priority" simply means that theological reflection is prioritized *first* for those who suffer, and *second* for all other matters (including perpetrators who may not be suffering), there would be less of a conflict here. However, in this instance one would then have to clarify what those "other matters" are within the field of pastoral theology, as well as their limits.

One may be tempted then to do away with human suffering as a locus for pastoral theological inquiry altogether. There are indications in Reich's description of the *cura animarum*, that the ancient care of souls tradition was not concerned primarily with suffering in itself. Amongst the examples of "helping acts" that Reich outlines within the tradition, only one—"compassionate consolation"—implies a response to existential suffering. The other acts—penitential reconciliation, and spiritual and moral guidance—do not necessarily imply the presence of physical or emotional

180 *Chapter 5*

distress.[7] If one goes the route of the *cura animarum*, then one must determine to what singular purpose this spectrum of activities aim that draw them together. It would not be enough to say that these helping acts are within the domain of pastoral theology without articulating why they are so.

One other implication of admitting sin as a pastoral theological issue (because it is sin and not because it is a cause of human suffering) is that *all* sins then become worthy of pastoral attention. Interestingly, no definition of moral injury, including my own, necessarily limits the possibility of such injury only to those who participate in war. Medical providers, however, will not likely be concerned with treating the moral injury of a man who exaggerates his charitable contributions to receive a higher tax return, despite the fact that it may be a "serious transgression" of a "deeply held moral belief." If the failure of human vocation is deemed a pastoral theological issue, however, then pastoral care providers cannot condone even those perceived lesser sins. That the medical world does so is a matter of practicality, but for the Church, to do so would be a theological inconsistency. The assumption of sin as a pastoral theological matter places within the pastor's responsibilities a greater concern for the moral integrity of the congregation in all aspects of life. Pastors then must determine thoughtful, theological responses not only to the "big" sins in life, but to the "little" ones as well.

Though not a significant priority for pastoral theological research today, this study posits that the matter of sin is a natural area of inquiry for the field. What has been pointed to here, however, is that a deeper commitment to reflect on sin may require a reconsideration of basic definitions and parameters for pastoral theology. What may not have been considered conventionally the domain of pastoral theology may now become relevant. These pursuits should prove fruitful not only for pastoral theology as a field of study, but also for the life of the Church that needs to know how better to countenance sin today. One of the ways that these chapters have proposed to do so is the use of ritual, and it is to this matter that I wish to turn next.

RITUAL AND PASTORAL THEOLOGY

What I hope to have conveyed in my exploration of ritual care is that it is not a specialized form of care reserved only for unique circumstances like moral injury. I also wish to cast ritual care not as just another tool amidst a plethora of tools at the pastor's disposal to be chosen according to preference or whim, but as a fundamental component of pastoral care as a whole. In this section I will summarize some of the aspects of rituals/liturgies that make them necessary in the Church's task of caring for her own.

Sin and Pastoral Theology 181

First, ritual care is uniquely holistic care as it attends to the body. Such is needed at this juncture as pastoral theology's close relationship to psychology over the years has resulted in little pastoral theological reflection on the body. This threatens a deep legacy of an explicitly Christian affirmation of the body. It is important to note, however, that the early Fathers did not affirm the body separately from the soul, but saw them as composite, as "entirely and indissociably both."[8] As such, the Fathers, according to Larchet, "contradicted the spiritualist conceptions" and "they opposed every form of materialism and naturalism."[9] The assumption of this anthropology as a foundation for pastoral care is what may distinguish it most from other forms of care within the world. So then, one of the questions for pastoral theology to investigate further is how the body can be used as the means by which the soul is cared for and vice versa. The answer proposed implicitly in this study is to appeal to rituals and the liturgy, as they attend holistically to both the body and the soul.

Liturgies also provide a way for imagining how care can be communal, both practically and theologically. In the modern Western milieu, professional care is most often equated with a private conference in an office somewhere. In general, people in need are administered *to*. That segment of the Church tradition revealed in this study invites envisioning a form of care that involves partaking in the plight of the sufferer. This entails not just empathy, imagining what it is like to be that person, but *knowing* that you are that person. St. Gregory's graded penitential rite provides just one map for moving into the space of solidarity with sufferers and sinners. Further reflection on liturgies from a pastoral theological perspective may lead to similar provisions for a modern world.

Third, ritual care is comprehensive care. If liturgies are administered pastorally, they make available a resource for care that is consistent and predictable. Liturgies also touch a broader range of occasions. Viewing rituals as a form of care reminds us that pastoral care should be not only for those moments of suffering, but also for joy. If, as suggested in chapter 4, rituals teach us how to mourn appropriately, they must also teach us how to celebrate appropriately. To include such celebrations as weddings within pastoral care, as Willimon does[10] potentially challenges McGarrah Sharp's prioritization of human suffering in pastoral theology. Ritual care's broad reach will continue to inspire further discussion regarding the scope of what pastoral theology entails.

Finally, rituals are a necessary feature of care because of the varying intellectual and linguistic capacities of people represented within the Church. If in order to receive pastoral care in a typical American church, one must be self-reflective, have basic reasoning and decision-making capabilities, and have the ability to communicate in English, a large swath of the population would be disqualified from it. More than likely, these are also the very people the Church is specifically tasked to reach. Liturgy does not require the same

182　　　　　　　　　　　　　　　　*Chapter 5*

intellectual prerequisites one needs to receive conventional counseling successfully. Ramshaw notes for instance how the rich sensations and symbols of liturgy can speak to the intellectually disabled.[11] John Swinton has drawn attention to the ways worship can tend to the pastoral needs of those suffering from dementia.[12] One need not look to such severe maladies alone to see the value in ritual care. Young children, non-English speakers, and people who are not intellectually disabled, but simply have a hard time reflecting deeply on their thoughts, feelings, and motives, are also good candidates for ritual care. A commitment to caring for all peoples demands that ritual be looked upon more intently as a fundamental vehicle for care within the Church.

To use the designation, "ritual care," that I do already begins to suggest that there is a separate category of rituals intended for care, or that ritual care is a sub-discipline of the more normative pastoral care. On the contrary, I affirm with Ramshaw that "ritual and pastoral care are not separate activities . . . they each involve the other necessarily."[13] What I am not saying by this is that it is enough simply to have worship, as all churches do this. The first two tasks of more fully integrating ritual as a form of care within the church is (1) to build the liturgical fluency of the church and (2) to be more intentional and thoughtful in the way that liturgies are shaped and conducted. My hope is that this book will have contributed to these tasks.

NOTES

1. Shira Maguen and Brett Litz, "Moral Injury in Veterans of War," *PTSD Research Quarterly* 23, no. 1 (2012): 1.
2. James N. Poling, "Child Sexual Abuse: A Rich Context for Thinking about God, Community, and Ministry." *The Journal of Pastoral Care* 42, no. 1 (Spring 1988): 58.
3. Melinda A. McGarrah Sharp, *Misunderstanding Stories: Toward a Postcolonial Pastoral Theology* (Eugene, OR: Pickwick Publications, 2013), 73.
4. Ibid.
5. Warren T. Reich, "History of the Notion of Care," *Georgetown University: History of Care*, accessed June 03, 2018, https://care.georgetown.edu/Classic%20Article.html. The text is taken from Warren T. Reich, ed., *Encyclopedia of Bioethics* (New York: Macmillan Pub. Co., 1995), 319–331.
6. Ibid.
7. Ibid.
8. Jean-Claude Larchet, *Mental Disorders & Spiritual Healing: Teachings from the Early Christian East* (Hillsdale, NY: Sophia Perennis, 2005), 16.
9. Larchet, *Mental Disorders and Spiritual Healing*, 16–17.
10. William H. Willimon, *Worship as Pastoral Care* (Nashville, TN: Abingdon, 1979), 130.

Sin and Pastoral Theology   183

11. Elaine Ramshaw, *Ritual and Pastoral Care* (Philadelphia: Fortress Press, 1987), 78.

12. John Swinton, "Gentle Discipleship: Theological Reflections on Dementia," *ABC: Religion & Ethics*, July 11, 2016, accessed March 21, 2018, https://www.abc.net.au/religion/gentle-discipleship-theological-reflections-on-dementia/10096784. See also Swinton, *Dementia: Living in the Memories of God.*

13. Elaine Ramshaw, "Ritual and Pastoral Care: The Vital Connection," in *Disciples at the Crossroads: Perspectives on Worship and Church Leadership*, ed. Eleanor Bernstein, C.S.J. (Collegeville, MN: The Liturgical Press, 1993), 92.

Appendix A

Solidarity in Sin in the Early Church

Early Christian penitential practices exhibit an aspect of sin often lost on the contemporary church. Prior to the development of private penance, public penance invited both confessor and congregation into the penitent's process of reconciliation. The modern western world may cringe at the thought of such a violation of one's privacy and individual freedom. Early and medieval Christian descriptions of these rites, however, do not present these events as the public shaming and condemnation of an individual some people today may perceive them to be. Underlying these practices is a corporate understanding of sin that would preclude any possibility of singling out of a community member in such a manner. Illustrations of this can be discovered throughout church history.

A common thread found in early penitential rites is a sense of solidarity between the penitent and the church in her sin. Penance according to Origen assumes excommunication or a handing-over-to-Satan for the destruction of the flesh.[1] This process of expiation, however, is not a solitary act. Palmer writes that Origen's church understood the process to be a communal one, one in which the whole church takes upon itself the sins of its members and undergoes expiation with them. Once the process is finished, the bishop may reconcile the penitent and he may rejoin the Body of Christ.[2]

Church leaders were known to model this solidarity with penitents. Sozomen the historian and Paulinus the Deacon, both writing in the fifth century, give accounts of bishops weeping and lying prostrate alongside penitents. Paulinus, speaking of St. Ambrose, commends the bishop's example to other confessors that they may follow his model as intercessors before God, rather than as accusers of men.[3] In Sozomen's account the congregation would in turn weep and groan along with the bishop and penitent.[4]

The biblical basis for this identification with penitents appears to be two Pauline texts—Romans 12:15 ("Rejoice with those who rejoice, weep with

186 *Appendix A*

those who weep") and 1 Corinthians 12:26 ("If one member suffers, all suffer together with it; if one member is honored, all rejoice together with it"). These texts are paraphrased or directly cited on a number of occasions where penance is discussed. As far back as the second and third centuries we have the witnesses of St. Cyprian and Tertullian. In his *On Penance*, Tertullian writes, "The body cannot rejoice over the misery of one of its members; rather the whole body must suffer and work together for a cure. The Church is present in one and the next, and the Church is truly Christ."[5] St. Cyprian cites Romans 12:15 almost directly in his letter to Antonian while appealing for moderation in response to the Novatian schism. He writes, "Considering his love and mercy, we ought not to be so bitter nor cruel nor inhuman in cherishing the brethren; rather, we ought to mourn with those that mourn, and to weep with those who weep, and as far as we can to raise them up with the comforting support of our love. Neither should we be too unmerciful and stubborn in repelling them from penance: nor, again, too lax and easy in rashly allowing them to communicate."[6] Both texts are written in the context of penance and both advocate for the assembly to identify with the suffering of the penitent, while taking responsibility for her rehabilitation. The prologue of the ninth-century *Roman Penitential* of Halitgar goes further in using 1 Cor. 12:26 to state that people should even fast alongside penitents for one to two weeks.[7]

The identification called for between penitent and community is not simply at the level of pity, as in one feeling sorry for another's misfortune. The Fathers remind the church of the connection between one's own fallenness and that of the penitent. The early tenth century *Penitential Canons* of Regino's *Ecclesiastical Discipline* states, "When bishops or presbyters receive the confessions of the faithful they ought to humble themselves and pray with groans of sorrow and with tears not only for their own faults but also for their brother's fall. For the Apostle saith: 'Who is weak and I am not weak?'"[8] The above-mentioned *Penitential* of Halitgar seems to follow in this line of thinking, stating, "No physician can treat the wounds of the sick unless he familiarizes himself with their foulness."[9]

Not only are we to recognize our own faults in the face of another's, there are places within the tradition that admonish Christians to view the suffering and faults of their brothers and sisters as their own. This may have been a perspective more explicit within the early monastic tradition, as expressed within the *Sayings of the Desert Fathers*: "The old men used to say that we should each of us look upon our neighbor's experiences as if they were our own. We should suffer with our neighbor in everything and weep with him, and should behave as if we were inside his body; and if any trouble befalls him, we should feel as much distress as we would for ourselves."[10] A sixth-century biography of St. Theodosius portrays a monk putting this principle into practice. The *Life of Theodosius* speaks to the saint's compassion for his

Solidarity in Sin in the Early Church 187

"brothers who had lost their minds," so much so that he assumes responsibility for their faults and partakes of their lot.[11] He speaks not only of the need for *their* salvation, but "our salvation" and enjoins upon himself whatever counsel or reproach is given to these afflicted members.[12] According to Jean-Claude Larchet, this act of implicating oneself in the instruction and reproofs of one's disciples is a common one in patristic literature.[13]

Similarly, St. Caesarius of Arles (d. 542 CE), a bishop and trained monk, saw something at stake for the wider community when an individual sinned. In one sermon, St. Caesarius distinguishes between the practices appropriate for remedying both "light" and "capital" sins. Regarding the graver offenses, the saint states, "[T]hese and similar actions cannot be entirely expiated by common and ordinary or secret satisfaction; but grave cases call for cures that are more grave and drastic and public; so that he who has ruined himself to the destruction of many, may in like manner redeem himself to the edification of many."[14] Here, the identification between one another is such that one's sins have ramifications for the wider community. Consequently, they ought to be addressed as such in a public and serious manner. In turn, the redemption of the one, presumably through some form of public penance, results in the edification of the community as a whole.

Gunstone believes that this radical form of solidarity in sin characterizes the church and its penitential practices. The congregation identifies with the penitent's need for mercy, shares in his sinful state, and so participates with him in his penitence and expiation.[15] What the liturgy of penance teaches us is that sin, even that of military service, is communal in nature.

NOTES

1. A reference to 1 Corinthians 5:5.

2. Paul E. Palmer, *Sacraments and Forgiveness* (Westminster, MD: Newman Press, 1961), 34–35.

3. Paulinus, *Vita S. Ambrosii*, 39.

4. Sozomen, *Ecclesiastical History*, 7, 16. St. Jerome's description of the penance of Fabiola similarly states that when the penitent lay prostrate before the bishop, "the presbyters and all the people" wept along with her. [*Epist.* 77, *To Oceanus.*]

5. Tertullian, *On Penance* 10, cited in Palmer, *Sacraments and Forgiveness*, 26–27.

6. St. Cyprian, *Letter to Antonian* 19, cited in Palmer, *Sacraments and Forgiveness*, 51–52.

7. Palmer, *Sacraments and Forgiveness*, 168.

8. John T. McNeil and Helena Gamer, *Medieval Handbooks of Penance* (New York: Columbia University Press, 1990), 315.

9. McNeill and Gamer, *Medieval Handbooks of Penance*, 46.

188   *Appendix A*

10. *The Sayings of the Desert Fathers*: in Paul Evergetinos, *Collection*, vol. iii, ed. Victor Matthaiou (Monastery of the Transfiguration, Athens, 1964), 497.

11. Theodore of Petra, *Life of St. Theodosius*, 42, cited in Jean-Claude Larchet, *Mental Disorders & Spiritual Healing: Teachings from the Early Christian East* (Hillsdale, NY: Sophia Perennis, 2005), 80.

12. Theodore of Petra, *Life of St. Theodosius*, 43, cited in Larchet, *Mental Disorders and Spiritual Healing*, 81.

13. Larchet, *Mental Disorders and Spiritual Healing*, 81 n. 3.

14. St. Caesarius of Arles, *Sermon 262* (PL, 39, 2229).

15. John Thomas Arthur Gunstone, *The Liturgy of Penance* (New York: Morehouse-Barlow, 1966), 31, 36–37, 77.

Appendix B

The Universality of Kill-Trauma

Here, I will demonstrate how moral injury is a nearly universal phenomenon, spanning time and culture, arising from a natural reluctance by humans to kill their own. The evidence below will show that the vast majority of warriors are reluctant to take a life when the enemy is in their sights and, if they do, most will suffer from pangs of remorse for having done so. A generally modern bias that pre-modern or tribal cultures tended to be more barbaric (or positively "medieval," as the expression goes) would presume that these cultures did not suffer from moral injury. The evidence, however, suggests that even pre-modern peoples did not kill wantonly, nor did they kill nearly at the rates the "civilized" do in the modern era. Though moral injury can result from a variety of experiences, for the sake of simplicity here, I am focusing primarily on moral injury resulting from the act of killing, in order to provide an easier comparison of such a phenomenon across various ages and locales. In any case, killing may be viewed as the paradigmatic act which leads to moral injury for veterans.[1] Though it is impossible to prove concretely the existence of moral injury across all eras and peoples, I will provide statistics and firsthand accounts from across history to suggest that moral injury and the aversion to killing is a common experience for warriors across time and cultures. First, I will paint a picture of people's reluctance to kill in America's wars of the nineteenth and twentieth centuries. Second, I will present the evidence of other cultures over roughly the same period. Third, I will present moral injury and the reluctance to kill as phenomena seen amongst ancient and medieval populations. Finally, I will address some counter arguments to this position before concluding this essay.

190 *Appendix B*

AMERICA'S RELUCTANCE TO KILL

One of the means by which Grossman argues for the normativity of humanity's inherent unwillingness to kill one of its own is by citing the firing rates of Americans in war. Grossman goes as far back as the Battle of Gettysburg during the American Civil War. No direct survey was conducted of Gettysburg soldiers regarding their firing rates, but the battlefield itself provided telling evidence in the aftermath of the conflict. In addition to the numerous corpses littering the field, 25,574 muskets were recovered. Of those rifles approximately 24,000 (or 87 percent) of them were fully loaded. Half of these loaded muskets were loaded more than once with six thousand of them having as much as three to ten rounds in a single barrel. Various explanations can be posited for this strange phenomenon, but the "obvious conclusion" Grossman arrives at is that most soldiers in Gettysburg were not trying to kill the enemy.[2] It appears many Gettysburg soldiers were loading their weapons, sometimes more than once at a time, to present the impression of engaging in battle without actually firing their weapons. Evidence on the battlefield further indicates that those who did pull the trigger often fired away from the enemy's general direction.[3]

Grossman's interpretation of the Gettysburg battlefield appears more plausible when looking at firing rates in the US wars of the twentieth century. The first direct study on the firing rates of American armed personnel began with World War II veterans. This was a landmark study conducted by S.L.A. Marshall, US Army historian and brigadier general. The results showed that only 15 to 20 percent of American riflemen in combat would fire at the enemy. These low rates persisted even when the combatants' own lives were at risk. Marshall's studies led him to believe that most combatants throughout history will find in that moment of truth—when they have their enemy in their sights—that they are in fact conscientious objectors.[4]

Marshall's statistics, however, scandalized Army leadership, and expectedly so. This led to the development of new techniques to override what seems to be this deep inhibition when it comes to taking human lives. What the Army leadership concocted was what they called "reflexive fire training." Through this training, the Army was able to condition soldiers to shoot *even before thinking*. According to Major Pete Kilner, "It becomes muscle memory. You don't think about it, you just do it."[5] The firing rates were raised to about 55 percent in the Korean War and 90 percent in Vietnam.[6] A 2004 study estimates that 77 percent to 87 percent of Operation Iraqi Freedom soldiers reported directing fire at the enemy.[7] What results is a reversal of the non-fire to firing ratio from World War II to today. From this perspective, the training was a resounding success.

The Universality of Kill-Trauma 191

Looking at the increasing firing rates alone, people may argue that in fact humans do not have an inherent reluctance to kill others. However, once the development of reflexive fire training is considered, as well as the traumatic fallout that has resulted from it, one sees a very different narrative. Grossman's perspective as a veteran, researcher, and therapist has led him to maintain that "[w]ar is an environment that will psychologically debilitate 98 percent of all who participate in it for any length of time. And the 2 percent who are not driven insane by war appear to have already been insane—aggressive psychopaths—before coming to the battlefield."[8] It is no wonder that the first American war with a 90 percent firing rate resulted in the recognition of Post Traumatic Stress Disorder as a mental disorder. Of course, hidden within this disorder is another injury revealed a couple of decades later. Kilner states, "The problem with reflexive fire training is that it does bypass, in some sense, [the soldiers'] moral decision-making process."[9] It is this "muscle memory," overriding any opportunity for moral deliberation, that leaves moral injury in its wake.

THE ARGUMENT OF CULTURES

The limitation of just detailing the firing rates of nineteenth and twentieth century US service persons is that one can simply come to the conclusion that modern Americans may be a uniquely dovish bunch. Grossman, however, preempts any such argument by turning to the studies of firing rates and casualties amongst other cultures. He claims that every available parallel scholarly study replicates Marshall's findings. Included in these parallel studies are Argentine firing rates in the Falklands War, the "extraordinary low killing rates" among Napoleonic War regiments, the British Army's laser reenactments of historical battles, and what Grossman calls "countless other individual and anecdotal observations."[10]

This is not just a feature of modern industrialized civilization either. Scholars have noted the importance of *posturing at the expense of fighting* in times of war amongst "primitive" tribesman. Stephenson writes that "warfare as practiced among indigenous peoples on the periphery of industrial society is said to be highly ritualized and, as a result, relatively harmless when compared with modern warfare of industrial civilization."[11] The historian of war, Gwynne Dyer, similarly relates that "almost all of [hunting-and-gathering societies] have the same attitude towards 'war': it is an important ritual, an exciting and dangerous game, and perhaps even as an opportunity for self-expression, but it is not about power in any modern sense of the word, and it is most certainly not about slaughter."[12] For example, American Indians saw "counting coup," or simply touching their enemy combatants as being

192 *Appendix B*

far more important than killing them. Interestingly, the New Guinea tribes were known even to take the feathers off their arrows when they went to war.[13] This is not unlike US soldiers who intentionally shot above the heads of their targets while in combat so as not to take responsibility for claiming the life of another.

It is also worthwhile to note that the paradigmatic villains of American historical lore, the "sub-human" Japanese (as depicted in American war posters) and the genocidal Germans, had no higher firing rates than their American counterparts during World War II.[14] Moreover, the Nazis do not appear to be immune from experiencing moral injury either. Simon Wiesenthal in his book *The Sunflower* recounts being called from his work detail at a Nazi concentration camp to come to the bedside of a dying SS soldier. Apparently, the soldier's conscience plagued him in his final moments, and he wanted to find a Jew to whom he could confess his war crimes and ask forgiveness. The soldier revealed to Wiesenthal his participation in herding Jewish men, women, and children into a house and then setting it aflame.[15] He recalled hearing "horrible" screams and having to shoot any persons that tried to escape the conflagration.[16] One particular moment left an indelible mark on the soldier's being:

> Behind the windows of the second floor, I saw a man with a small child in his arms. His clothes were alight. By his side stood a woman, doubtless the mother of the child. With his free hand the man covered the child's eyes . . . then he jumped into the street. Seconds later the mother followed. Then from the other windows fell burning bodies. . . . We shot . . . Oh God! . . . I don't know how many tried to jump out of the windows but that one family I shall never forget—least of all the child. It had black hair and dark eyes.[17]

Finally, the reason for the Nazi's invitation to his bedside became apparent as he pleaded with Wiesenthal: "I want to die in peace. . . . In the long nights while I have been waiting for death, time and time again I have longed to talk about it to a Jew and beg forgiveness from him. Only I didn't know whether there were any Jews left. . . . I know that what I am asking is almost too much for you, but without your answer I cannot die in peace."[18] This SS soldier, though capable of unspeakable crimes against humanity, still could hardly withstand the pain of moral injury upon his mind, body, and soul.

THE EVIDENCE OF PRE-MODERN PEOPLES

The majority of our evidence of humanity's reluctance to kill comes from the modern era where such statistics and anecdotes are readily available. As it is

The Universality of Kill-Trauma 193

easy to look at American statistics alone and assume the more delicate sensibilities of industrialized Western cultures over those of others, it is just as easy to look at modern cases alone and presume ancient and medieval peoples must have been more violent and barbaric. While there is comparatively less information regarding the killing experiences of pre-modern warriors, even the modest amount of evidence available does reveal some continuity.

Looking first to the ancient world, Grossman cites Harvard classicist and theologian, Arthur Nock, who was known to assert that wars between the Greek city-states "were only slightly more dangerous than American football." Contributing to this picture is the statistic that Alexander the Great, for all his years of conquest, lost only seven hundred men to the sword.[19] Though we have statistics like these, there is admittedly little qualitative evidence regarding the impact of killing on the psyche of ancient peoples. Given the evidence above and that which will follow, one could infer, however, that the ancient combatant's inefficiency at killing at close range[20] (where ancient combat almost always took place) may have been partly by design.

Later antiquity provides us with a bit more of the personal conflict attached to war. Church Fathers, like St. Augustine for instance, were not unfamiliar with violent conflict in their lifetime. The great Doctor of the Church commented upon war in the *City of God*, stating, "And so everyone who reflects with sorrow on such grievous evils, in all their horror and cruelty, must acknowledge the misery of them. And yet a man who experiences such evils, or even thinks about them, without heartfelt grief, is assuredly in a far more pitiable condition, if he thinks himself happy simply because he has lost all human feeling."[21]

In this quotation, Augustine seems to present "heartfelt grief" and "sorrow" as normative responses to the "horror and cruelty" of war. Those "without heartfelt grief" are people who have lost all "human feeling." These may be people who are—as Grossman describes them—sociopaths, or those who have had to suppress their emotions to countenance the reality of war. In either case, neither would represent a normative state for a human, but instead a "pitiable condition."[22]

The Middle Ages is far more generous in its accounts of the human response to war. According to Verkamp, "There is . . . considerable evidence to suggest that the medieval warrior did in fact have frequent misgivings about the killing he was doing on the battlefield."[23] Verkamp considers for instance Louis the Pious who was so distraught over the "shedding of Christian blood" at Stellinga in 842 that he had resolved from then on "nothing could induce him to condemn anyone else to death."[24] There is also documentation of "countless medieval knights" who have retired from fighting to spend the rest of their days in monasteries. It would not be overly presumptuous to assume that these knights were at the very least motivated in part by

194 *Appendix B*

feelings of shame over killing.[25] There would certainly be a precedent for this. In the ancient desert tradition, for instance, monks viewed themselves, in effect, as "permanent penitents."[26] Moreover, the Gelasian Sacramentary, one of the earliest detailed descriptions of the rite of penance and reconciliation, describes penitents being remanded to a monastery as a means of performing their penance.[27]

In the High Middle Ages, William of Poitiers's recounting of the Battle of Hastings notes that William the Conqueror returned to the "blood-stained battle ground . . . covered with the flower of the youth and nobility of England."[28] He writes that the Norman king "could not gaze without pity on the carnage, although the slain were evil men, and although it is good and glorious in a just war to kill a tyrant."[29] Notice here the tension between one's sense of duty conflicting with what seems to be an innate disinclination or aversion to killing, even that of "evil men." This is not unlike the response of armed personnel today exhibiting moral injury.

A few hundred years later, the man who would become the venerable St. Francis of Assisi would also return from battle exhibiting symptoms of trauma. A biographer described his behavior at the time as "wandering listlessly about the house," "taking no joy in the beauties of nature that had previously delighted him."[30] He was moody, self-absorbed, emotionally numb, his old pleasures no longer having attraction to him.[31] It is also said that he had strange dreams and war-related flashbacks. Could these be the signs of someone with traditional PTSD, moral injury, or both? Though no one can know for certain the precise nature of Francis's experiences in war, his actions following his return were quite telling. Thompson describes a peculiar pattern of behavior that follows the traditional works of penance for the age. Francis began engaging in almsgiving, prayer, and bodily mortification. Thompson writes, "When out of the house, Francis gave alms to any beggar who asked. When money ran out, he literally gave the shirt off his back. He secretly purchased furnishings for poor churches and had them delivered anonymously to the priests serving them. It seems that these alms were an attempt to buy himself back into divine favor."[32] Though Francis's behavior broadly exhibits the marks of PTSD, the penitential acts more narrowly indicate one who is racked with guilt for past actions.

THE ARGUMENT AGAINST THE PREVALENCE OF PRE-MODERN KILL-TRAUMA

Aislinn Melchior offers the most directed arguments *against* the theory that the ancients had experiences of war trauma comparable to those of modern warriors. Melchior does not rule out the possibility that Roman soldiers may

The Universality of Kill-Trauma 195

have experienced PTSD, but she argues that if they did, it would be at a lower frequency than that experienced by armed personnel today. Melchior's conception of PTSD here includes this present study's understanding of MI as it includes the act of killing as a known source of PTSD.[33] Her argument is founded on two main points: First, PTSD is often the product of shelling and explosions, phenomena non-existent in the ancient world;[34] and second, violence and death were much more part of the day-to-day world of Romans, making the experience of combat less traumatic.[35] As Heebøll-Holm notes, given the nature of Melchior's argument, equal skepticism could be levied against any notion of PTSD in the Middle Ages.[36] But do these arguments hold water?

Melchior's first point is the easier of the two to dismiss. One of the occasions for writing her article was a then recently released study that correlated concussive injuries amongst soldiers with higher rates of PTSD. Melchior's argument is that since concussive injuries are typically caused by explosives, there would have to be lower instances of PTSD amongst ancient peoples who had no recourse to such technologies. I, however, side with Heebøll-Holm who writes that "there is reason to doubt the effect of concussions as the major cause of PTSD (which would make it an almost exclusively gun-powder era affliction)." Researchers today would not doubt that bombs and IEDs contribute to the instances of PTSD in combatants, but as Heebøll-Holm avers, many would doubt it is the "major cause" that Melchior insists it is. He adds, "Recent studies on war-related PTSD shows that a rather large number of other factors in the experience of war cause trauma."[37] The PTSD literature surveyed in this study points to the same conclusion. In this regard, Melchior stakes too much on a single study, whose results she admits are only "preliminary."[38] This one argument is all the more irrelevant to this present study as exposure to explosives is not a known cause of MI.

In support of her second point, Melchior cites a "widening chasm" that exists between the realm of combat and the civilian world today.[39] This is in contrast to the ancient Romans who regularly saw death and violence whether it be that of animal slaughter or the executioner. The conceit then is that because quotidian Roman living was not sheltered from various forms of death, those who bore the sword were likely desensitized to the actions of war in ways modern combatants are not. This is a cogent argument with which I do not entirely disagree. It is likely the average Roman was more acquainted with death and violence than the average US citizen is. However, one could argue that the ubiquity of communication technologies, broadcasting both staged and actual violence at all hours of the day and night, contributes significantly to the imagination of the modern individual. Watching a video may not be as intimate as watching an execution or losing multiple family

196   *Appendix B*

members to early deaths, but depictions of death and violence are readily available to people of all ages today.

Moreover, I would have to contend again that Melchior's argument relies on comparing rates of PTSD, *narrowly conceived* (as in Shay's "simple PTSD"). It may be the case that one is less likely to carry *fear-based* trauma upon leaving the battlefield if death and violence were ubiquitous in one's civilian life. Yet the argument would seem a bit tenuous when speaking of moral injury (or "complex PTSD"). Watching the execution of a condemned criminal does not necessarily prepare one for the traumatic experience of taking a life. This is a notable oversight as the author does in fact include killing as a possible trigger for PTSD.[40] In the end, I will not dispute that ancient and medieval peoples may have had lower instances of PTSD (narrowly conceived), but I will maintain given the evidence outlined above that the rates of moral injury amongst those who killed should be comparable to those today.

This brief excursus on the universality of kill-trauma contends that the trauma of killing, and moral injury in general, is not merely a phenomenon of a modern Western industrialized culture. Evidence demonstrates that non-Western, non-industrialized, and pre-modern peoples also exhibit an inherent reluctance to kill, as well as remorse (at times life-changing guilt) for taking the life of another person. This insight is necessary for this study for two reasons: First, the evidence posits an understanding of the human creature whose reluctance to kill is a foundational aspect of its being, and not *solely* a product of cultural conditioning. For this reason, chapter 1 suggests that moral injury is not relative to how one thinks or feels about a particular act. It is not about "transgressing *one's* [personal] moral beliefs" but about transgressing the nature of the human creature.[41] I once spoke with a veteran who shared with me that he was ordered to kill the lone survivor of a Vietnamese village that had been razed on a "search and destroy" mission. Decades later the veteran still continues to be troubled by that moment. His experience of ending another man's life has led him to believe, "God did not make us to kill one another. . . . Killing goes against our nature." This section further affirms that point.

The second reason this essay pursues this line of reasoning is that it places early Christian post-war rituals into perspective. If, as Grossman argues, war will "psychologically debilitate 98 percent of all who participate in it,"[42] then one can presume that even our ancient veteran ancestors were for the most part not indifferent participants in these penitential rites. This study seeks to argue that the shape of these rites not only fulfilled some theological or ritual necessity for addressing sin, but also satisfied a pastoral necessity for addressing trauma amongst the veteran population. Moreover, such "pastoral" rituals are not to be seen as occasional or exceptional forms of Christian ritual. These ancient liturgies are not placed in a separate category of rites designated for "pastoral" use. Part of the challenge of this study is to see in what way traditional liturgies inherently serve a pastoral purpose, even for those, like veterans, suffering from moral injury.

NOTES

1. Nieuwsma et al., "Possibilities within Acceptance and Commitment Therapy for Approaching Moral Injury," *Current Psychiatry Reviews* vol. 11 (2015): 194.

2. David Grossman, *On Killing: The Psychological Cost of Learning to Kill in War and Society* (Boston: Little, Brown, 1996), 22.

3. Grossman, *On Killing*, 21–22.

4. Rita Nakashima Brock and Gabriella Lettini, *Soul Repair: Recovering from Moral Injury after War* (Boston, MA: Beacon Press, 2013), 17; and Grossman, *On Killing*, xv, 4.

5. Documentary *Soldiers of Conscience* cited in Brock, *Soul Repair*, 18.

6. Grossman, *On Killing*, 35. Brock, *Soul Repair*, 18.

7. Shira Maguen's *Killing in War* presentation to VA personnel, 2016.

8. Grossman, *On Killing*, 50.

9. Cited in Brock, *Soul Repair*, 18.

10. Grossman, *On Killing*, xv.

11. Barry Stephenson, *Ritual: A Very Short Introduction* (Oxford: Oxford University Press, 2015), 18.

12. Gwynne Dyer, *War* (New York: Crown, 1985), 6.

13. Grossman, *On Killing*, 12.

14. Ibid., 16.

15. Simon Wiesenthal, *The Sunflower: On the Possibilities and Limits of Forgiveness* (New York: Shocken books, 1998), 41. This narrative demonstrates again the sensual nature of trauma, with vivid descriptions of sights, sounds and other sensations—at one point the soldier recalls choking on the smoke.

16. Ibid., 42.

17. Ibid., 43.

18. Ibid., 54.

19. Grossman, *On Killing*, 12.

20. Grossman in *On Killing* and Maguen in "The Impact of Direct and Indirect Killing" (*Journal of Traumatic Stress*, 23) speak to the difficulty and trauma of killing at close range.

21. Augustine, *City of God*, 19.7.

22. This goes back to my point in chapter 1 regarding the hypothetical few who may be able to harm another and appear unaffected by it. As I have said, a veteran who is able to kill in war and go on living life as usual is not likely to concern medical professionals, but from a pastoral perspective such a response may exhibit a more grievous condition or "injury." Yet, as Grossman would argue, for a person to kill and be truly unaffected by it is highly unlikely and virtually unseen given his research. It is unclear from Augustine's text whether these people are sincerely unmoved or

198 *Appendix B*

simply numb following exposure to war. Moreover, the point I sought to make in chapter 1 is that the "diagnosing" of moral injury cannot be based purely upon the outward symptoms of distress.

23. Bernard Joseph Verkamp, *The Moral Treatment of Returning Warriors in Early Medieval and Modern Times* (Scranton, PA: Univ. of Scranton Press, 1993), 41.

24. Ibid.

25. Ibid.

26. William Harmless, *Desert Christians: An Introduction to the Literature of Early Monasticism* (New York: Oxford University Press, 2004), 239.

27. Palmer, *Sacraments and Forgiveness*, 120.

28. Verkamp, *Moral Treatment*, 41, citing Douglas and Greenway's *English Historical Documents*, 229.

29. Ibid.

30. Augustine Thompson, *Francis of Assisi: A New Biography* (Ithaca: Cornell University Press, 2012), 10.

31. Thompson, *Francis of Assisi*, 12.

32. Ibid., 12.

33. Aislinn Melchior, "Caesar in Vietnam: Did Roman Soldiers Suffer from Post-Traumatic Stress Disorder?" *Greece and Rome* 58, no. 2 (2011): 217.

34. Melchior, "Caesar in Vietnam," 218–20.

35. Ibid., 221.

36. Thomas Kristian Heebøll-Holm, "Apocalypse Then? The First Crusade, Trauma of War and Thomas de Marle," in *Denmark and Europe in the Middle Ages: C. 1000–1525; Essays in Honour of Professor Michael H. Gelting*, edited by Kerstin Hundahl, Lars Kjær, and Niels Lund (Farnham: Ashgate, 2014), 244.

37. Heebøll-Holm, "Apocalypse Then? The First Crusade, Trauma of War and Thomas de Marle," 244.

38. Melchior, "Caesar in Vietnam," 219.

39. Ibid., 221.

40. Specifically, Melchior refers to "the act of killing—especially close kills where the reality of one's responsibility cannot be doubted." [Melchior, "Caesar in Vietnam," 217.]

41. Stanley Hauerwas writes, "Indeed, I will argue that the greatest sacrifice of war is not the sacrifice of life, great as such a sacrifice may be, but rather the sacrifice of our unwillingness to kill. That sacrifice of our unwillingness to kill is why war is at once so morally compelling and morally perverse." [Stanley Hauerwas, *War and the American Difference: Theological Reflections on Violence and National Identity* (Grand Rapids, MI: Baker Academic, 2011), 56.]

42. Grossman, *On Killing*, 50.

Bibliography

Anderson, Herbert, and Edward Foley. *Mighty Stories, Dangerous Rituals: Weaving Together the Human and the Divine*. San Francisco: Jossey-Bass, 2001.

Bell, Catherine M., and Aslan, Reza. *Ritual: Perspectives and Dimensions*. Cary: Oxford University Press USA—OSO, 2009. Accessed May 14, 2018. ProQuest Ebook Central.

Bell, Catherine M. *Ritual Theory, Ritual Practice*. New York: Oxford University Press, 2010.

Bernstein, Eleanor, and John F. Baldovin, eds. *Disciples at the Crossroads: Perspectives on Worship and Church Leadership*. Collegeville MN: Liturgical Press, 1993.

Bradshaw, Paul F., Maxwell E. Johnson, and L. Edward Phillips. *The Apostolic Tradition: A Commentary*. Minneapolis, MN: Fortress Press, 2002.

Breslau, Naomi, Edward L. Peterson, and Lonni R. Schultz. "A Second Look at Prior Trauma and the Posttraumatic Stress Disorder Effects of Subsequent Trauma." *Archives of General Psychiatry* 65, no. 4 (2008): 431–37.

Brock, Rita Nakashima, and Gabriella Lettini. *Soul Repair: Recovering from Moral Injury after War*. Boston: Beacon Press, 2013.

Campbell, Joseph. *The Hero with a Thousand Faces*. Novato: New World Library, 2008.

Capps, Walter H., ed. *The Vietnam Reader*. New York: Routledge, 1991.

Cavanaugh, William T. "An End to Every War: The Politics of the Eucharist and . . ." *ABC: Religion & Ethics*. January 19, 2016. Accessed March 21, 2018. http://www.abc.net.au/religion/articles/2016/01/19/4390491.htm.

Cavanaugh, William T. *Field Hospital: The Church's Engagement with a Wounded World*. Grand Rapids, MI: William B. Eerdmans Publishing Company, 2016.

Diagnostic and Statistical Manual of Mental Disorders: DSM-5. Washington, DC: American Psychiatric Association, 2013.

Drescher, Kent D., David W. Foy, Caroline Kelly, Anna Leshner, Kerrie Schutz, and Brett Litz. "An Exploration of the Viability and Usefulness of the Construct of Moral Injury in War Veterans." *Traumatology* 17, no. 1 (2011): 8–13.

Dyer, Gwynne. *War*. New York: Crown, 1985.

Emert, Rick. "Lodge Offers Traditional Ceremonies." www.army.mil. Accessed March 16, 2018. https://www.army.mil/article/43370/lodge_offers_traditional_ceremonies.

Farley, Lawrence. "Conclusion: 'The Doors! The Doors! In Wisdom Let Us Attend.'" *Orthodox Christian Network.* July 14, 2014. Accessed March 21, 2018. http://myocn.net/conclusion-exclusion-the-doors-the-doors-in-wisdom-let-us-attend/.

Fredriksen, Paula. *Sin: The Early History of an Idea.* Princeton, NJ: Princeton University Press, 2014.

Freedman, Jill, and Gene Combs. *Narrative Therapy: The Social Construction of Preferred Realities.* New York: W. W. Norton & Company, 1996.

Friedman, Edwin H. *Generation to Generation: Family Process in Church and Synagogue.* New York: Guilford Press, 2011.

Friedman, Matthew J., and Laurie B. Slone. *After the War Zone: A Practical Guide for Returning Troops and Their Families.* Cambridge, MA: Da Capo Lifelong, 2008.

Freud, Sigmund, Alix Strachey, and Alan Tyson. *The Standard Edition of the Complete Psychological Works of Sigmund Freud / On the History of the Psychoanalytic Movement; Papers on Metapsychology.* London: Hogarth Press, 1957.

Fritts, Paul D. *Adaptive Disclosure: Critique of a Descriptive Intervention Modified for the Normative Problem of Moral Injury in Combat Veterans.* Seminar paper. Yale Divinity School, April 29, 2013.

Gabriel, Richard A. *No More Heroes: Madness & Psychiatry in War.* New York: Farrar, Straus and Giroux, 1988.

Granjo, Paulo. "The Homecomer: Postwar Cleansing Rituals of Mozambique." *Armed Forces & Society* 33, no. 3 (2007): 382–95.

Gray, Matt J., Yonit Schorr, William Nash, Leslie Lebowitz, Amy Amidon, Amy Lansing, Melissa Maglione, Ariel J. Lang, and Brett T. Litz. "Adaptive Disclosure: An Open Trial of a Novel Exposure-Based Intervention for Service Members With Combat Related Psychological Stress Injuries." *Behavior Therapy* 43, no. 2 (2012): 407–415.

Grossman, David. *On Killing: The Psychological Cost of Learning to Kill in War and Society.* Boston: Little, Brown, 1996.

Grundy, Christopher. "Basic Retraining: The Role of Congregational Ritual in the Care of Returning Veterans." *Liturgy* 27, no. 4 (2012): 27–36.

Gunstone, John Thomas Arthur. *The Liturgy of Penance.* New York: Morehouse-Barlow, 1966.

Harmless, William. *Desert Christians: An Introduction to the Literature of Early Monasticism.* New York: Oxford University Press, 2004.

Hauerwas, Stanley. *War and the American Difference: Theological Reflections on Violence and National Identity.* Grand Rapids, MI: Baker Academic, 2011.

Hayes, Tara O'Neill. "The Economic Costs of the U.S. Criminal Justice System." *American Action Forum.* July 16, 2020. Accessed October 3, 2023. https://www.american-actionforum.org/research/the-economic-costs-of-the-u-s-criminal-justice-system/.

Herman, Judith Lewis. *Trauma and Recovery: The Aftermath of Violence, from Domestic Abuse to Political Terror.* New York: Basic Books, 2015.

Hogue, David. *Remembering the Future, Imagining the Past: Story, Ritual and the Human Brain.* Eugene, OR: Wipf & Stock, 2009.

Holmes, Richard. *Acts of War: The Behavior of Men in Battle.* New York: Free Press, 1989.

Bibliography

Hopko, Thomas. "The Orthodox Faith—Volume II—Worship—The Divine Liturgy— Love and Faith." *Orthodox Church in America*. Accessed March 21, 2018. https: //oca.org/orthodoxy/the-orthodox-faith/worship/the-divine-liturgy/love-and-faith.

Horowitz, Mardi J., and George F. Solomon. "A Prediction of Delayed Stress Response Syndromes in Vietnam Veterans." *Journal of Social Issues* 31, no. 4 (1975): 67–80.

"How Common Is PTSD? *PTSD: National Center for PTSD*. Accessed October 3, 2023. https://www.ptsd.va.gov/understand/common/common_adults.asp.

Hundahl, Kerstin, Lars Kjær, and Niels Lund, eds. *Denmark and Europe in the Middle Ages: C. 1000–1525; Essays in Honour of Professor Michael H. Gelting*. Farnham: Ashgate, 2014.

Hunsinger, Deborah van Deusen. *Theology and Pastoral Counseling: A New Interdisciplinary Approach*. Grand Rapids, MI: Eerdmans, 1995.

Johnson, Todd. E., ed. *The Conviction of Things Not Seen: Worship and Ministry in the 21st Century*. Grand Rapids, MI: Brazos Press, 2002.

Junger, Sebastian. "Veterans Need to Share the Moral Burden of War." *The Washington Post*, May 26, 2013. Accessed March 11, 2018.

Kang, Han K., Tim A. Bullman, Derek J. Smolenski, Nancy A. Skopp, Gregory A. Gahm, and Mark A. Reger. "Suicide Risk among 1.3 Million Veterans Who Were on Active Duty during the Iraq and Afghanistan Wars." *Annals of Epidemiology* 25, no. 2 (2015): 96–100.

Kinghorn, Warren. "Combat Trauma and Moral Fragmentation: A Theological Account of Moral Injury." *Journal of the Society of Christian Ethics* 32, no. 2 (Fall/Winter 2012): 57–74.

Kline, Anna, Marc D. Weiner, Alejandro Interian, Anton Shcherbakov, and Lauren St. Hill. "Morbid Thoughts and Suicidal Ideation in Iraq War Veterans: The Role of Direct and Indirect Killing in Combat." *Depression and Anxiety* 33, no. 6 (2016): 473–482.

Koenig, Harold G., Donna Ames, Nagy A. Youssef, John P. Oliver, Fred Volk, Ellen J. Teng, Kerry Haynes, Zachary D. Erickson, et al. "The Moral Injury Symptom Scale-Military Version." *Journal of Religion & Health* 52, no. 3 (September 2013): 1–17 (Author's copy).

Kupfer, David. "Like Wandering Ghosts." *The Sun Magazine*. June 2008. Accessed April 04, 2018. https://www.thesunmagazine.org/issues/390/like-wandering -ghosts.

Larchet, Jean-Claude. *Mental Disorders & Spiritual Healing: Teachings from the Early Christian East*. Hillsdale, NY: Sophia Perennis, 2005.

"Layout of Rooms—Back To The Walls, Doors In View." My PTSD Forum. February 6, 2007. Accessed March 21, 2018. https://www.myptsd.com/threads/layout-of -rooms-back-to-the-walls-doors-in-view.1563/.

Litz, Brett. *The Viability and Usefulness of the Construct of Moral Injury in War Veterans* [PowerPoint slides]. 2014.

Litz, Brett T., Nathan Stein, Eileen Delaney, Leslie Lebowitz, William P. Nash, Caroline Silva, and Shira Maguen. "Moral Injury and Moral Repair in War

Veterans: A Preliminary Model and Intervention Strategy." *Clinical Psychology Review* 29, no. 8 (2009): 695–706.

Loewenstein, Rudolph, et al., eds. *Psychoanalysis: A General Psychology*. New York: International Universities Press, 1966.

MacIntyre, Alasdair C. *After Virtue: A Study in Moral Theory*. Notre Dame: University of Notre Dame Press, 1981.

Maguen, Shira. "Killing in War: Research and Treatment." PowerPoint presentation, San Francisco VA Medical Center, 2016.

Maguen, Shira, "Moral Injury and Killing in Combat Veterans: Research & Clinical Implications." Cyber seminar transcript, November 19, 2015.

Maguen, Shira, and Brett Litz. "Moral Injury in Veterans of War." *PTSD Research Quarterly* 23, no. 1 (2012): 1–3.

Maguen, Shira, and Brett Litz. "Moral Injury in the Context of War." *PTSD: National Center for PTSD*. December 23, 2011. Accessed March 18, 2018. http://www.ptsd.va.gov/professional/co-occurring/moral_injury_at_war.asp.

Maguen, Shira, Kristine Burkman, Erin Madden, Julie Dinh, Jeane Bosch, Jessica Keyser, Martha Schmitz, and Thomas C. Neylan. "Impact of Killing in War: A Randomized, Controlled Pilot Trial." *Journal of Clinical Psychology* 73, no. 9 (March 10, 2017): 997–1012.

Martin, Phillip. "Why So Many Iraqis Hate Us? Try 'Towel Head' On for Size." *The Huffington Post*. May 25, 2011. Accessed April 09, 2018. https://www.huffingtonpost.com/phillip-martin/why-so-many-iraqis-hateu_b_96330.html.

Matsakis, Aphrodite. *Back from the Front: Combat Trauma, Love, and the Family*. Baltimore, MD: Sidran Institute Press, 2007.

McGarrah Sharp, Melinda A. *Misunderstanding Stories: Toward a Postcolonial Pastoral Theology*. Eugene, OR: Pickwick Publications, 2013.

McGuckin, John. "Nonviolence and Peace Traditions in Early & Eastern Christianity." *In Communion*. December 29, 2014. Accessed March 18, 2018. http://incommunion.org/2004/12/29/nonviolence-and-peace-traditions/.

McNeil, John T., and Helena Gamer. *Medieval Handbooks of Penance*. New York: Columbia University Press, 1990.

Melchior, Aislinn. "Caesar in Vietnam: Did Roman Soldiers Suffer from Post-Traumatic Stress Disorder?" *Greece and Rome* 58, no. 2 (2011): 209–23.

"Military Sexual Trauma." *PTSD: National Center for PTSD*. Accessed October 3, 2023. https://www.ptsd.va.gov/understand/types/violence/sexual-trauma-military.asp.

Morris, David J. "War Is Hell, and the Hell Rubs Off." *Slate Magazine*. April 17, 2014. Accessed March 16, 2018. http://www.slate.com/articles/health_and_science/medical_examiner/2014/04/ptsd_an_violence_by_veterans_increased_murder_rates_related_to_war_experience.html.

Neuger, Christie Cozad. *Counseling Women: A Narrative, Pastoral Approach*. Minneapolis, MN: Fortress Press, 2004.

Nieuwsma, Jason, Robyn Walser, Jacob Farnsworth, Kent Drescher, Keith Meador, and William Nash. "Possibilities within Acceptance and Commitment Therapy for Approaching Moral Injury." *Current Psychiatry Reviews* 11, no. 3 (2015): 193–206.

Bibliography

Nünning, Vera, ed. *Ritual and Narrative: Theoretical Explorations and Historical Case Studies*. Bielefeld: Transcript-Verlag, 2014.

Palmer, Paul E. *Sacraments and Forgiveness: History and Doctrinal Development of Penance, Extreme Unction and Indulgences*. Westminster, MD: Newman Press, 1961.

Payne, Martin. *Narrative Therapy*. Thousand Oaks: Sage Publications, 2006.

Poling, James N. "Child Sexual Abuse: A Rich Context for Thinking about God, Community, and Ministry." *The Journal of Pastoral Care* 42 no. 1 (Spring 1988): 58–61.

Poling, James N. "Issues in the Psychotherapy of Child Molesters." *The Journal of Pastoral Care* 43, no. 1 (Spring 1989): 25–32.

"PTSD and Substance Abuse in Veterans." *PTSD: National Center for PTSD*. Accessed October 3, 2023. https://www.ptsd.va.gov/understand/related/substance_abuse_vet.asp.

Ramshaw, Elaine. *Ritual and Pastoral Care*. Philadelphia: Fortress Press, 1987.

Reich, Warren T., ed. *Encyclopedia of Bioethics*. New York: Macmillan Pub. Co., 1995.

Renner, H.P.V. "The Use of Ritual in Pastoral Care." *Journal of Pastoral Care & Counseling* 33, no. 3 (1979): 164–77.

Ruger, William, Sven E. Wilson, and Shawn L. Waddoups. "Warfare and Welfare: Military Service, Combat, and Marital Dissolution." *Armed Forces & Society* 29, no. 1 (2002): 85–107.

Saint Basil. *Letters: Volume 2 (186–368)*. Translated by Sister Agnes Clare Way with notes by Roy J. Deferrari. Washington, DC: Catholic University of America Press, 2008.

Saint Gregory. *St. Gregory Thaumaturgus: Life and Works (Fathers of the Church; v. 98)*. Translated by Michael Slusser. Washington, DC: Catholic University of America Press, 1998.

Sax, William Sturman, Johannes Quack, and Jan Weinhold (eds.). *The Problem of Ritual Efficacy*. Oxford: Oxford University Press, 2010.

Schmemann, Alexander. *For the Life of the World: Sacraments and Orthodoxy*. Yonkers, NY: St. Vladimir's Seminary Press, 1973.

Searle, Mark. "Active Participation" (Editorial). *Assembly* 6, no. 2 (1979): 65, 72.

Seligman, Adam B. *Ritual and Its Consequences: An Essay on the Limits of Sincerity*. Oxford: Oxford University Press, 2008.

Shay, Jonathan. *Achilles in Vietnam Combat Trauma and the Undoing of Character*. New York: Scribner, 2003.

Shay, Jonathan. "Casualties." *Daedalus* 140, no. 3 (2011): 179–88.

Shay, Jonathan. *Odysseus in America: Combat Trauma and the Trials of Homecoming*. New York: Scribner, 2010.

Shay, Jonathan. "Moral Injury." Webinar transcript, 2016.

Sherman, Nancy. *Afterwar: Healing the Moral Injuries of Our Soldiers*. New York: Oxford University Press, 2015.

204 *Bibliography*

Sippola, John, Amy Blumenshine, Donald A. Tubesing, and Valerie Yancey. *Welcome Them Home, Help Them Heal: Pastoral Care and Ministry with Service Members Returning from War*. Duluth, MN: Whole Person Associates, 2009.

Smith, James K. A. *Desiring the Kingdom: Worship, Worldview, and Cultural Formation*. Grand Rapids, MI: Baker Academic, 2009.

Smith, Jonathan Z. *Imagining Religion: From Babylon to Jonestown*. Chicago: University of Chicago Press, 2013.

Smith, Susan Marie. *Caring Liturgies: The Pastoral Power of Christian Ritual*. Minneapolis: Fortress Press, 2012.

Stephenson, Barry. *Ritual: A Very Short Introduction*. Oxford: Oxford University Press, 2015.

Stewart-Sykes, Alistair, trans. *The Didascalia Apostolorum: An English Version*. Turnhout, Belgium: Brepols Publishers, 2009.

Swinton, John. "Gentle Discipleship: Theological Reflections on Dementia." *ABC: Religion & Ethics*. July 11, 2016. Accessed March 21, 2018. http://www.abc .net.au/religion/articles/2016/07/11/4498510.htm.

Swinton, John, and Harriet Mowat. *Practical Theology and Qualitative Research*. London: SCM Press, 2011.

Thompson, Augustine. *Francis of Assisi: A New Biography*. Ithaca: Cornell University Press, 2012.

Thompson, David A., and Darlene F. Wetterstrom. *Beyond the Yellow Ribbon: Ministering to Returning Combat Veterans*. Nashville, TN: Abingdon Press, 2009.

Tick, Edward. "Healing the Wounds of War." *Parabola Magazine*, October 31, 2014.

Tick, Edward. *War and the Soul: Healing our Nation's Veterans from Post-Traumatic Stress Disorder*. Wheaton, IL: Quest Books, 2005.

Tick, Edward. *Warrior's Return: Restoring the Soul after War*. Louisville, CO: Sounds True, 2014.

Van der Kolk, Bessel. *The Body Keeps the Score: Brain, Mind and Body in the Healing of Trauma*. New York: Penguin Books, 2015.

Verkamp, Bernard Joseph. *The Moral Treatment of Returning Warriors in Early Medieval and Modern Times*. Scranton, PA: Univ. of Scranton Press, 1993.

Vogler, Christopher. *The Writer's Journey: Mythic Structure for Storytellers and Screenwriters*. Studio City: Michael Wiese Productions, 2007.

White, Michael, and David Epston. *Narrative Means to Therapeutic Ends*. New York: Norton, 1990.

Wiesenthal, Simon, et al. *The Sunflower: On the Possibilities and Limits of Forgiveness*. New York: Shocken Books, 1998.

Wilbricht, Stephen S. *Rehearsing God's Just Kingdom: The Eucharistic Vision of Mark Searle*. Collegeville, MN: Liturgical Press, 2013.

Willimon, William H. *Worship as Pastoral Care*. Nashville: Abingdon, 1979.

Wilson, Timothy D. *Strangers to Ourselves: Discovering the Adaptive Unconscious*. Cambridge, MA: Belknap, 2004.

Bibliography

Wright, N. T. "Romans 2:17–3:9: A Hidden Clue to the Meaning of Romans?" *Journal for the Study of Paul and His Letters* 1, no. 2 (2011): 1–35.

Wright, N. T. *The Day the Revolution Began: Reconsidering the Meaning of Jesus's Crucifixion.* San Francisco: HarperOne, 2016.

Index

Page numbers in italics refer to tables.

Acceptance and Commitment Therapy (ACT), 82, 83, 86, 122, 123, 125
ACT. *See* Acceptance and Commitment Therapy
AD. *See* Adaptive Disclosure
Adaptive Disclosure (AD), 82–84, 119
American Civil War, 190
Anderson, Herbert, 69, 88, 90, 91, 145, 146, 148, 152
Anselm, 86
Aquinas, Thomas, 93, 165n13
Aristotle, 62, 133, 168n66
Athanasius, 169n72
Augustine, 47n146, 115, 171n121, 193, 197n22

Basil the Great, 112–16, 128, 134
Bourdieu, Pierre, 67
Brock, Rita, 2, 3, 22–25, 30, 40, 63, 111, 128

Caesarius of Arles, 187
Campbell, Joseph, 145, 146, 173n158
Canon 13, 113, 114. *See also* Basil the Great

Canonical Epistle, 112, 118, 125, 130, 140, 143, 176n248. *See also* Gregory the Wonderworker
Canons of Hippolytus, 113, 114, 116, 118, 121
care of souls, 36, 52, 161, 178–80
Catechism of the Catholic Church, 39, 47n147, 113, 168n64
Catholic. *See* Roman Catholic
Catholic Worker, 136, 137
Cavanaugh, William T., 6, 136, 137, 151
CBT. *See* Cognitive Behavioral Therapy
Cognitive Behavioral Therapy (CBT), 80, 82
confession, 3, 4, 8n2, 9n2, 9n7, 49, 63, 84, 112, 118–20, 122, 128, 157, 162, 166n30, 167n30, 186
Contra Celsum, 114. *See also* Origen
counter-narratives, 147–49, 150–52, 162
Crossan, John Dominic, 88
cura animarum. See care of souls
Cyprian, 169n74, 186

Day, Dorothy, 136, 137, 152
De Corona, 114. *See also* Tertullian
Didascalia, 112, 118, 121, 125–27, 132, 149, 152

208 *Index*

Drescher, Kent, 22, 23, 26, 27, 30, 31, 34, 37, 134
Driver, Tom, 89, 97
Dyer, Gwynne, 191

Eastern Orthodox, 6, 51, 69, 101, 143, 176n248; Church, 6, 143, 167n30
Ecclesiastical Discipline, 186
Ecclesiastical History, 135
Erikson, Erik, 68
Eucharist, 33, 52, 63, 92–94, 100–2, 108n116, 109n117, 109n124, 110n125, 112, 113, 129, 139, 144, 147, 151, 152, 159, 161, 163, 164, 171n102, 175n212, 176n249
Eucharistic consciousness, 94, 97, 100, 164
exomologesis, 122, 125. *See also* confession

Fabiola, 166n30, 187n4
Farley, Lawrence, 143
Foley, Edward, 69, 88, 90, 91, 145, 146, 148, 152
Francis of Assisi, 194
Freud, Sigmund, 141
Friedman, Matthew, 4, 28, 56, 79
Fritts, Paul D., 32, 84–86

Gabriel, Richard A., 64
Grade of Audience, 130, 158, 162, 166n20
Grade of Participation, 152, 162
Grade of Standing with, 144, 145, 147, 162
Grade of Submission, 140, 162
Grade of Weeping, 120, 121, 129, 147, 156, 157, 162
Granjo, Paul, 4
Gray, Matt, 82, 83, 86
Gregory of Nyssa, 8n1, 35, 36
Gregory the Wonderworker, 7, 111–13, 117, 118, 121, 122, 124, 125, 130–32, 134, 140, 143–47, 149, 152, 155,

157–64, 168n64, 173n158, 175n212, 176n248, 179, 181
Grossman, Dave, 3, 4, 18, 27, 28, 30, 36, 38, 39, 63, 124, 190, 191, 193, 196, 197n22
Grundy, Christopher, 2, 4, 111
guilt, 3, 4, 7, 8n2, 12, 27, 28, 30, 31, 34, 39, 40, 45n102, 53, 64, 67, 70n8, 72n35, 74n71, 77–81, 83–85, 103, 115–17, 123, 124, 127, 128, 134–40, 166, 171n102, 177, 179, 194, 196; definition of, 78, 79
Gunstone, John, 63, 167n30, 187

Hadley, Arthur, 3, 63, 64
Halitgar. *See Roman Penitential*
Hauerwas, Stanley, 46n139, 116, 151, 165n19, 198n41
healing, 10n18, 12, 21, 41, 53, 54, 62, 70, 131, 132, 134, 138, 154, 155, 157, 159, 160, 161, 178; pastoral theological understanding of, 41, 175n229
Heebøll-Holm, Thomas, 195
Herman, Judith, 152–56, 158–60
hermeneutics, 92, 94, 100–3, 108n116, 120, 129, 143, 146, 171n102, 173n165; pastoral ritual, 94, 99, 100, 117, 130, 141, 142, 164, 176n244
Hogue, David, 73n69, 88–91, 95–99, 107n95, 139
Holmes, Richard, 133

Impact of Killing (IOK), 81, 84, 86
IOK. *See* Impact of Killing
Irenaeus, 93, 122
Isidore of Pelusium, 114, 115, 117, 134, 169n72

James, William, 125
Junger, Sebastian, 3

Kilner, Peter, 190, 191
Kinghorn, Warren, 3, 4, 21, 22, 34, 56, 85, 86, 104n32, 111, 134, 168n56

Index

Korean War, *15*, 74n72, 190

Larchet, Jean-Claude, 36, 102, 170n98, 181, 187
leitourgia. See liturgy
Lettini, Gabriella, 3, 22, 24, 30, 40, 63
Life of St. Ambrose, 135, 167n30, 185
Life of Theodosius, 104n32, 170n98, 186, 187
liturgy, 2, 6, 7, 10n22, 49–51, 65–70, 78, 87–97, 99, 100–3, 105n45, 105n55, 107n93, 107n95, 107n97, 109n119, 109n123, 109n124, 111, 116, 118, 121, 123, 124, 126, 129, 130, 136, 139, 140, 143–47, 149, 151, 152, 157, 160–64, 168n64, 168n67, 169n81, 173n165, 180–82, 187, 196, 197; Divine, 6, 143, 176n248; Eucharistic, 34, 51, 52, 94, 97, 99, 100, 102, 103, 107n90, 108n116, 109n121, 117, 120, 139, 140, 151, 152, 164, 175n212, 176n248; humanistic, 10n22, 92, 95–97, 100, 102, 163; theocentric, 6, 92, 163
Litz, Brett, 15, 20, 21, 22, 24, 30, 31, 34, 40, 45n102, 46n126, 47n143, 60, 80–86, 119, 134, 150, 151, 153–60
Louis the Pious, 193

MacIntyre, Alasdair, 148
Maguen, Shira, 24, 31, 40, 81, 86
Marin, Peter, 138, 139, 166n20, 168n59
Marshall, S. L. A., 39, 190, 191
Matsakis, Aphrodite, 26, 27, 79, 80, 84, 138, 139, 153
McGuckin, John, 114, 165n12
Medieval. *See* Middle Ages
Melchior, Aislinn, 194–96
Middle Ages, 63, 124, 135, 185, 189, 193, 195, 196; High, 127, 194
moral injury, definition of, 5, 7, 11, 22, 23, 29, 31, 32, 40, 41, 46n126, 78, 180
Moral Injury Symptom Scale, 131

Mystical Body of Christ, 136, 137

Narrative Therapy, 91, 145, 148, 149, 152, 154, 174n195
Nash, William P., 24
Neuger, Christie, 149
Nieuwsma, Jason A., 82–84, 86, 123, 124
Nock, Arthur, 193
Nünning, Vera, 145, 148, 151

On Penance, 186. *See also* Tertullian
Operation Enduring Freedom, *15*, 16
Operation Iraqi Freedom, *15*, 16, 190
Origen, 114, 185
Orthodox. *See* Eastern Orthodox

pastoral care, 1, 5–7, 11, 49–53, 55, 58, 61, 62, 64, 65, 70, 78, 84, 87–90, 93, 99, 102, 105n55, 111, 116, 118, 121, 123, 124, 131, 134, 142, 147, 161–63, 177, 178, 180–82
pastoral theology, 1, 6, 8, 12, 35, 40, 49, 50, 52, 53, 55, 79, 123, 134, 177–81
Paulinus, 135, 167n30, 185
penance, 3, 8n2, 35, 63, 112–18, 121, 124, 126–28, 132, 134–37, 140, 146, 158, 164, 169n74, 175n212, 185–87, 187n4, 194
Penitential Canons. See Ecclesiastical Discipline
Poling, James Newton, 53–55, 84, 85, 178, 179
Post Traumatic Stress Disorder (PTSD), 1, 2, 12–19, 26, 28–31, 41n1, 45n102, 45n105, 55, 59, 84, 119, 138, 141, 142, 170n88, 191, 194–96; complex, 29, 196; simple, 29, 30, 153, 196
Pruyser, Paul, 62
PTSD. *See* Post Traumatic Stress Disorder

Quack, Johannes, 67

Ramshaw, Elaine, 50, 51, 70n8, 88–93, 100, 105n55, 108n104, 121, 122, 173n165, 182
Reich, Warren, 178, 179
Renner, H. P. V., 139
ritual, definition of, 50
ritual care, 2, 5–7, 11–13, 49, 50, 78, 79, 86–89, 91–97, 99–103, 107n93, 108n116, 109n124, 116, 118, 121, 122, 124, 129, 130, 140, 141, 143, 145, 146, 149, 152–54, 160, 161, 163, 164, 171n102, 173n165, 176n249, 177, 180–82
ritual honesty, 49, 88, 91–93, 99, 100, 102, 111, 162, 163
Roman Catholic, 3, 5, 6, 9n7, 47n147, 51, 124; Church, 4, 6, 8n2, 9n7, 167n30
Roman Penitential, 135, 186

Sayings of the Desert Fathers, 136, 186
Schmemann, Alexander, 5, 6, 33, 34, 69, 99, 101, 106n88, 107n93, 107n95, 109n121, 123, 142, 170n95
Searle, Mark, 124, 147
Seligman, Adam, 68, 73n62, 107n95, 150, 167n42, 169n67, 169n73
Sharp, Melinda McGarrah, 178, 179, 181
Shay, Jonathan, 3, 4, 8n2, 11, 15, 18, 23–26, 29, 30, 36, 38, 41n1, 55, 56, 59, 61, 62, 119, 138, 153, 166n22, 196
Sherman, Nancy, 137
sin, 7, 12, 28, 32–35, 39, 40, 41, 47n147, 50, 52–55, 62–64, 69, 70n8, 112–22, 125, 127, 129–32, 134–38, 156–58, 162, 166n20, 166n22, 167n30, 168n64, 177–80, 185, 187, 196; definition of, 32
Sippola, John, 27, 28, 38
Slone, Laurie, 4, 28, 56, 79
Smith, James K. A., 65–68, 107n97, 145, 147
Smith, Jonathan Z., 69

Smith, Susan, 67, 69, 89–91, 107n95, 128, 129, 139
solidarity, 35, 39, 130–40, 144, 158, 161, 181, 185, 187
Sozomen, 135, 185
Stephenson, Barry, 66, 191
suicide, 14, 16
The Sunflower, 192
Swinton, John, 6, 175n229, 182

Tertullian, 114, 122, 125, 186
Theodosius, 104n32, 170n98, 186
theological anthropology, 33, 35, 54, 106n88
Thompson, Augustine, 194
Thompson, David, 28, 38
Tick, Edward, 4, 11, 25, 26, 29, 62, 63, 132

VA. *See* Veterans Affairs, Department of
Van Gennep, Arnold, 89
Verkamp, Bernard J., 115, 116, 124, 193
Veterans Affairs (VA), Department of, 1, 17, 18, 23, 38, 45n102, 45n105, 46n126, 54, 56, 58, 59, 70, 116, 125, 127, 141
Van der Kolk, Bessel, 1, 17, 45n105, 60, 65, 66
Van Deusen Hunsinger, Deborah, 6
Vietnam: veteran, 54, 59, 72n34, 74n71, 116, 128, 133, 138, 196; War, *15*, 18, 138, 190
vocation, 32–35, 37, 41, 54, 55, 85, 93, 115–17, 126, 159, 160, 161, 175n229, 180
Vogler, Christopher, 145–47, 173n158

Wetterstrom, Darlene, 28, 38
Wiesenthal, Simon, 192
William of Poitiers, 194
William the Conqueror, 194
Willimon, William, 87–93, 98, 100, 102, 103, 105n45, 123, 124, 161, 169n81, 181

Index

Wilson, Timothy, 108n117, 109n117, 125, 148, 168n66

Wittgenstein, Ludwig, 62, 67, 107n93

World War II, *15*, 190, 192

worship, 7, 32–34, 37, 41, 50, 52, 54, 62, 65, 78, 87–89, 90–94, 97–102, 106n88, 107n90, 109n119, 109n121, 109n124, 110n125, 112, 116, 117, 120, 123, 124, 139, 140, 142, 144, 146, 151, 159–61, 164, 165n19, 166n20, 166n22, 169n67, 169n81, 175n212, 175n229, 182; definition of, 52

Wright, N. T., 32, 33, 34, 166n22

About the Author

Johann Choi (PhD, Emory University) is a chaplain with the Veterans Health Administration and a former US Air Force chaplain. He is ordained and endorsed by the Anglican Church in North America.